NO
PATTERNS
NEEDED

LAURENCE KING

First published in 2016
by Laurence King Publishing Ltd
361–373 City Road
London EC1V 1LR
Tel: +44 20 7841 6900
Fax: +44 20 7841 6910
email: enquiries@laurenceking.com
www.laurenceking.com

A catalogue record for this book is
available from the British Library

ISBN: 978 1 78067 828 3

Design: Evelin Kasikov

Photography of models by
Victoria Siddle

Hair and make-up: Haleigh Maskall

Models: Courtney Graham,
Karishma Kumar, Melody Marsh,
Mairead McDaid, Linda Peterkopa
and Kristina Pringle

All other photographs,
and step-by-step illustrations,
by Rosie Martin

Illustrations on pages 14–15, 80–81
and 142–143 by Danielle Doobay

Drawings on page 5 by
Evelin Kasikov

Printed in China

ROSIE MARTIN

NO

PATTERNS

NEEDED

DIY COUTURE
from Simple Shapes

Laurence King Publishing

CONTENTS

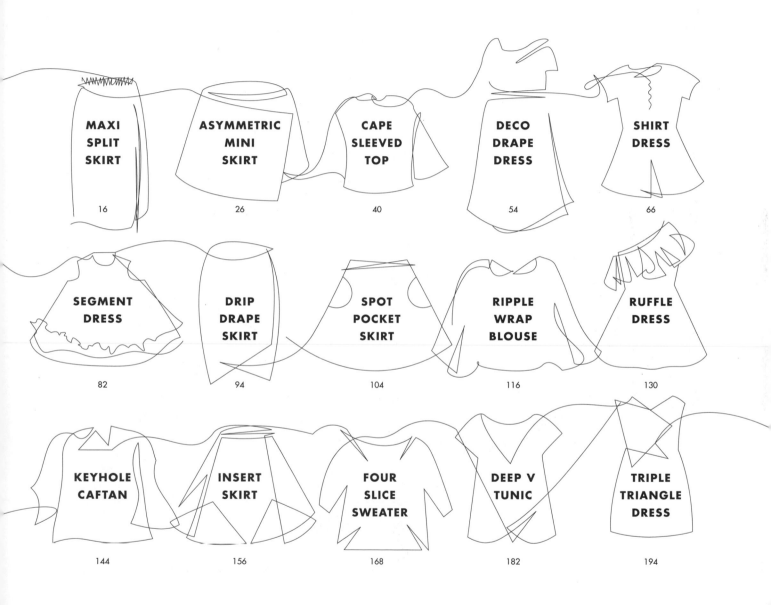

INTRODUCTION

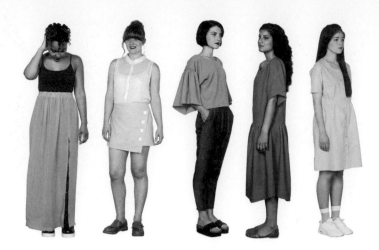

This book contains 15 visual tutorials that show you how to create clothing from scratch. Each of the 15 designs is based on one of the three simplest geometric shapes: the rectangle, the circle or the triangle. The tutorials do not involve the use of premade paper sewing patterns. Instead, they demonstrate how to mark out the simple shapes needed to construct these garments so that they fit your body. All of the garments in the rectangles section are made using rectangular pieces of fabric. All of the garments in the circles section are made by using full- or part-circle-shaped pieces of fabric. The triangles section gets more playful, with some designs stemming from distinct triangular pieces, and some using the triangle to form negative space.

We start with the rectangle

Humans love to build with rectangles. From buildings made of bricks to books made of humble pieces of paper, we like the stability of a four-cornered shape. Look around you… What can you see that is rectangular? My manmade world is crammed full of objects built out of this simple, balanced form – the computer I'm writing on, the desk it sits on, the fish tank in the corner of the room and the window I can see out of.

Our five 'rectangle' designs all begin with this stable, reassuring shape. We treat the rectangle as a blank page. You and I are not built from rectangles, but we can force flat expanses of fabric into 3D shapes that complement our human irregularities. Just as the sculptor chips away at a rectangular block of marble to reveal a beautiful flowing form, or the artist paints onto a rectangular canvas until the shape of the canvas disappears and it's the image we are concerned with, we will manipulate this basic shape to create clothing with beauty that far exceeds its unassuming origins.

We move on to circles

This section presents five tutorials that harness the unconstrained, organic power of the circle. The circle is a wilder shape than the rectangle. It has no corners, therefore it can roll away. The circle has its own energy, as it has no flat side on which to rest. In nature, planet earth spins, taking us along for the ride without asking us if we want a ticket. In the manmade world, wheels turn faster and faster, transporting us to other places. Humans have the urge to control the circle. We mark the perimeter of a circle with notches and map time onto it in the form of a clock. We use a wheel to cut a round pizza up into manageable chunks.

In our circle tutorials we are going to tame the circle by cutting circular pieces of fabric into segments like a pie and using them to make clothes. We will also harness its flowing organic power and learn to embrace the waves and ripples that arise from a circular shape.

We transcend through the triangle

The triangle has the stability of the rectangle – it can rest on a flat side – and some of the dynamic properties of the circle – it points upwards and appears to be able to take off like a spacecraft. In this section of the book we let this intriguing shape speak for itself.

From love triangles to the Holy Trinity, this pointy shape is often used to denote a space or situation that humans cannot master. The greatest structures on earth to embrace the triangle must surely be the ancient Egyptian pyramids. Though ancient, they seem to conjure up the spectre of the futuristic and otherworldly. Triangles are also employed in mystical symbolism, representing gateways to higher spiritual understanding, or the irresistible door to other worlds or dimensions. The Bermuda Triangle is thought to be a hole into which matter can literally disappear, never to be seen again.

Some of the designs in this section employ the positive power of this commanding shape, building clothes from triangular pieces of fabric and using their angular lines to create cutting-edge designs. Others use the triangle as an absence, employing it to create negative space. Will we ever understand the triangle? Perhaps not, but we can wear it!

WHY SHAPES?

Curiosity and learning, freedom and play

Not long after we are born, we learn to recognize shapes. We are excited and naturally curious about the strange and overwhelming environment we have been placed in. Learning to identify simple geometric shapes helps us to organize visual information and apply logic to a diverse world. We learn to name shapes and colours before we learn our alphabet or how to count to ten. Being able to grasp these shapes means we are able to take action on our curiosity; it is the beginning of understanding and interacting with our world. Understanding brings freedom. Once we can apply logic to what we can see, we are at liberty to explore it and to make it work for us. True freedom is empowering, as it is the ability to articulate and to choose.

We can also think about this in terms of making clothes. Most of us have worn premade garments our whole lives. Many of us then experience a moment when we become curious about the possibility of constructing our own clothing from scratch. When you're new to making clothes, curiosity is your spark, but sewing is a new world, with its own set of customs and a language that may seem strange and overwhelming.

By using simple shapes as a starting point, this book will help your curiosity flourish into action so that you can achieve your goal – a finished, wearable garment. The visual tutorials will help you get to grips with making clothing, without needing to study sewing vocabulary.

Being able to make clothing provides the freedom to wear what you want in terms of colour and style. For those who already make their own clothes, as well as those new to sewing, I hope that the direct, pattern-free approach in this book brings new freedoms; the freedom to create a garment that fits your own unique body shape, and the freedom to play with design. As you are sketching your own shapes, you can exercise choice over key elements such as necklines and sleeve length. You can even take bits from one tutorial – a collar here, a fastening there – and blend them with another.

With knowledge of basic techniques and processes, and with the confidence to play and experiment, I hope that this book can help you approach clothes-making boldly and creatively.

Beauty

As children we grasp at geometric shapes as a way of understanding the visual world, and as adults we compose with them. Art, architecture, fashion and furniture design agree that the balance present in simple shapes is pleasing to the eye. Shapes transcend cultures and the passage of time.

I hope that using the instructions in this book will bring you skills, determination and freedom, and some really nice clothes.

Rosie Martin

TECHNIQUES

How to make a piece of clothing

Whichever design you choose to make from this book, you'll be working through an essential construction process that varies remarkably little from garment to garment.

You will begin with choosing the fabric you're going to use (more on this on page 13), then move on to marking and cutting the pieces, joining them together and finally finishing the rough garment so it becomes something polished and wearable.

Here is a closer look at the steps you'll take.

Marking out

This book aims to equip you to make clothing without relying on premade paper patterns. By marking out your own shapes, you can make each of the designs specifically tailored to your size and shape. Each set of instructions will recommend using your body measurements or a guide garment – or a combination of the two – to help you mark out your fabric pieces. Use the information on page 12 to take your body measurements, then you can refer to them whenever you need them. You'll find a maths section at the beginning of each tutorial. Use your measurements and a calculator to complete this, then you have it to hand as you work through the instructions.

I also recommend some essential tools – nothing too fancy – for marking out your shapes. See pages 10–11.

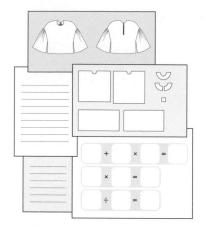

You'll be marking out your shapes either directly onto your fabric, or onto newspaper. Sometimes I recommend using newspaper for the best results. Sometimes it's up to you which method you choose.

The benefits of marking straight onto fabric are that it is a direct, straightforward approach and it allows you to make different design choices every time you use the same set of instructions. Marking onto paper can help if your fabric is flimsy or drapey and wouldn't take well to being drawn on with chalk. It also gives you a template that can be used to create more versions of the same garment in the future.

When marking your shapes you'll be adding extra fabric for ease and for seam allowance. Ease is how much space there will be between your finished garment and your body. Unless you are sewing a swimsuit or leggings, you'll almost always want to add ease to your garment or you won't be able to move around. We add ease to your measurements in the maths bit at the beginning of each tutorial.

You can also play with the ease, adding more or less to make your garments looser or tighter.

When you join your pieces together, you'll be sewing a little way inside the raw edge of the fabric pieces. The distance between the cut edge of the fabric and your stitches is called the seam allowance and, unless the instructions state otherwise, it is assumed to be a standard 1.5cm (⅝in). We ask you to add this in the maths bit at the start of each tutorial.

Sewing

With your pieces cut, you need to join them together. Straight stitch is the main stitch you'll be relying on to attach one piece of fabric to another, with your stitches sitting 1.5cm (⅝in) from the edge of the fabric. Whenever you start a line of straight stitch, begin with your needle positioned slightly 'inland', then sew a couple of stitches backwards until you reach the very edge of the fabric. From there, you can sew merrily forwards until you get to the end of whatever you're sewing. Once there, again, you'll need to do a couple of stitches in reverse mode, sewing right over the stitches that are already in place. This reverse stitch is called backstitching and holds the entire line of stitching in place, ensuring it doesn't unravel at a later date.

For garments made of stretchy fabric, you'll need to use zigzag instead of straight stitch. Zigzag stitch allows a seam to stretch without snapping the thread. Choose a shallow zigzag stitch for sewing seams on stretch fabric, and backstitch whenever you start and finish a line of stitching.

Pressing

The iron is as crucial to making clothes as the sewing machine.

The first thing you'll do is iron the fabric, so you'll be marking your shapes onto a flat surface.

From then on, you will be using your iron as a pressing tool, using steam, heat and pressure to force parts of your garment to sit where you want them. You'll use your iron to press seams open so that they lie flat (see page 46), to create sharp details on your garment (see page 45) and to make neat necklines and crisp hems.

You'll also press creases into your pieces as a way of marking specific points, and use the iron to join fusible interfacing to fabric and prepare bias binding to be joined to garments.

Snipping and clipping

As pressing assists sewing, snipping assists pressing. In order to release tension in seams so they can be pressed flat, you will often need to snip into them. For examples of this see pages 47 and 60. For concave curves that will become convex when they are turned out, make single snips that stop just before the line of stitching. For convex curves that will become concave – such as the edge of the collar on the Ripple Wrap Blouse, shown on page 123 – snip out little triangles of fabric to release tension and reduce bulk. For any right-angled corners, such as those under the armpit of our Deco Drape Dress (see page 63), snip out triangles of fabric that break apart the underarm seam and the side seam, allowing them to be pressed flat.

Finishing

Aside from the main construction of your garment, you'll need to 'finish' all the remaining edges (though this is not necessarily done at the end!).

You'll have raw edges at the neck, the sleeve end or armhole and the bottom edge of your garment. Curved edges and straight edges require different finishing techniques. For sleeve ends and the straight hems of skirts, you can simply press up a single or double fold of even depth all the way around the edge you are finishing and then sew it into place.

For curved neck- and armholes, you'll need to use facing or bias binding to neaten the edges. For examples of this see pages 47 and 89.

As you construct your garment, you'll be creating space for fastenings and, if zips are required, adding them as you go. In the last moments of construction, you'll be hand sewing any fastenings like press studs, buttons, and hooks and eyes that are needed to make your beautiful piece of handmade clothing stay on your body!

WHAT DOES IT MEAN?

'Square a line…'

By squaring a line, we mean drawing a line that is at a right angle to either a chalk line you have already drawn or the edge of the fabric. You can do this simply with a piece of paper, using the edges to line up your ruler, or by making a DIY set square like our cardboard version used throughout the book. For an example, see page 28.

'Finish with zigzag stitch.'

On non-stretchy fabric, you'll use zigzag stitch to finish or neaten raw edges. Whenever you see the phrase 'Finish/ neaten with zigzag stitch', set your machine to sew a wide zigzag stitch and sew over one single raw edge of your fabric. The needle should hit your fabric when it moves to the left and land on air when it moves to the right. In this way, the zigzag stitch is binding or sealing the edge of the fabric so that it doesn't dissolve into a mess of loose threads over time.

'Press to the inside…'

When pressing a facing or strip of bias binding to the inside, you need to roll it so the join – where your line of stitching is holding the two pieces of fabric together – sits on the inside, just below the finished edge of the garment. By the power of pressing, you are forcing your facing or bias binding to be hidden from the outside of your garment and are creating a neat, clean edge. For an example, see page 76.

TOOLS

To start making your own clothes, you'll need a few basic tools.

MARKING OUT

Tape
Tape multiple pieces of newspaper together to make bigger pieces.

String
For marking out circular shapes.

Tailor's chalk
For making marks on fabric.

Paper scissors
For cutting out your paper shapes.

Pencil
For sketching shapes on paper.

Coloured pens
Also useful for marking on paper. Use different colours to distinguish between lines you want to cut along and marks you want to transfer to the fabric.

DIY set square
A set square will help you mark out shapes with 90 degree corners. You don't need an actual set square for this. We've used a right-angled triangle made of cardboard, but you can use anything that has a perfectly square corner, such as a piece of A4 paper (see step 24 on page 161 for a photo).

Newspaper
You can mark out your shapes onto newspaper so that you have a template you can use again.

Ruler
A ruler is useful for accurately marking out small distances, such as the depth of facing or width of a dart.

Tape measure
Mostly to be used for taking body measurements but sometimes for measuring curved edges.

Metre (or yard) stick
Many of the designs in this book start life as rectangular pieces of fabric. The metre stick will be your best friend when marking these out.

Sewing machine
You don't need a flashy machine in order to make your own clothes, just one that can do straight stitch and zigzag stitch.

Hand-sewing needles
For making the final touches such as adding buttons and securing facing in place. Also for transferring markings from paper to fabric using tailor's tacks.

Regular machine foot
For doing the majority of your sewing.

Zipper foot
For sewing regular or invisible zips. You can also buy a special 'invisible zipper foot' for sewing invisible zips, if you like.

Seam ripper
For carefully unpicking stitches, and for slicing into fabric when making buttonholes.

Snips
It's very useful to have a pair of small, sharp scissors for cutting threads as you sew and for making small snips into seam allowances to release tension.

Pins
Mainly for holding pieces of fabric together, but also used as an alternative to chalk to mark specific points on fabric. For example, you can fold a piece of fabric in half to find the centre, then mark that point by slipping a pin in.

Thread
Pick a thread that matches the main colour of your fabric.

Ironing board
You'll spend almost as much time at your ironing board as you will at your sewing machine.

Bobbins
To be wound with the same thread used in the needle.

Fabric scissors
Dedicate these to cutting fabric only, so they stay reliably sharp.

Iron
An essential tool for pressing seams open and hems up.

Seam gauge
Not a vital tool but useful to have for measuring the depth of hems easily as you press them up.

BODY MEASUREMENTS

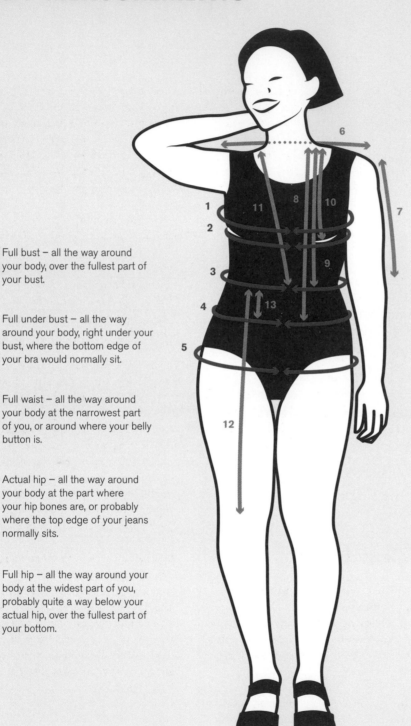

6 Shoulder peak to shoulder peak – from the pointy tip of one shoulder across the back of your neck to the pointy tip of the other shoulder.

7 Shoulder peak to elbow – from the pointy tip of your shoulder down your arm to the point of your elbow.

8 Nape of neck to actual hip – from the point where your neck roughly meets your shoulder line, down your front to your actual hip.

9 Nape of neck to waist – from the point where your neck meets your shoulder line down to your waist.

10 Nape of neck to under bust – from the point where your neck meets your shoulder line down over the curve of your bust to your under bust.

11 Nape of neck to belly button – from the point where your neck meets your shoulder line, diagonally down across your body to your belly button.

12 Waist to knee – from your waist down to roughly the middle of your knee.

13 Waist to hip – from your waist down to your actual hip.

14 Nape of neck to waist down back – from the point where your neck meets your shoulder line down your back to your waist. (Not shown.)

1 Full bust – all the way around your body, over the fullest part of your bust.

2 Full under bust – all the way around your body, right under your bust, where the bottom edge of your bra would normally sit.

3 Full waist – all the way around your body at the narrowest part of you, or around where your belly button is.

4 Actual hip – all the way around your body at the part where your hip bones are, or probably where the top edge of your jeans normally sits.

5 Full hip – all the way around your body at the widest part of you, probably quite a way below your actual hip, over the fullest part of your bottom.

NO PATTERNS NEEDED

A NOTE ABOUT FABRICS

Which fabric?

The fabric you choose will influence the appearance of your finished garment. Most obviously, the colour and print of the fabric will affect how your garment looks. At a deeper level, the physical properties of the fabric will exercise their power over the piece of clothing you make. These properties are found not just in the look, but in the feel of the fabric.

Throughout the book, we show three variations of each garment, made using different fabrics to help you visualize how the basic design can be interpreted.

We give some recommendations of specific fabrics using their technical names, which can help – particularly when buying material online.

We also give some recommendations by describing properties, focusing on the weight and drape of fabrics. These descriptions are aimed at helping you buy fabric in the real 3D world, where you can reach out and feel fabric and don't necessarily need to know what to call it.

The only recommendation that should be strictly adhered to is the advice to use knitted fabric for the Drip Drape Skirt and Four Slice Sweater. Knit fabric is stretchy, and these garments are designed specifically to work with fabrics that have a bit of stretch.

Making clothes is experimental and there is a vast, exciting world of delicious fabric out there, so feel free to buy whatever fabric you love, as loving it is the best start and you'll no doubt learn something useful by using it.

How much?

How much fabric to buy depends on your design choices and how big you are. Use the body measurement chart opposite, then do the maths bit at the beginning of the tutorial you are using. Read through the cutting process of the tutorial and look at how wide the fabric that you're buying is. Fabric can vary in width and will often be either 150cm (60in) wide or 115cm (45in) wide.

As a rough guide 1.5m (1⅝yd) will often be plenty for a top or slim-fitting skirt. For fuller skirts, loose dresses or something with a large gathered section, you will most likely need more. If you can't be bothered to do all the maths and don't mind having leftovers, 3m (3¼yd) will almost always be ample.

Once you've bought your fabric, take it home and wash it straight away. All fabric needs to be washed before it is cut up and turned into clothing as it may shrink substantially. It's much better that it shrinks before you have made a perfectly fitted garment than afterwards.

Cutting out

When marking out the pieces for your garment it helps to think of your fabric as a blank page. The page has a top and a bottom and two sides. All your pieces should sit square to the edges of the page of fabric.

Your fabric is made of threads that are woven in a tight grid. In the factory, the fabric will be made in a really long strip that is then wound into a roll. The long edges of the fabric strip are sealed so the threads don't unravel, and these sealed edges are called the selvage edges. The person cutting your fabric will cut across the roll of fabric from selvage to selvage, creating a fresh edge that runs at a right angle to the selvage edges.

When you are laying out your fabric to mark your pieces, the fresh edge will be the 'top' of the page you are working with. The imaginary horizontal lines that run across your body – the waist, the hips, the shoulders – should all be running parallel to this fresh edge of the fabric.

The direction the selvage runs in is called the grain line. As a general rule, you want the grain line to run up and down your garment from top to bottom. However, most important is to cut your pieces square, rather than at a crazy sloping or diagonal angle, so if you want to cut some of your pieces with the grain line running from side to side instead of up and down in order to make best use of your fabric, that is fine too.

Most fabrics have a right and a wrong side. The wrong side of fabric is really the back of the fabric. I show this with a paler colour in the illustrations. This will end up on the inside of your garments. The right side is the one that is meant to show on the outside of your garment. I show this with the stronger colour in all the illustrations.

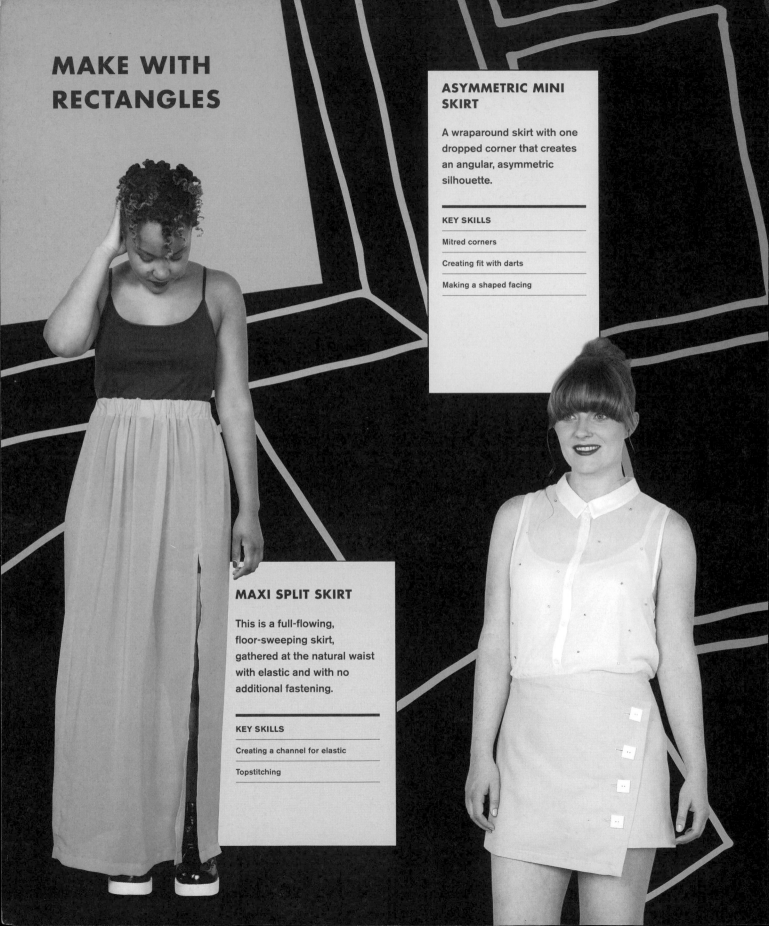

MAKE WITH RECTANGLES

ASYMMETRIC MINI SKIRT

A wraparound skirt with one dropped corner that creates an angular, asymmetric silhouette.

KEY SKILLS

Mitred corners

Creating fit with darts

Making a shaped facing

MAXI SPLIT SKIRT

This is a full-flowing, floor-sweeping skirt, gathered at the natural waist with elastic and with no additional fastening.

KEY SKILLS

Creating a channel for elastic

Topstitching

CAPE SLEEVED TOP

This is a boxy but flowing top with dropped shoulders and a relaxed fit.

KEY SKILLS

Gathering

Inserting an exposed zip

Facing

SHIRT DRESS

A smart, button-up dress with a central front placket, this features a semi-fitted bodice with six tucks across the waist edge, kimono sleeves and a gathered skirt.

KEY SKILLS

Making a placket

Creating tucks

Gathering

Using body measurements to create a paper template

Using bias binding to finish an edge

DECO DRAPE DRESS

Inspired by a bold independence reflected in women's clothing of the 1920s, this dress has a loose bodice with kimono sleeves, a dropped waistline and a simple rectangular skirt shaped by slashing and sections of gathering.

KEY SKILLS

Gathering

Sewing a neckline facing

Creating kimono sleeves

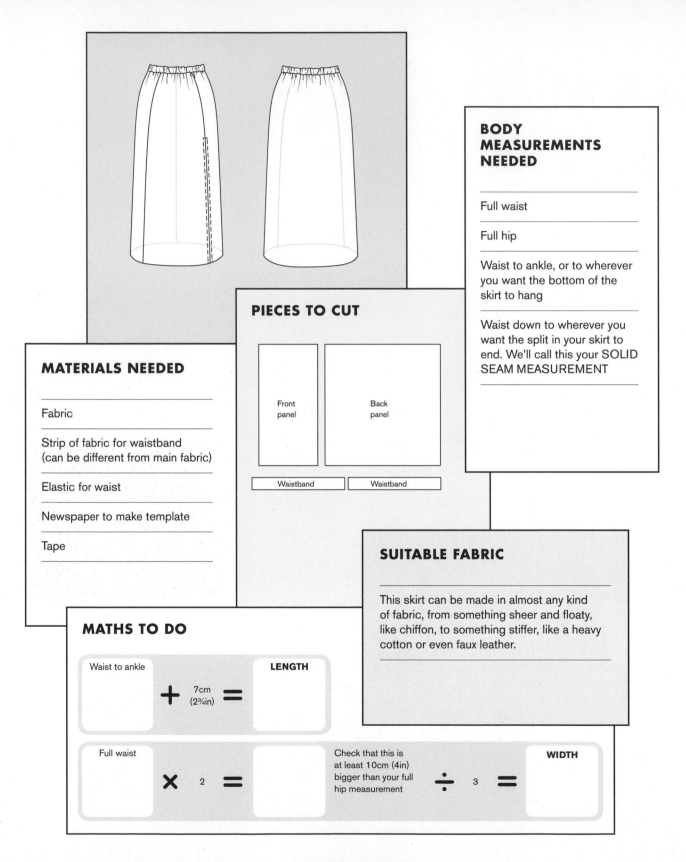

BODY MEASUREMENTS NEEDED

Full waist

Full hip

Waist to ankle, or to wherever you want the bottom of the skirt to hang

Waist down to wherever you want the split in your skirt to end. We'll call this your SOLID SEAM MEASUREMENT

MATERIALS NEEDED

Fabric

Strip of fabric for waistband (can be different from main fabric)

Elastic for waist

Newspaper to make template

Tape

PIECES TO CUT

Front panel

Back panel

Waistband

Waistband

SUITABLE FABRIC

This skirt can be made in almost any kind of fabric, from something sheer and floaty, like chiffon, to something stiffer, like a heavy cotton or even faux leather.

MATHS TO DO

Waist to ankle **+** 7cm (2¾in) **=** LENGTH

Full waist **×** 2 **=** Check that this is at least 10cm (4in) bigger than your full hip measurement **÷** 3 **=** WIDTH

MAXI SPLIT SKIRT

This skirt is made of just two rectangular panels, a large one wrapping around the back and a narrow one sitting at the centre front. The skirt can be made with a thigh-high split up one or both sides of the centre front panel. Make the skirt knee-length in stiffer fabric and with a shorter front panel for a more angular, austere silhouette.

01

RECTANGLES

You are going to make two rectangles that will form the main body of your skirt. One smaller rectangle will form the front panel of the skirt and a larger one will form the sides and back of the skirt. We will start by marking out the front panel.

You can mark the first rectangle straight onto your fabric (as in the Asymmetric Mini Skirt tutorial on page 28), but if your fabric is delicate or wobbly you might want to follow these instructions for making a template from newspaper.

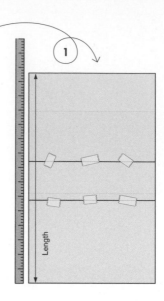

①

Length

Tape two or three pieces of newspaper together so that they are the same height as your LENGTH measurement. Make sure you are taping them square with one another!

②

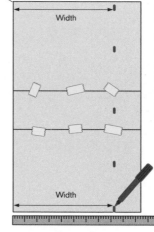

③ Draw a line joining all your marks using your metre stick.

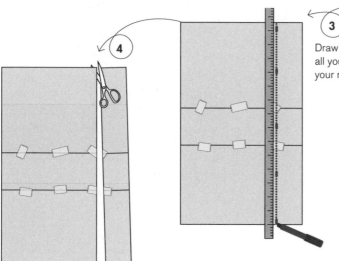

Width

Width

Measure your WIDTH across the bottom edge of your newspaper and make a mark. Do the same thing a few more times, measuring across from the vertical edge each time.

④

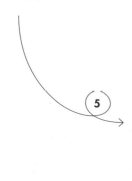

Cut along the line creating a big rectangle of newspaper.

⑤

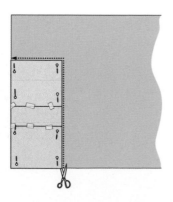

Pin the newspaper to your fabric, or if your fabric is very unstable, lay it on top and weigh it down with books or a pair of shoes. Then cut around it. This is your front piece.

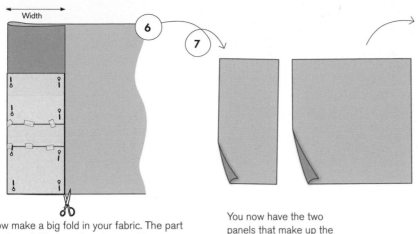

Width

Now make a big fold in your fabric. The part you have folded needs to be as wide as your WIDTH measurement. Lay your newspaper on top of it, bumping the edge of the newspaper up to the fold so it sits right on top of it, then pin or weigh the paper down and cut around it, cutting through the two layers of fabric. This is your back piece.

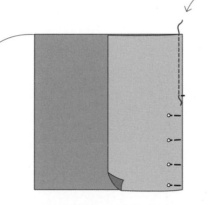

You now have the two panels that make up the main body of your skirt.

Now join your large back panel to your centre front panel.

Lay out your back panel with the front panel on top, right sides together. Pin them together down one side.

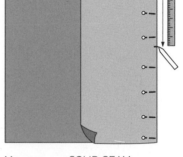

Solid seam measurement

Measure your SOLID SEAM MEASUREMENT down from the top and mark this point with a pin or with chalk.

Lift your machine needle, cut your thread and set your straight stitch to a longer setting – about 3.5mm (⅛in) long. Start a new line of stitching exactly where your last line finished. Manually lower your needle into your fabric so you are sure it is hitting the exact spot where your last line of stitching finished.

Sew down to this point from the top with straight stitch, with your stitches 1.5cm (⅝in) from the edge. Run your stitches backwards at the start and end of your line of stitching to secure them.

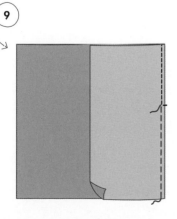

Sew down from this point but don't run your stitching backwards at the beginning and end as you normally would, as you are going to unpick these stitches later to create your split. This is a kind of stitch called tacking or basting, which holds the seam in place temporarily.

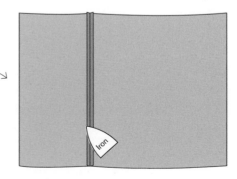

Iron

Press open the seam you have just created.

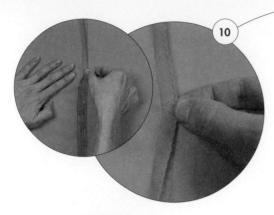

10

You're going to do some stitching to hold this seam open around the split. Before you start stitching, find the point where your basting stitch stops and your regular stitch begins. Make a mark here with chalk — or by slipping a pin in — on the wrong side of your skirt.

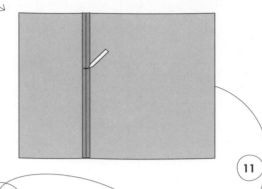

11

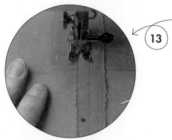

13

Pivot the skirt again with the needle in the down position, then sew your straight stitch back down to the bottom of the skirt, at the edge of the opposite seam flap.

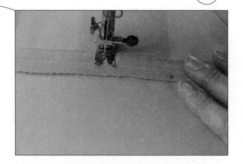

12

With the needle in the down position, raise the machine foot and twist your skirt clockwise by 90 degrees. Lower the foot again and stitch over the seam to the edge of the other seam flap.

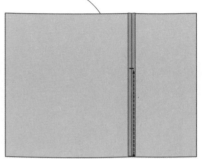

Pin your seam flaps so they lie open and flat. Now, beginning with your needle at what will be the bottom of your skirt, sew a line of straight stitch up the outer edge of the seam flap on the left, until you reach the mark you just made.

Now it is time to prepare a channel at the waist edge of your skirt, which you will be threading elastic through. You need to cut two long rectangles of fabric for this.

14

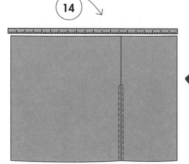

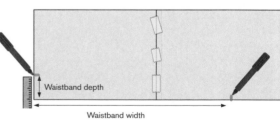

Waistband depth

Waistband width

These rectangles need to be as deep as the elastic you are going to be using plus 3cm (1⅛in). Measure the depth of your elastic and add 3cm (1⅛in). This is your WAISTBAND DEPTH. Mark this distance up the side of a piece of newspaper.

Measure the full distance across the waist edge of your skirt. Halve this then add 1.5cm (⅝in) to that measurement. We'll call this your WAISTBAND WIDTH. Mark that along the bottom of your newspaper. You might need to tape two pieces of paper together.

TUTORIAL

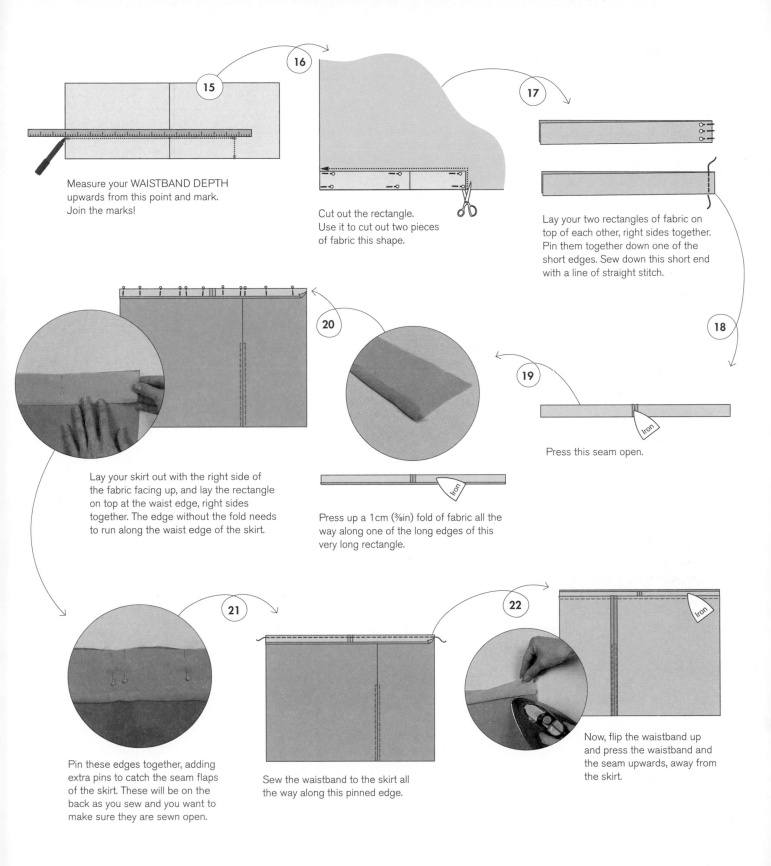

15 Measure your WAISTBAND DEPTH upwards from this point and mark. Join the marks!

16 Cut out the rectangle. Use it to cut out two pieces of fabric this shape.

17 Lay your two rectangles of fabric on top of each other, right sides together. Pin them together down one of the short edges. Sew down this short end with a line of straight stitch.

18

19 Press this seam open.

20 Press up a 1cm (⅜in) fold of fabric all the way along one of the long edges of this very long rectangle.

Lay your skirt out with the right side of the fabric facing up, and lay the rectangle on top at the waist edge, right sides together. The edge without the fold needs to run along the waist edge of the skirt.

21 Pin these edges together, adding extra pins to catch the seam flaps of the skirt. These will be on the back as you sew and you want to make sure they are sewn open.

Sew the waistband to the skirt all the way along this pinned edge.

22 Now, flip the waistband up and press the waistband and the seam upwards, away from the skirt.

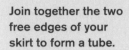

Join together the two free edges of your skirt to form a tube.

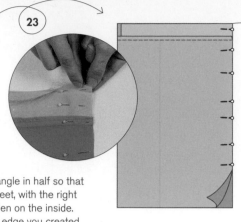

(23)

Fold your large rectangle in half so that the vertical edges meet, with the right side of the skirt hidden on the inside. Open out the ironed edge you created at the top of the waistband. Pin the edges together.

(24)

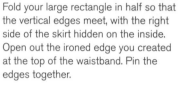

If you are creating a second split in your skirt, repeat the joining process from step 8, sewing normal-length stitches down as far as your SOLID SEAM MEASUREMENT then tacking. If you are only adding one split, sew with a regular-length straight stitch all the way from top to bottom.

(26)

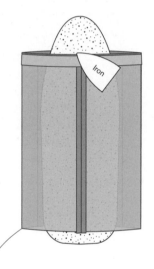

Fold your waistband down towards the hem of your skirt and press it so it sits about 1–2mm (¹⁄₁₆in) below the top edge of your skirt.

Create your gathered waistband.

(25)

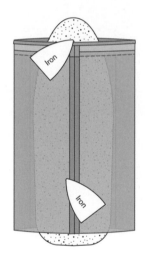

Press this seam open. Neaten the raw edge on each seam flap with zigzag stitch. Repress the fold into the top edge of your waistband.

(27)

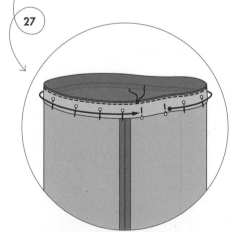

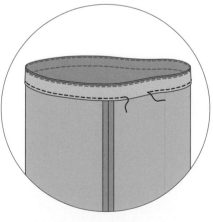

Pin it to the skirt in this position. Sew the waistband into place all the way around, with your line of stitches sitting about 3mm (¹⁄₈in) away from the top edge.

You're going to sew a second line of stitching along the bottom edge of the waistband, with your stitches sitting 2 or 3mm (¹⁄₈in) away from the pressed edge. You need to stop your stitches about 6cm (2⅜in) before they get back to where you started, so mark out a starting and stopping point with pins to remind yourself to stop sewing.

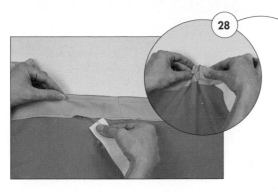 **28**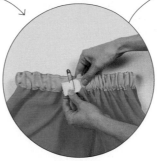

 **29**

30

Cut a piece of elastic as long as your waist measurement and push it through the waistband channel with a safety pin. Make sure the tail end doesn't disappear!

When the safety pin emerges, use it to pin the two ends of the elastic together, checking the elastic isn't twisted anywhere.

Try the skirt on to check the fit, then sew the pinned ends of the elastic together.

Check the fit again, then sew up the gap in the channel with straight stitch.

31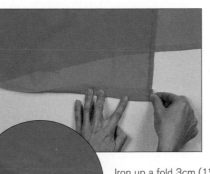

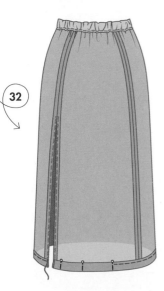

All that's left to do now is to hem your skirt.

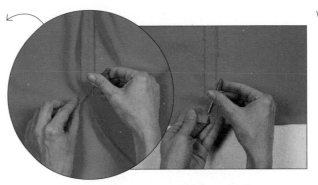

Iron up a fold 3cm (1⅛in) deep at the bottom edge of your skirt all around, then iron up a second fold 3cm (1⅛in) deep.

Now you can carefully unpick the tacking you did a long time ago.

32

Pin the fold in place and check that it is hanging at the same level on both sides of your split or splits.

Sew it all the way around near the inner folded edge. If you have two splits, you will be sewing your hem in two sections.

YOU HAVE MADE A MAXI SPLIT SKIRT!

Maxi split skirt

1

Kristina wears a cropped version of the skirt, with the narrow front panel cut even shorter to create a geometric detail at the hemline. The front panel is made of slightly shiny leatherette, which contrasts subtly with the matt medium-weight polycotton the rest of the skirt is made from. The skirt has a split up both sides of the front panel.

2

Karishma wears a full-length Maxi Split Skirt in semi-sheer polyester chiffon. This skirt is much fuller than the pink version photographed throughout the tutorial as we used the full hip rather than the waist measurement to determine the WIDTH measurement. This means there is much more gathering at the waist, and the skirt is more voluminous all over.

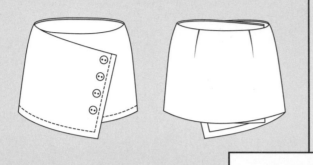

SUITABLE FABRIC

This skirt suits fabrics that hold their shape. You can make it in anything from a crisp cotton to a thicker wool or a stiff leatherette. Thinner fabrics will produce satisfyingly pointed corners. The facing can be made in a scrap fabric; try to use the same weight, or lighter, than the fabric used for the skirt.

MATERIALS NEEDED

Fabric

Fabric for facing

Short open-ended zip, or buttons

Strong press studs (snaps) x 2

BODY MEASUREMENTS NEEDED

Full hip

Desired length of the skirt, from the hip, waist or wherever the top of the skirt will sit, downwards

From where the top of the skirt will sit, down to full hip

MATHS TO DO

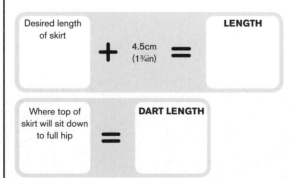

| Desired length of skirt | + | 4.5cm (1¾in) | = | LENGTH |

| Where top of skirt will sit down to full hip | = | DART LENGTH |

PIECES TO CUT

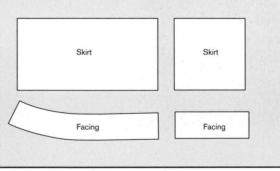

Skirt

Skirt

Facing

Facing

ASYMMETRIC MINI SKIRT

This mini can be fastened at the front with buttons for a 1960s look, or with an exposed zip for an edgier, contemporary look. The skirt is shaped at the rear with darts and finished at the edges with double-turned hems and mitred corners. For a clean, minimalist finish, eschew visible fastenings in favour of hand-sewn press studs.

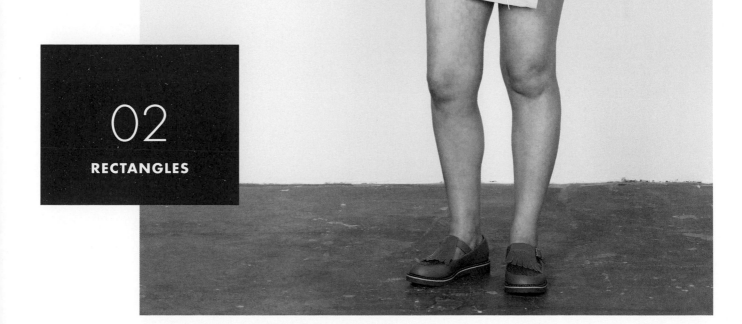

02
RECTANGLES

The Asymmetric Mini Skirt is made of two main rectangular pieces of fabric. You're going to start by cutting the larger rectangle, the one that will wrap around your body and show at the back and one side of your skirt once finished.

1

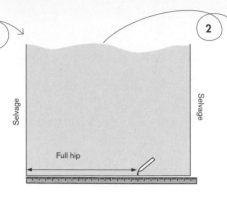

Measure your full hip measurement out along the bottom edge of your fabric and mark that point with chalk.

2

Measure your LENGTH upwards from this point and square a line to that point with chalk.

4

Cut out this rectangle.

Then join that mark to the top of the chalk line you have drawn.

3

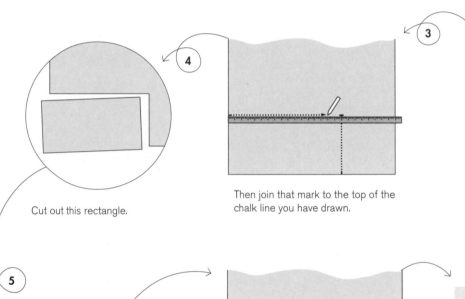

Measure your LENGTH up the side of your fabric, too, and mark that point.

5

Fold this rectangle in half and lay it on your fabric. You are going to cut out the small rectangle that will show at the front of your skirt. You might like to use a different fabric.

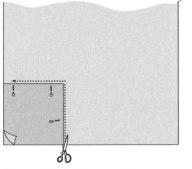

Pin your folded fabric down then cut around it.

You are going make a facing to neaten the top edge of your skirt. Your facing will be made of two parts, just like your skirt. The facing should be made of a fabric that isn't too heavy; a polycotton or cotton would work well. You can make one part of your facing now.

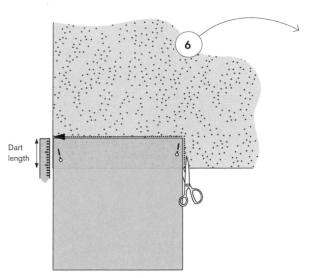

6

Lay your facing fabric out and lay your smaller skirt rectangle on top of it. This piece of facing is just a strip of fabric as wide as your skirt rectangle and as deep as your DART LENGTH. Position your skirt piece so the top of it is your DART LENGTH above the bottom edge of your facing. Put a couple of pins in to hold it in place. Cut around your skirt piece to create your strip of facing, then take your pins out and put the facing to one side for now.

Dart length

Join your two main rectangles together.

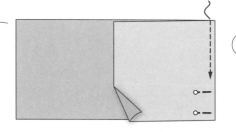

8

7

Wrap the strip of fabric around your body, fitting it to your full hip. Start with the top corner of the larger rectangle sitting at your right hip on the side seam of whatever trousers/skirt you are wearing. Wrap it across the front of your body, over to the left hip. Tilt the piece slightly so that the side of the skirt slopes out at the bottom.

Keep wrapping the piece across your back until you get to the right hip. The seam joining the two rectangles should be sitting here, roughly on top of the side seam of the garment you are wearing.

Lay out your larger skirt rectangle with the smaller one on top of it, right sides together. Match up the edges, pin them together then sew them together with a line of straight stitch. You have made one long strip of fabric.

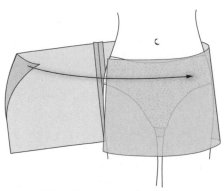

C

Tilt

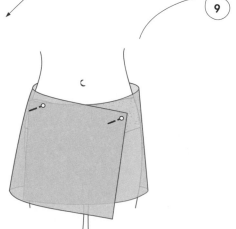

C

Bring the remaining flap of fabric across the front of your body, angling the top edge downwards until it's sitting in a way you like and is hiding the bottom corner at the start of your rectangle. Pin it down here, pinning it to your clothing to keep it up!

9

There will be quite a bit of fabric gaping around the waist edge. Pinch all this fabric up in one big pinch at the back, roughly in the middle. Pinch it tight and pin as close to the base of the pinch as possible. This will tighten the fabric around your hips at the side.

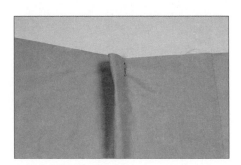

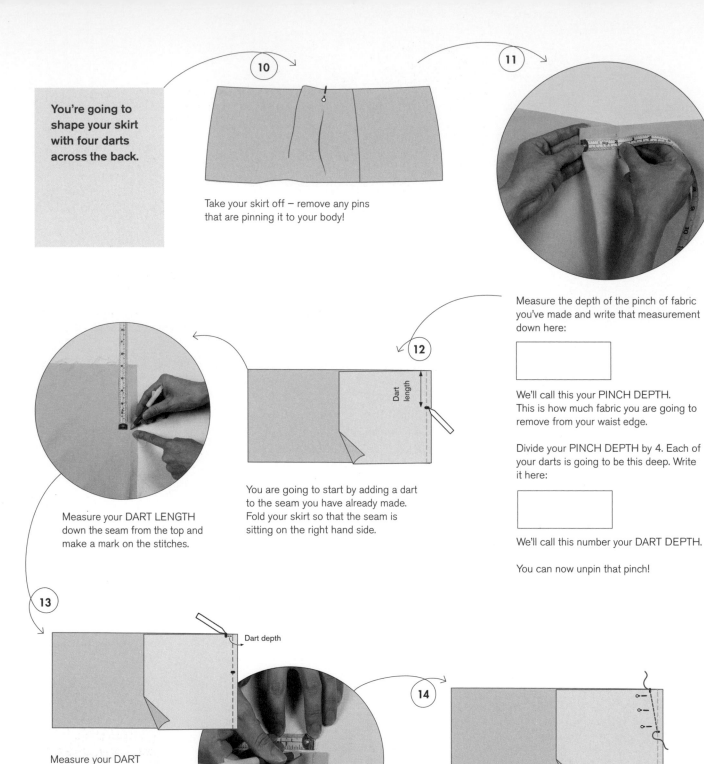

You're going to shape your skirt with four darts across the back.

10 Take your skirt off – remove any pins that are pinning it to your body!

11

12 Measure the depth of the pinch of fabric you've made and write that measurement down here:

We'll call this your PINCH DEPTH. This is how much fabric you are going to remove from your waist edge.

Divide your PINCH DEPTH by 4. Each of your darts is going to be this deep. Write it here:

We'll call this number your DART DEPTH.

You can now unpin that pinch!

You are going to start by adding a dart to the seam you have already made. Fold your skirt so that the seam is sitting on the right hand side.

Dart length

Measure your DART LENGTH down the seam from the top and make a mark on the stitches.

13 Measure your DART DEPTH from the stitch line inwards and make a mark.

Dart depth

14 Sew a line of straight stitch between the two marks.

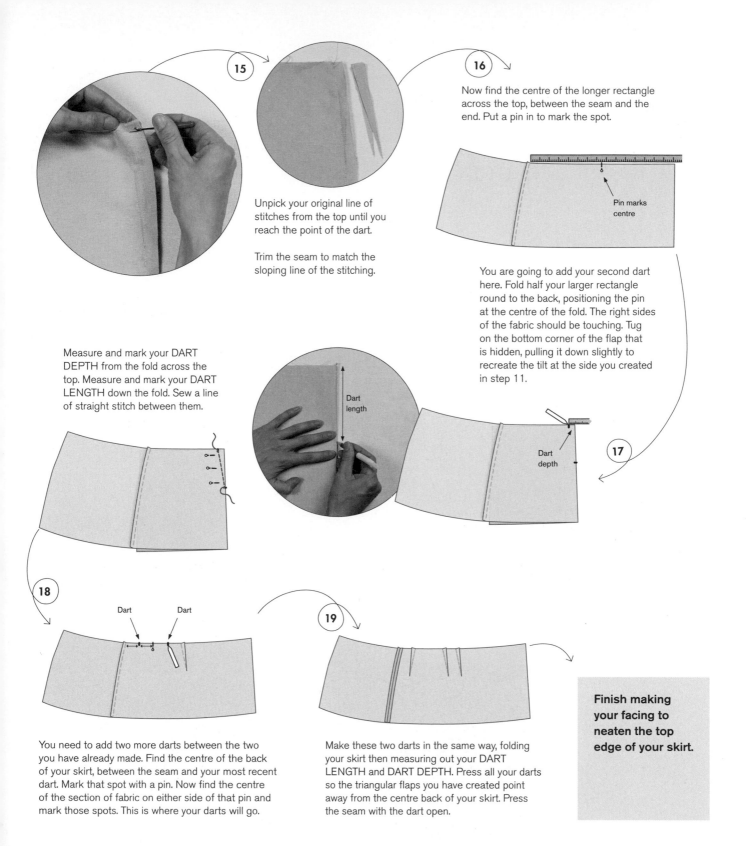

15

Unpick your original line of stitches from the top until you reach the point of the dart.

Trim the seam to match the sloping line of the stitching.

16

Now find the centre of the longer rectangle across the top, between the seam and the end. Put a pin in to mark the spot.

Pin marks centre

You are going to add your second dart here. Fold half your larger rectangle round to the back, positioning the pin at the centre of the fold. The right sides of the fabric should be touching. Tug on the bottom corner of the flap that is hidden, pulling it down slightly to recreate the tilt at the side you created in step 11.

17

Dart depth

Measure and mark your DART DEPTH from the fold across the top. Measure and mark your DART LENGTH down the fold. Sew a line of straight stitch between them.

Dart length

18

Dart   Dart

You need to add two more darts between the two you have already made. Find the centre of the back of your skirt, between the seam and your most recent dart. Mark that spot with a pin. Now find the centre of the section of fabric on either side of that pin and mark those spots. This is where your darts will go.

19

Make these two darts in the same way, folding your skirt then measuring out your DART LENGTH and DART DEPTH. Press all your darts so the triangular flaps you have created point away from the centre back of your skirt. Press the seam with the dart open.

Finish making your facing to neaten the top edge of your skirt.

Mark out your second, longer piece of facing. This will sit inside the edge of your skirt where you have added the darts. The darts have pinched up your fabric, so the top edge will now be curved rather than straight. Your facing needs to be curved, too.

Lay out your facing fabric again and lay your skirt on top of it, wrong sides together, with the straight vertical end of your skirt sitting roughly over the straight edge of your fabric. Spread out the first part of your skirt as flat as possible and draw along the top edge with chalk.

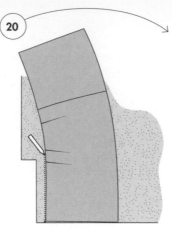

Keep spreading the skirt flat, section by section, continuing your chalk line. The skirt will swivel as you go, so that the part you started drawing will no longer be sitting next to your chalk line. That is fine. Draw until you get to the seam joining the two rectangles. Stick a pin into the seam, level with the bottom of one of your darts.

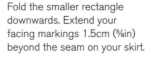

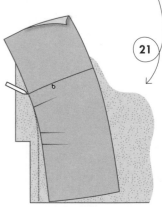

Fold the smaller rectangle downwards. Extend your facing markings 1.5cm (⅝in) beyond the seam on your skirt.

For the facing length, measure your DART LENGTH down from the line you've just drawn, marking it at intervals. Join the marks then cut out the facing.

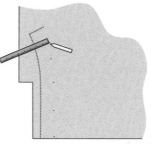

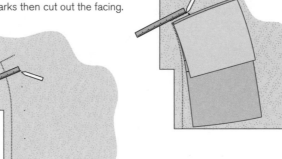

Place the short rectangle of facing on top of the curved end of the longer piece, right sides together, and pin in place. Mark the DART DEPTH + 1.5cm (⅝in) from the end on the top edge, and just 1.5cm (⅝in) on the bottom edge. Sew between the two marks with straight stitch then trim this seam and press open.

Dart depth + 1.5cm (⅝in)

1.5cm (⅝in)

Neaten the long bottom edge of the facing by trimming it with pinking shears or sewing over the raw edge with zigzag stitch.

Join your facing to your skirt.

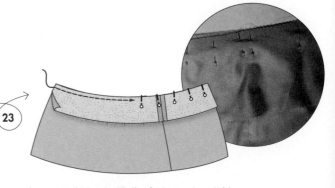

Lay your skirt out with the facing on top, right sides together. Pin them together across the top, matching up the seams, then sew them together with a long line of straight stitch, sitting just 1cm (⅜in) away from the edge.

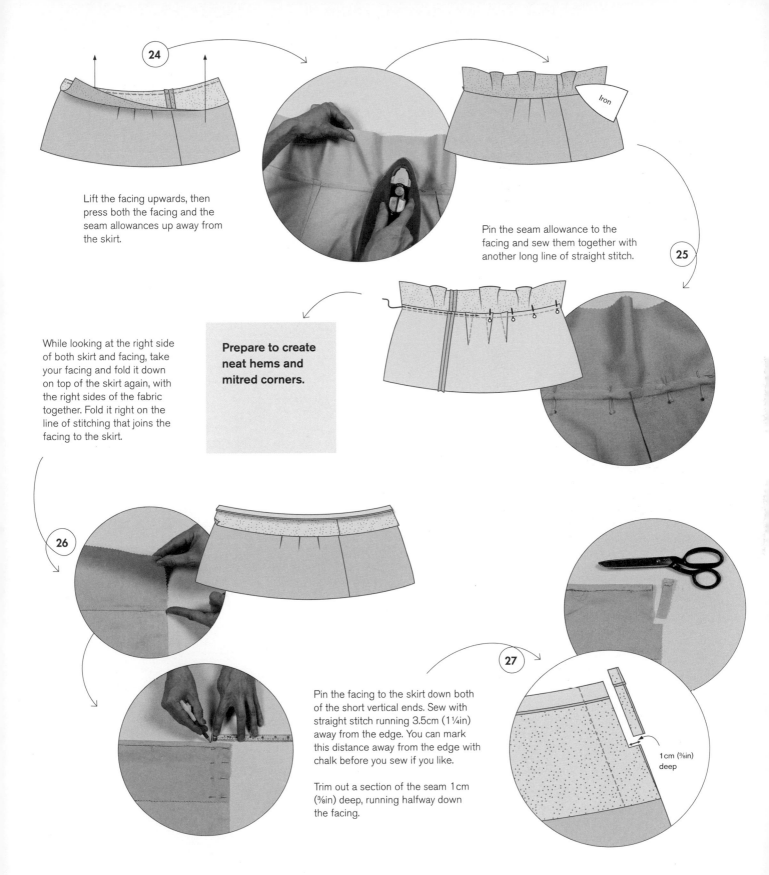

24

Lift the facing upwards, then press both the facing and the seam allowances up away from the skirt.

Pin the seam allowance to the facing and sew them together with another long line of straight stitch.

25

While looking at the right side of both skirt and facing, take your facing and fold it down on top of the skirt again, with the right sides of the fabric together. Fold it right on the line of stitching that joins the facing to the skirt.

Prepare to create neat hems and mitred corners.

26

27

Pin the facing to the skirt down both of the short vertical ends. Sew with straight stitch running 3.5cm (1¼in) away from the edge. You can mark this distance away from the edge with chalk before you sew if you like.

Trim out a section of the seam 1cm (⅜in) deep, running halfway down the facing.

1cm (⅜in) deep

Iron

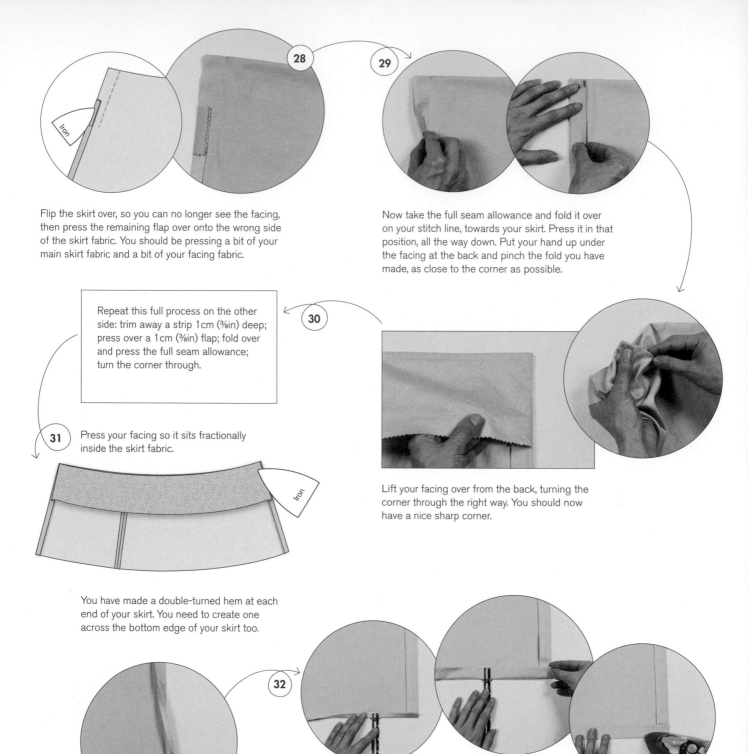

Flip the skirt over, so you can no longer see the facing, then press the remaining flap over onto the wrong side of the skirt fabric. You should be pressing a bit of your main skirt fabric and a bit of your facing fabric.

Now take the full seam allowance and fold it over on your stitch line, towards your skirt. Press it in that position, all the way down. Put your hand up under the facing at the back and pinch the fold you have made, as close to the corner as possible.

Repeat this full process on the other side: trim away a strip 1cm (⅜in) deep; press over a 1cm (⅜in) flap; fold over and press the full seam allowance; turn the corner through.

Press your facing so it sits fractionally inside the skirt fabric.

Lift your facing over from the back, turning the corner through the right way. You should now have a nice sharp corner.

You have made a double-turned hem at each end of your skirt. You need to create one across the bottom edge of your skirt too.

Press a 1cm (⅜in) fold up all the way along the bottom. Then turn that up 2.5cm (1in) and press again. Let the fabric cool to ensure the creases stay.

TUTORIAL

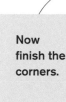

Now finish the corners.

(33)

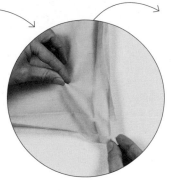

Open out all the turns you've pressed at one corner. You should be looking at the wrong side of the fabric.

Pinch the fabric, right sides together, to make a diagonal fold sloping up from the corner.

Match up the two sides so the lines created by the ironed creases sit directly on top of one another.

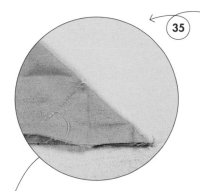

(35)

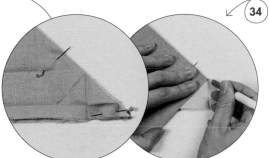

(34)

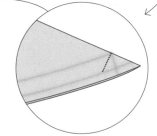

Stick a few pins in to hold the two sides together, then sew along the marked line, stopping your stitches right on the crease.

The stitching must sit at a right angle to the folded edge. Use a piece of paper or anything with a 90 degree corner to check this and draw the line in with chalk so that you can follow it when you sew.

You are going to sew a very short line of stitching, shown by the dotted line in this illustration.

(36)

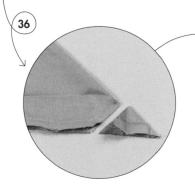

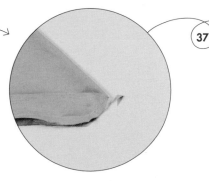

(37)

Once sewn, trim off the corner of fabric, 3 or 4mm (⅛in) away from your stitching.

Then snip off the very corner, getting as close to your stitching as you dare. This will allow you to open up that tiny seam and press it flat, in the next step.

Now open up the corner and turn the double-pressed hems over towards the back of the skirt. Press the corner. Look how beautiful it is!

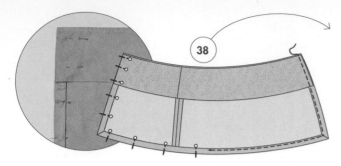

38

Rearrange the ironed hems and pin them down all the way round. Sew them down with a line of straight stitch that runs next to the inner folded edge. You will also be sewing over your facing, which will help to keep it where it should be.

All that's left to do is make a fastening for your skirt.

You need to sew a press stud to your skirt at the point where the smaller rectangle starts to overlap the long rectangle when wrapped around you.

Put your skirt on and pin it into the position you would like it to sit. Put a big stitch with long thread through both layers of your skirt where the front layer overlaps the top corner of the back layer. Pull the front layer away slowly and snip the threads between the layers, so some bits of thread remain stuck through both layers of the skirt. Take the skirt off.

39

40

Hand sew the second half of the press stud on top of the other marker stitch. This one will be sitting somewhere near the corner that you positioned on your hip in step 8 and will be on the finished side of the skirt.

You need to sew it to the inside of the skirt. Try to sew it so that your stitches go through the facing and just catch the main fabric, so they don't show on the outside.

Your stitch shows you where you need to position the first half of your press stud. It will be on the smaller of the two skirt rectangles, fairly near the seam that joins the two.

You also need to fasten the sloping edge of the small rectangle to the main body of the skirt. You can do this with buttons, a zip or with press studs that are invisible from the outside. If you are doing this with press studs, just hand sew two or three down the tilting front edge of the smaller rectangle, so they can't be seen from the outside.

41

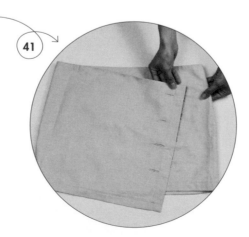

To fasten with buttons
Create your buttonholes fairly close to the edge of the smaller rectangle at the front. See also page 77 of the Shirt Dress tutorial.

Put the skirt on again and fasten the press stud. Tilt the front rectangle to the position you want it and put a line of pins running along this edge, but on the back layer of the skirt. The pins are just a rough sketch to indicate where you want your front flap to sit. Take the skirt off and reposition the front part, using the pins as a guide.

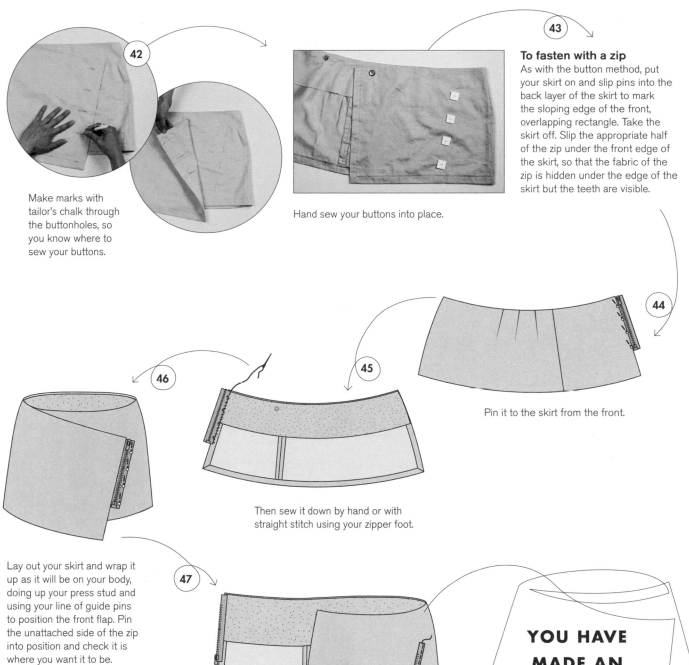

42

Make marks with tailor's chalk through the buttonholes, so you know where to sew your buttons.

Hand sew your buttons into place.

43

To fasten with a zip

As with the button method, put your skirt on and slip pins into the back layer of the skirt to mark the sloping edge of the front, overlapping rectangle. Take the skirt off. Slip the appropriate half of the zip under the front edge of the skirt, so that the fabric of the zip is hidden under the edge of the skirt but the teeth are visible.

44

Pin it to the skirt from the front.

45

Then sew it down by hand or with straight stitch using your zipper foot.

46

Lay out your skirt and wrap it up as it will be on your body, doing up your press stud and using your line of guide pins to position the front flap. Pin the unattached side of the zip into position and check it is where you want it to be.

47

Undo your open-ended zip completely, so it is in two halves, and sew the second half of the zip into place with a line of straight stitch using your zipper foot.

YOU HAVE MADE AN ASYMMETRIC MINI SKIRT!

Asymmetric mini skirt

1

Linda wears an Asymmetric Mini Skirt made with a stiff pale blue leatherette and a contrasting black wool. The skirt sits above her natural hip, almost at her waistline. The skirt has no visible fastening and is instead held closed with a series of press studs running along the top and down the front edge of the overlapping fabrics.

2

Kristina wears a longer version
of the Asymmetric Mini Skirt,
made in a heavy wool. The front,
overlapping side of the skirt
has been tilted sharply to create
a large overhang at the bottom
edge. The skirt fastens with a
contrasting exposed zip.

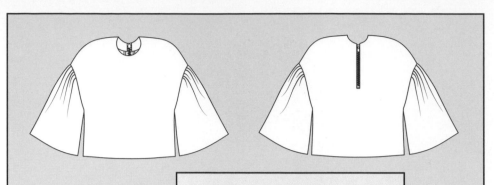

MATERIALS NEEDED

Fabric

Fabric for facing

Small square of fusible interfacing

Zip: 15 or 18cm (6 or 7in)

Guide garment (for neckline)

SUITABLE FABRIC

Most non-stretchy fabrics will work for this top. Crisp, thin cotton, thicker, heavier fabric or something floppy with drape will all work. Something stiff will give it structure, something drapey will let it hang more loosely. Avoid transparent fabrics.

BODY MEASUREMENTS NEEDED

Full bust

Shoulder peak to shoulder peak

Nape of neck to actual hip

Nape of neck to under bust

PIECES TO CUT

Front   Back

Facings

Sleeve

Sleeve

Zip facing

MATHS TO DO

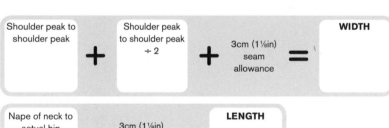

Shoulder peak to shoulder peak **+** Shoulder peak to shoulder peak ÷ 2 **+** 3cm (1⅛in) seam allowance **=** **WIDTH**

Nape of neck to actual hip **+** 3cm (1⅛in) for hem and seam allowance **=** **LENGTH**

Nape of neck to under bust **×** 3 **=** **SLEEVE WIDTH**

CAPE SLEEVED TOP

This flowing top has wide sleeves that are gathered at the top and cropped to hang in line with the hem, to create a cape-like illusion. The neckline is finished with bias binding or a facing; it can fit closely if the optional zip opening at the back is added, or it can be made wide so that it doesn't require a zip. This top can be made so long that it becomes a dress.

03

RECTANGLES

You're going to begin by cutting the rectangle that will form the front of the top.

1

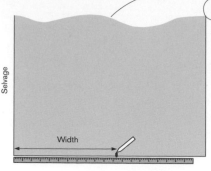

Measure your WIDTH along the bottom edge of your fabric and mark that point with chalk.

2

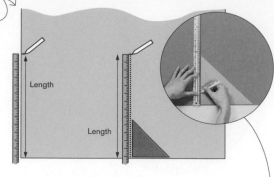

Measure the LENGTH upwards from that mark and square a line up to that point with chalk. Measure the LENGTH up the selvage edge of the fabric, too, and mark.

3

Now you're going to cut a neckline in your front piece. You can cut a small neckline in the top if you're adding a zip at the back, as that will allow your head to fit through. If you're cutting a large neck opening you don't need to add a zip, so skip steps 7 to 26.

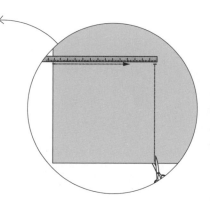

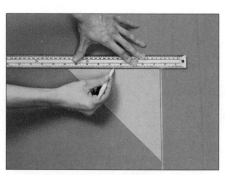

Lay your metre stick out so it touches both LENGTH marks and square a line with chalk that joins the two, forming a rectangle. Cut out your rectangle.

4

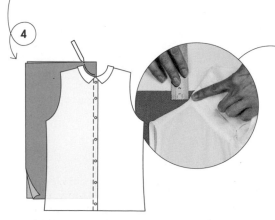

Fold your front piece in half and position your guide garment on top of it, so the fold of the fabric is sitting beneath the centre of your guide garment and the neck sits about 1.5cm (⅝in) below the top edge of your fabric.

Mark the position of the top of the neckline seam onto your fabric with chalk, and the bottom of the scoop of the neckline.

You can either sketch out a neckline following the one on your guide garment, or remove the guide garment and draw a round neckline using a bowl or plate.

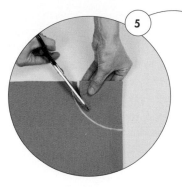

5

Cut away just inside the line you have drawn.

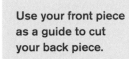

6

Use your front piece as a guide to cut your back piece.

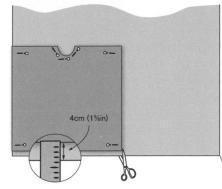

4cm (1⅝in)

Lay your front piece on your fabric so that the bottom edge sits 4cm (1⅝in) above the bottom edge of your fabric. Pin it down to keep it in place and cut around it.

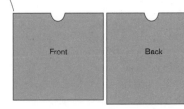

Front   Back

Now you have a front piece and a slightly longer back piece.

7

You can add a zip to the back piece.

Cut a small square of fabric 6 x 6cm (2⅜ x 2⅜in). Cut a piece of fusible interfacing the same size and iron them so they stick together.

8

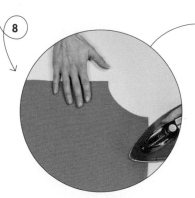

9

Fold your back piece in half vertically, with wrong sides together. Press the fold at the top to form a crease.

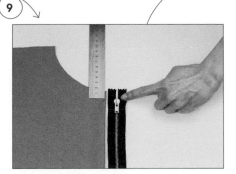

Lay your zip next to the fold so the zip pull sits about 1cm (⅜in) below the top edge.

10

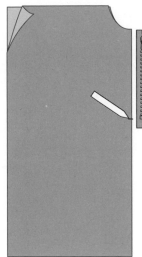

Mark with chalk the point where the bottom metal stopper of your zip sits. You're going to position your square of fabric right over this mark.

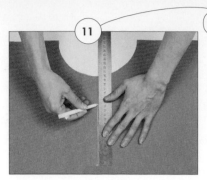
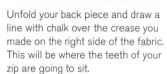

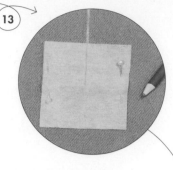

Unfold your back piece and draw a line with chalk over the crease you made on the right side of the fabric. This will be where the teeth of your zip are going to sit.

Fold your little square in half and in half again and position the centre folded point over the bottom point of your chalk line.

Unfold it in this position and pin it down. Re-draw the bottom of your chalk line. You are going to sew a three-sided rectangle around the chalk line, creating a hole for your zip teeth to stick out of.

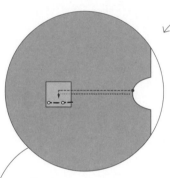
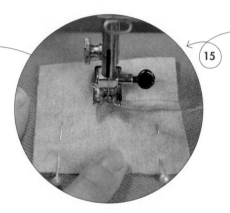
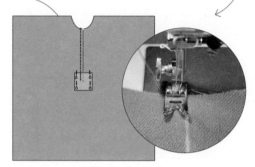

Put the foot down again and sew across the chalk line until your needle is 5mm (³⁄₁₆in) away from it on the other side.

Sew down until your stitching is parallel with the bottom of the chalk line, then with the needle in the down position, lift the machine foot and swivel your fabric 90 degrees.

Start your line of stitching at your neckline, with the needle sitting 5mm (³⁄₁₆in) away from your chalk line.

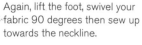
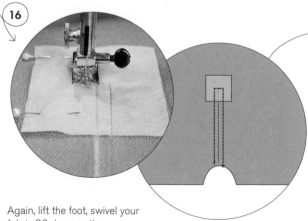
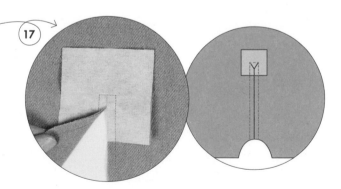

Again, lift the foot, swivel your fabric 90 degrees then sew up towards the neckline.

Snip into your fabric along the chalk line, but stop cutting about 1.5cm (⅝in) from the bottom stitches. Snip diagonally outwards from the end of your snipped line, towards the corners of the stitched rectangle you have made. Stop your snipping just before you hit your stitches.

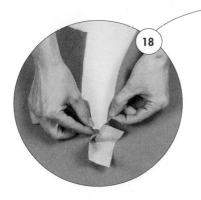

18

Now grab the little square of fabric and push it towards the wrong side of your fabric.

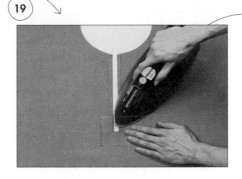

19

Flip your fabric piece over so you're looking at the wrong side and pull the square all the way through. Press it down, pressing an even fold of fabric on each side of the gap, so the stitching is just visible on this side.

Before you insert the zip, you're going to mark and cut the facing, which will finish off your neckline.

20

You need to cut three pieces of facing, two for the back and one for the front. Use the instructions on page 59 of the Deco Drape Dress tutorial to mark and cut your front facing piece.

For the back facing pieces:

Fold one corner out of the way and rest the back piece on your facing fabric, with right sides together and the pressed edge sitting 2cm (¾in) away from the edge of your facing fabric. Then cut out the same neckline shape.

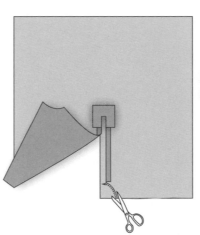

21

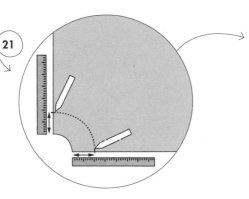

Use your ruler to make several marks 8cm (3⅛in) away from the cut neck edge, then sketch a curved chalk line joining the marks. Cut along the curved line. Flip this first piece over and use it as a guide to cut a second piece that is a mirror image of the first.

Put your facing pieces to one side now – it's time to insert the zip.

22

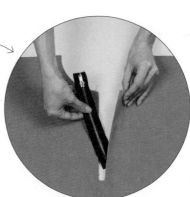

With your back piece right side up, slip your zip under the rectangular gap.

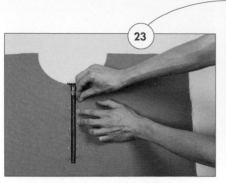

23

Pin it into place, keeping the opening the same width all the way up. Roughly hand sew your zip in place with big stitches and remove the pins. You will unpick these stitches later.

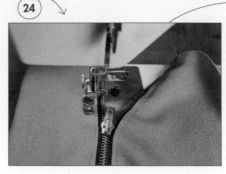

24

Put the zipper foot onto your sewing machine and sew around the zip. Start at the top left with the zip partially unzipped.

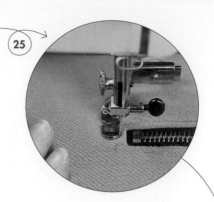

25

Sew down to the zip pull then with the needle in the down position, lift the foot and manoeuvre the zip pull upwards past the foot, closing the zip. Continue sewing downwards until you are just past the zip stopper. Pivot your garment and sew over the end of the zip.

26

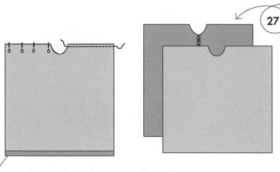

27

Lay the back piece out with the front piece on top, right sides together. Pin them together along the shoulder edges and sew with straight stitch, running 1.5cm (⅝in) away from the edge.

Now join your front piece to your back piece at the shoulder seams.

Pivot again and sew towards your neckline, pausing below the zip pull to manoeuvre it below your machine foot, then continue sewing to the very top.

28

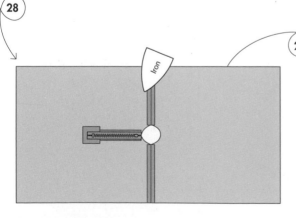

Press the seams open.

Iron

29

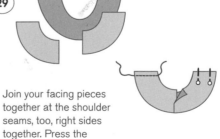

Join your facing pieces together at the shoulder seams, too, right sides together. Press the seams open.

Now join your facing to your main garment.

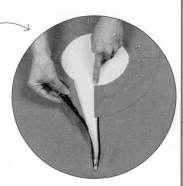

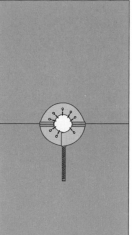

30

Lay your garment out with the right side facing up and unzip the zip. Position the facing on top of the neckhole, right sides together.

Try to match the shoulder seams if possible. There should be a bit of facing fabric extending beyond the zip teeth on both sides.

31

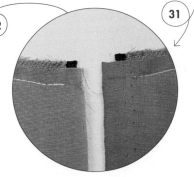

Sew the facing to the garment all the way around the neckline, starting your stitching just slightly inland of the zip teeth, so you're not sewing over them.

32

Run your stitches 1cm (⅜in) away from the raw edge, stopping them just before the zip teeth at the other side. Trim the seam down so it's about 5mm (³⁄₁₆in) deep and snip into it to release the tension.

33

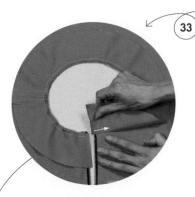

Lift the facing and stitch it to the snipped seam allowance. For more detailed instructions on this, see the Deco Drape Dress, step 32, on page 61.

34

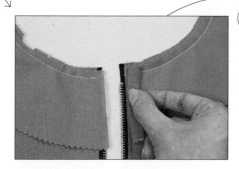

Tuck the ends of the facing in so they sit behind the zip teeth, then fold the facing up over the neckhole so it sits on the wrong side of the garment.

35

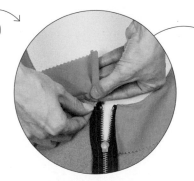

Press it in that position, with the ends tucked under. Hand stitch the folded ends just behind the zip teeth.

Now you are going to cut the two rectangles that will become your sleeves and prepare your top for attaching them.

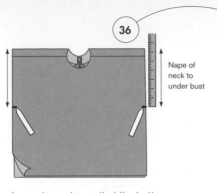

36

Nape of neck to under bust

Lay out your top so that the bottom edges sit on top of one another, wrong sides together. You will need to drag the front piece downwards, making the shoulder seams sit slightly towards the front. Measure your nape of neck to under bust downwards from the top fold and mark that point in chalk on both sides.

37

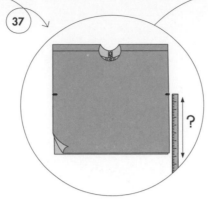

?

Measure how far the mark is from the bottom edge of your top and write that down here.

38

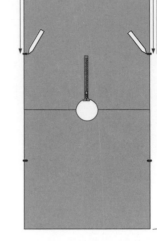

Open your top out and measure this distance upwards from the bottom edges of the garment at the back, marking these points in chalk.

Prepare your sleeves by gathering them at the top, then attach them to the main garment.

To work out the sleeve length, take that measurement you wrote down in step 37. Divide that by four, then add that to the original number. This is your SLEEVE LENGTH.

Mark out two sleeve rectangles using your SLEEVE LENGTH and SLEEVE WIDTH (from page 40) and cut. Yes, they are very wide!

39

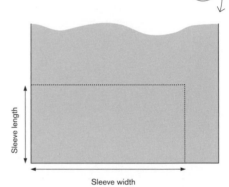

Sleeve length

Sleeve width

40

Neaten all four edges of your sleeves with zigzag stitch. Divide your SLEEVE WIDTH by four. Measure that distance inwards from each side of your sleeve and make a chalk mark. You are going to gather the section of fabric between these two marks.

41

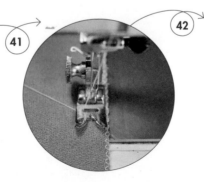

Set your machine to sew the longest straight stitch possible and sew two parallel lines between the two marks. Sew the first line so the edge of your machine foot runs along the raw edge of your fabric.

42

If your fabric has naturally gathered after sewing the first line, spread it out again so you are not sewing your second line of stitching onto gathered fabric. Sew your second line with the edge of the machine foot running along your first line of stitches. Repeat on your other sleeve.

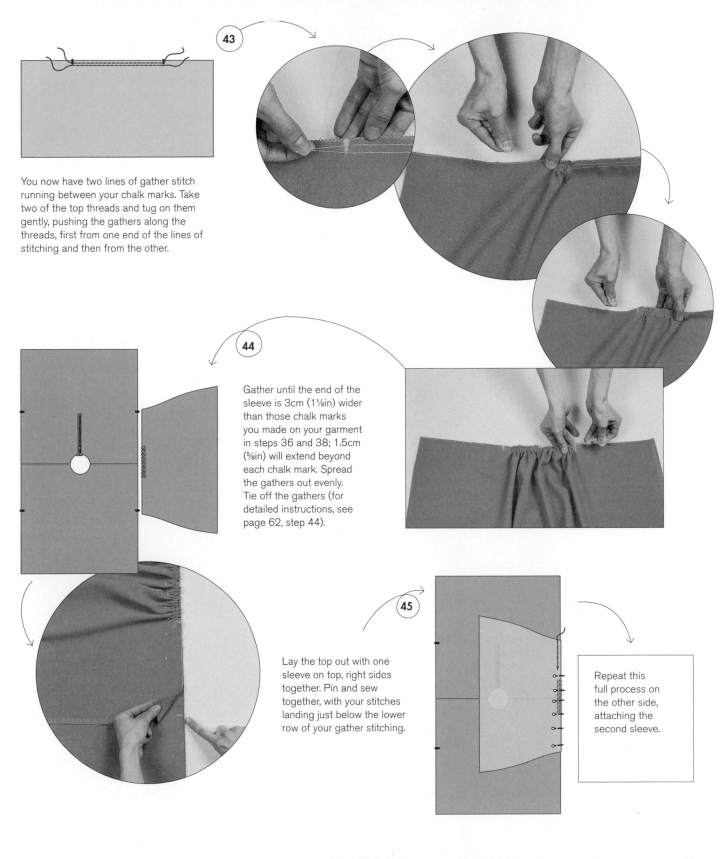

43

You now have two lines of gather stitch running between your chalk marks. Take two of the top threads and tug on them gently, pushing the gathers along the threads, first from one end of the lines of stitching and then from the other.

44

Gather until the end of the sleeve is 3cm (1⅛in) wider than those chalk marks you made on your garment in steps 36 and 38; 1.5cm (⅝in) will extend beyond each chalk mark. Spread the gathers out evenly. Tie off the gathers (for detailed instructions, see page 62, step 44).

45

Lay the top out with one sleeve on top, right sides together. Pin and sew together, with your stitches landing just below the lower row of your gather stitching.

Repeat this full process on the other side, attaching the second sleeve.

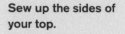

Sew up the sides of your top.

Fold the top so that the bottom edges and the bottom edges of the sleeves are aligned, right sides together. You're going to sew a 4cm- (1⅝in-) deep seam on both sides. It makes sense to sew from the bottom edge towards the armpits on both sides, so place your pins so that you'll be able to remove them as you sew.

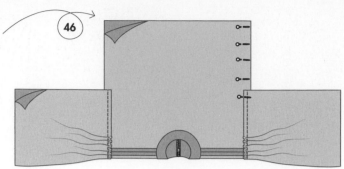

(46)

(47)

Mark a point with chalk 4cm (1⅝in) inland from the edge, so you know where to start your line of stitching.

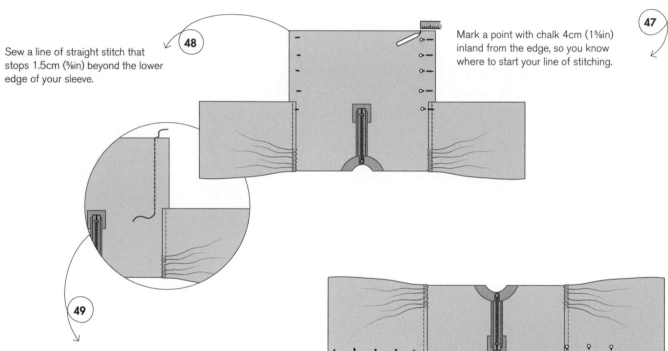

(48)

Sew a line of straight stitch that stops 1.5cm (⅝in) beyond the lower edge of your sleeve.

(49)

You're going to sew a line of straight stitch from the end of each sleeve until you reach the end of the lines of stitching you just made. Most importantly, you are going to sew over the seam that joins the sleeve to the top so that it folds towards the top on both sides (the side you can see and the side that is hidden!). Press this seam with the iron to help it sit that way.

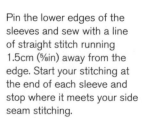

(50)

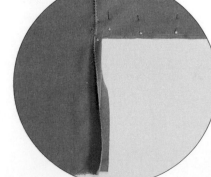

Pin the lower edges of the sleeves and sew with a line of straight stitch running 1.5cm (⅝in) away from the edge. Start your stitching at the end of each sleeve and stop where it meets your side seam stitching.

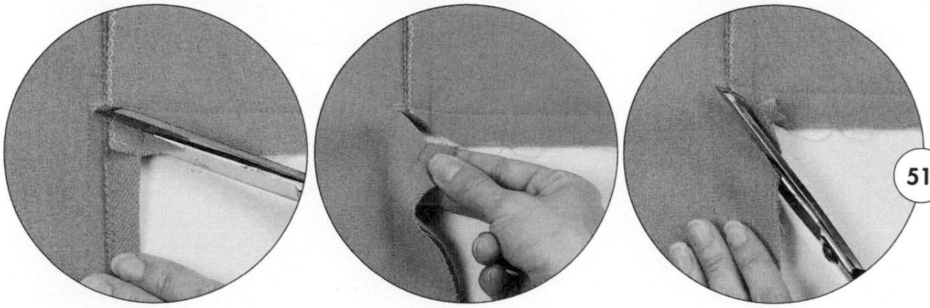

Snip a triangle of fabric away at the armpit corner of each sleeve.

51

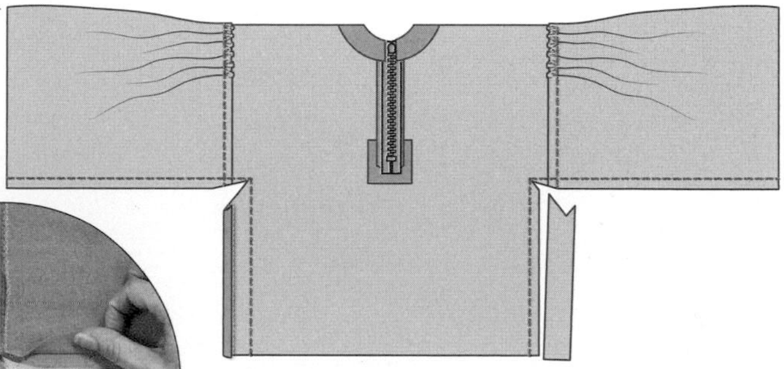

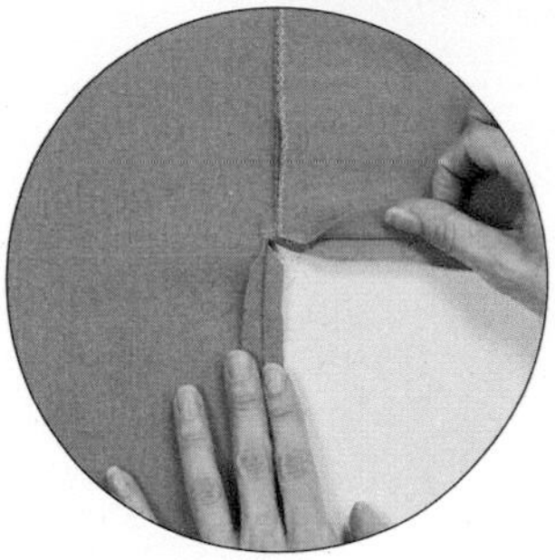

52

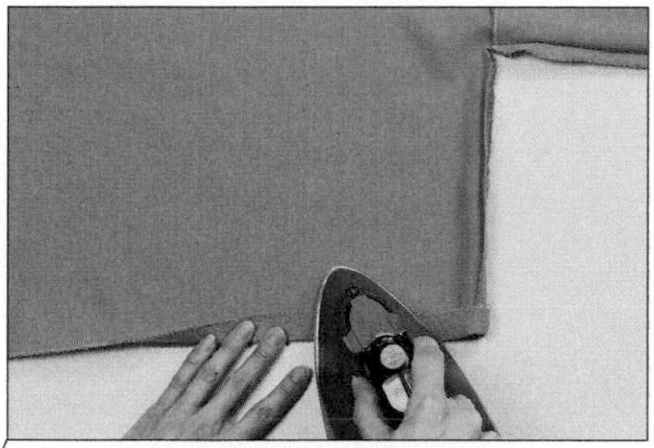

Zigzag the raw edge at the bottom of your top and press up a 1.5cm (⅝in) fold all the way around. Pin and sew the fold in place, with your stitches running close to the zigzagged edge.

This will allow you to open out the side seams and trim off a strip of fabric so you are left with a 1.5cm (⅝in) seam allowance. Then iron your side and underarm seams open and zigzag all the raw edges.

53

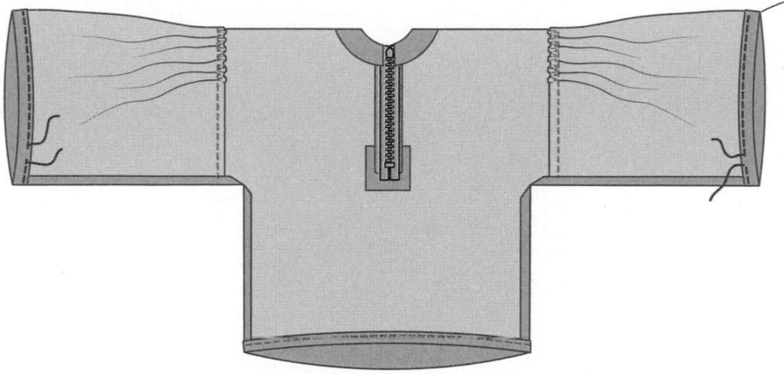

Try your top on and look at the sleeve length. This top looks best when the end of the sleeve nearest to your body hangs at exactly the same level as the main hem of your garment. Decide how much fabric you need to fold up to make this happen, then press up a single or double hem at the ends of your sleeves and sew in place.

YOU HAVE MADE A CAPE SLEEVED TOP!

Cape sleeved top

1

Courtney wears a version of the Cape Sleeved Top made in a bold, patterned soft satin. It has been cut so long that it has become a dress. The neckline is wide and scooped so there is no zip at the back.

2

Mairead's version of the top is made in quilting-weight cotton. The top has a narrow neckline and a contrasting zip at the centre back.

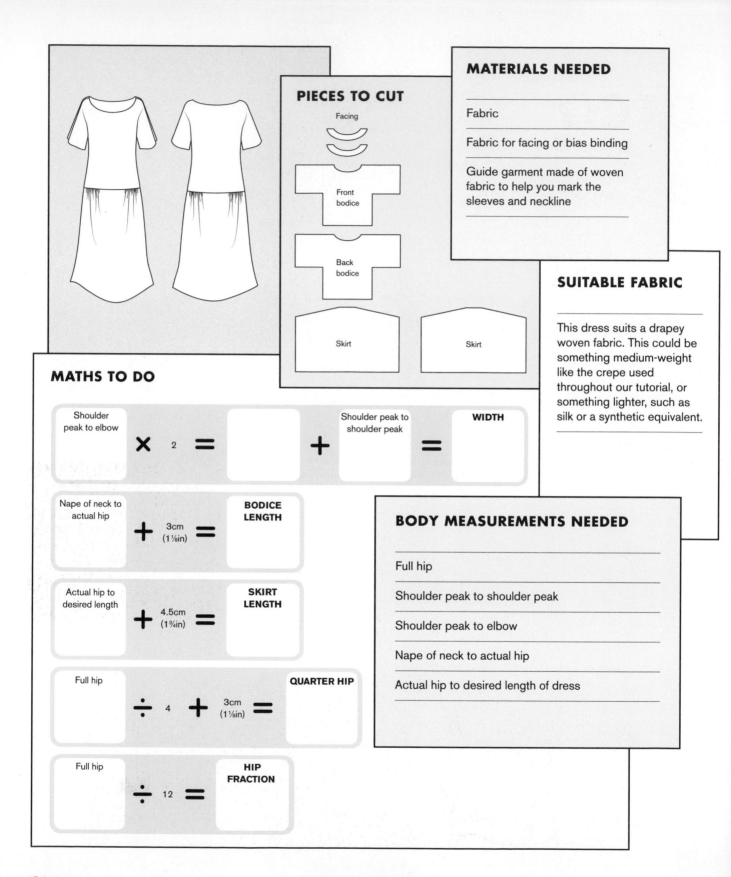

PIECES TO CUT

Facing

Front bodice

Back bodice

Skirt

Skirt

MATERIALS NEEDED

Fabric

Fabric for facing or bias binding

Guide garment made of woven fabric to help you mark the sleeves and neckline

SUITABLE FABRIC

This dress suits a drapey woven fabric. This could be something medium-weight like the crepe used throughout our tutorial, or something lighter, such as silk or a synthetic equivalent.

MATHS TO DO

| Shoulder peak to elbow | ✕ 2 | = | | + | Shoulder peak to shoulder peak | = | WIDTH |

| Nape of neck to actual hip | + 3cm (1⅛in) | = | BODICE LENGTH |

| Actual hip to desired length | + 4.5cm (1¾in) | = | SKIRT LENGTH |

| Full hip | ÷ 4 | + 3cm (1⅛in) | = | QUARTER HIP |

| Full hip | ÷ 12 | = | HIP FRACTION |

BODY MEASUREMENTS NEEDED

Full hip

Shoulder peak to shoulder peak

Shoulder peak to elbow

Nape of neck to actual hip

Actual hip to desired length of dress

DECO DRAPE DRESS

This dress features a wide neckline that can be finished with a facing or bias binding. It can be made as a midi, a mini or a maxi, and can have optional split sleeves. The skirt can be made with an asymmetric hem.

04

RECTANGLES

First you're going to make your front bodice piece.

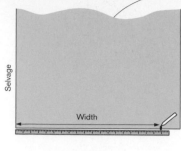

1 Measure your WIDTH across one edge of your fabric and make a mark there with chalk.

2 Measure your BODICE LENGTH upwards from that mark, squaring a line with chalk up to that point. Measure your BODICE LENGTH up the side of your fabric too, making a mark, then draw a line joining this mark with the tip of the vertical chalk line you have made.

While you're cutting rectangles, you may as well cut out the two rectangles that form your skirt.

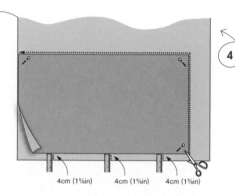

4 Lay your fabric out again and lay your first rectangle on top of it. Position it 4cm (1⅝in) above the bottom edge of your fabric. Your back piece is going to be longer than your front piece. Cut around the rectangle, including that extra depth. Put the deeper rectangle to one side for now.

4cm (1⅝in)   4cm (1⅝in)   4cm (1⅝in)

3 Cut out the rectangle you have drawn.

This rectangle is the beginning of your front bodice piece.

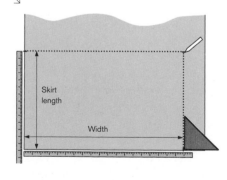

5 Each skirt piece uses the same WIDTH measurement as your bodice pieces, so begin in the same way, measuring the WIDTH out along the bottom edge of your fabric. Square a line upwards that is as long as your SKIRT LENGTH.

Skirt length

Width

As before, mark this distance up the side of your fabric too, square across then cut out the rectangle. Use your first rectangle as a guide to cut out an identical second rectangle. Fold these pieces up and put them to one side for now.

You're going to shape your front bodice piece to form sleeves, by cutting away a small rectangle from each bottom corner.

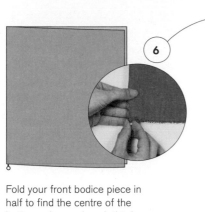

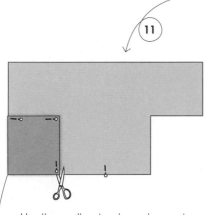

Fold your front bodice piece in half to find the centre of the bottom edge, and mark this by slipping a pin in.

6

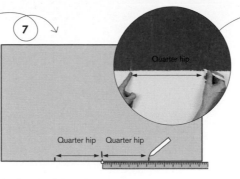

7

Unfold the fabric, then measure your QUARTER HIP out from the marker pin on both sides, marking those points with chalk.

8

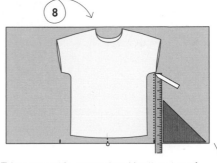

Take your guide garment and lay it on top of your rectangle, positioning it centrally. Square a line upwards from one of your quarter-hip chalk marks until it is level with the armpit point of your guide garment.

9

10

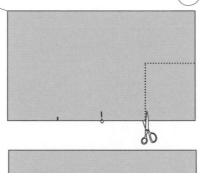

Put the guide garment to one side. Cut along these two lines.

11

Use the small rectangle you have cut away as a guide to cut a rectangle exactly the same size on the other side of your fabric piece.

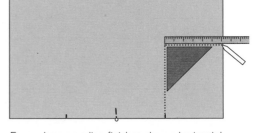

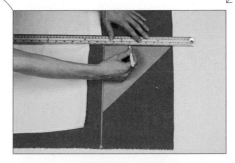

From where your line finishes, draw a horizontal line out to the edge of your fabric.

Now you are going to mark out a neckline.

We demonstrate how to mark out a wide, low neckline, but you can choose to make a smaller neckline, like the one on the Segment Dress on page 83.

12

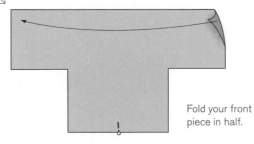

Fold your front piece in half.

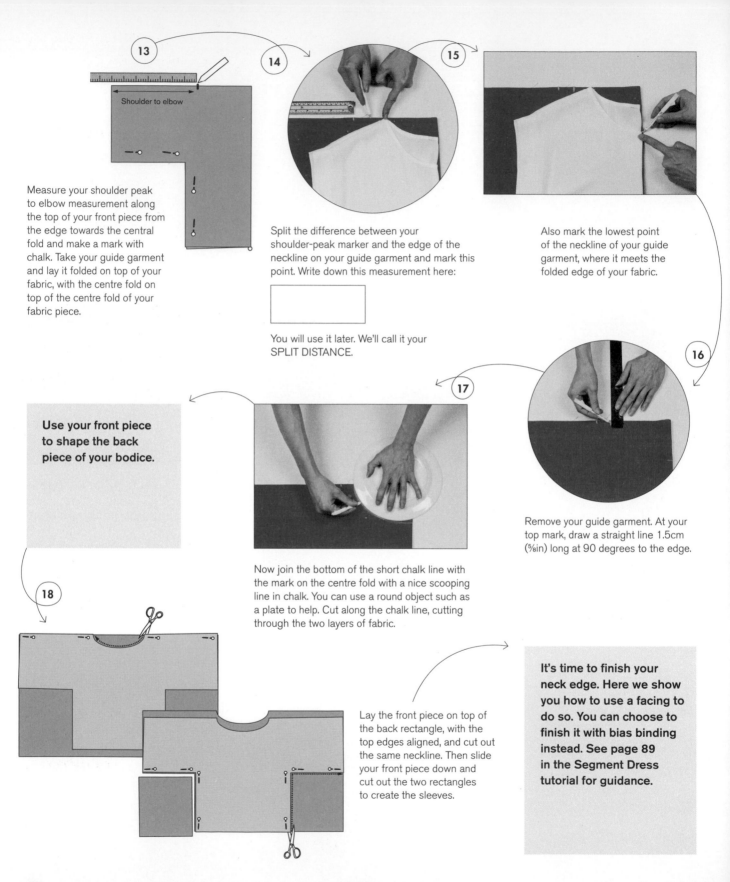

13

Shoulder to elbow

Measure your shoulder peak to elbow measurement along the top of your front piece from the edge towards the central fold and make a mark with chalk. Take your guide garment and lay it folded on top of your fabric, with the centre fold on top of the centre fold of your fabric piece.

14

Split the difference between your shoulder-peak marker and the edge of the neckline on your guide garment and mark this point. Write down this measurement here:

You will use it later. We'll call it your SPLIT DISTANCE.

15

Also mark the lowest point of the neckline of your guide garment, where it meets the folded edge of your fabric.

16

Remove your guide garment. At your top mark, draw a straight line 1.5cm (⅝in) long at 90 degrees to the edge.

17

Now join the bottom of the short chalk line with the mark on the centre fold with a nice scooping line in chalk. You can use a round object such as a plate to help. Cut along the chalk line, cutting through the two layers of fabric.

Use your front piece to shape the back piece of your bodice.

18

Lay the front piece on top of the back rectangle, with the top edges aligned, and cut out the same neckline. Then slide your front piece down and cut out the two rectangles to create the sleeves.

It's time to finish your neck edge. Here we show you how to use a facing to do so. You can choose to finish it with bias binding instead. See page 89 in the Segment Dress tutorial for guidance.

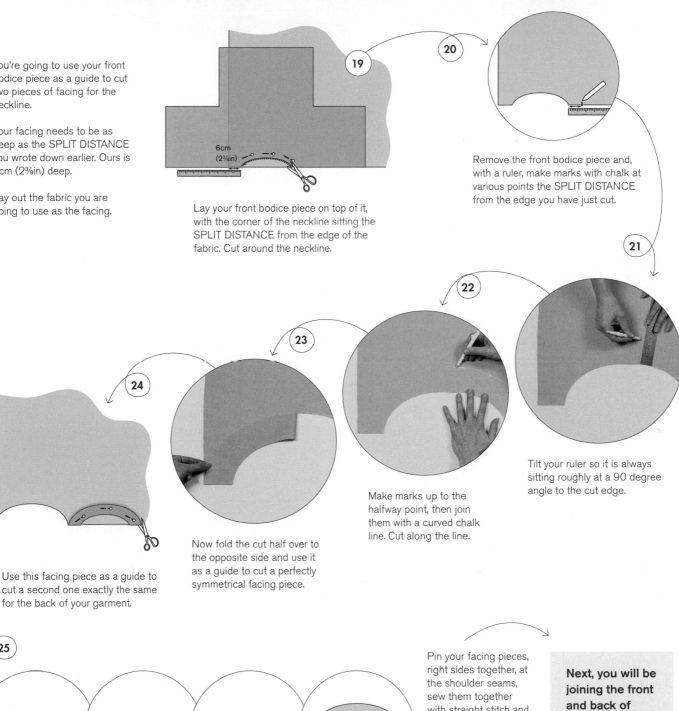

You're going to use your front bodice piece as a guide to cut two pieces of facing for the neckline.

Your facing needs to be as deep as the SPLIT DISTANCE you wrote down earlier. Ours is 6cm (2⅜in) deep.

Lay out the fabric you are going to use as the facing.

19

6cm
(2⅜in)

Lay your front bodice piece on top of it, with the corner of the neckline sitting the SPLIT DISTANCE from the edge of the fabric. Cut around the neckline.

20

Remove the front bodice piece and, with a ruler, make marks with chalk at various points the SPLIT DISTANCE from the edge you have just cut.

21

22

Tilt your ruler so it is always sitting roughly at a 90 degree angle to the cut edge.

23

Make marks up to the halfway point, then join them with a curved chalk line. Cut along the line.

24

Now fold the cut half over to the opposite side and use it as a guide to cut a perfectly symmetrical facing piece.

Use this facing piece as a guide to cut a second one exactly the same for the back of your garment.

25

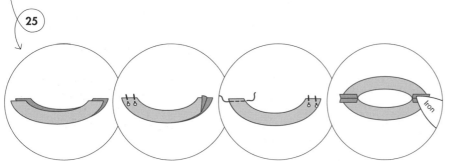

Pin your facing pieces, right sides together, at the shoulder seams, sew them together with straight stitch and press the seams open. Zigzag all the way round the outer edge of your facing.

Next, you will be joining the front and back of your bodice at the shoulders.

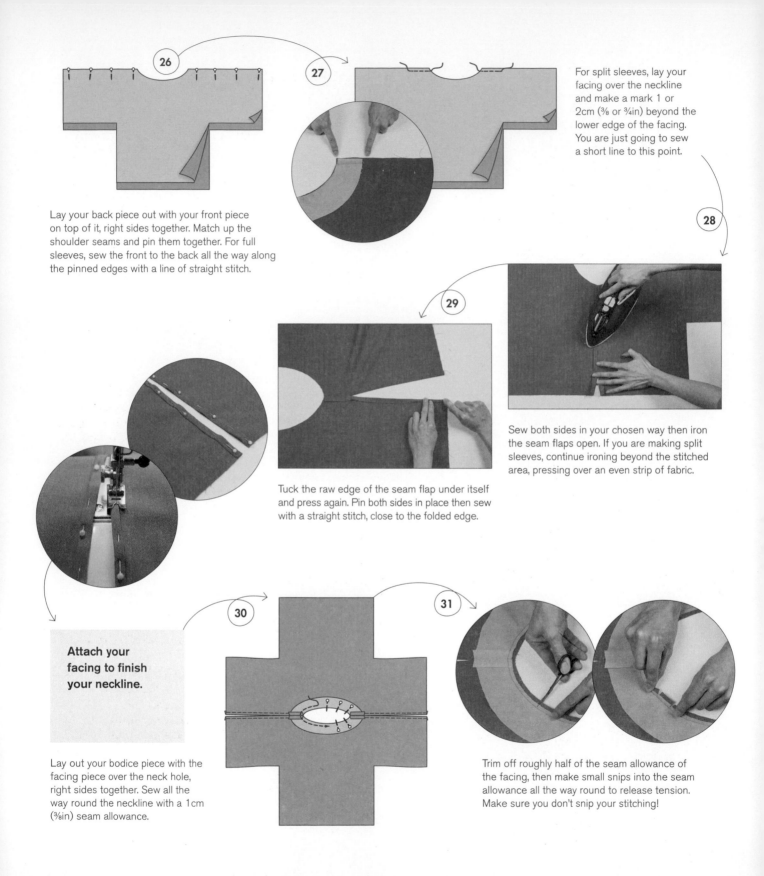

Lay your back piece out with your front piece on top of it, right sides together. Match up the shoulder seams and pin them together. For full sleeves, sew the front to the back all the way along the pinned edges with a line of straight stitch.

For split sleeves, lay your facing over the neckline and make a mark 1 or 2cm (⅜ or ¾in) beyond the lower edge of the facing. You are just going to sew a short line to this point.

Sew both sides in your chosen way then iron the seam flaps open. If you are making split sleeves, continue ironing beyond the stitched area, pressing over an even strip of fabric.

Tuck the raw edge of the seam flap under itself and press again. Pin both sides in place then sew with a straight stitch, close to the folded edge.

Attach your facing to finish your neckline.

Lay out your bodice piece with the facing piece over the neck hole, right sides together. Sew all the way round the neckline with a 1cm (⅜in) seam allowance.

Trim off roughly half of the seam allowance of the facing, then make small snips into the seam allowance all the way round to release tension. Make sure you don't snip your stitching!

TUTORIAL

You're going to sew your facing to the seam allowance to help it sit neatly hidden on the inside of your garment.

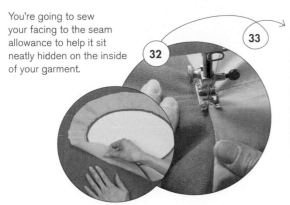

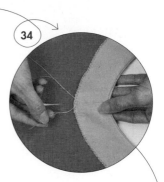

Pull the facing upwards away from the garment and position it over the arm of your sewing machine. The seam allowance should be sitting underneath the facing. Sew all the way round the neckline on the facing fabric with straight stitch, close to the seam that joins the facing to the main garment.

Lay your bodice out, wrong side up, and pull your facing through to this side. Press it so it can't be seen from the outside of the dress.

Put a few stitches in by hand at the shoulder seams on each side, catching the facing so it won't flip to the outside of your dress when you wear it.

You also need to make a mark down the unfolded vertical edge of the piece. This will determine how high you raise your hemline at the sides, so the bigger you make it, the more scooped your hem will appear and the bigger the folds will be on your skirt piece. We marked 12cm (4¾in) on this dress.

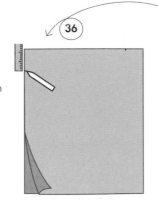

Take one of your skirt pieces and fold it in half down the middle. From the folded edge, measure your HIP FRACTION along the top edge and make a mark.

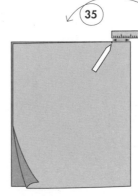

Now, prepare your skirt pieces ready to join them to the bodice.

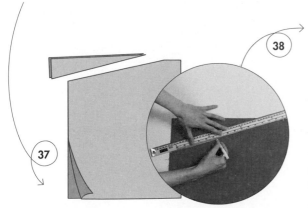

Use a metre stick to draw a straight line joining the two marks you have just made. Cut along that line.

Take the fabric triangles you just snipped away and use them as guides to cut away the same amount of fabric from your back skirt piece.

Zigzag along these top edges of your skirt pieces. While you're zigzagging, you can zigzag the bottom edges of your bodice pieces too.

You are going to sew two lines of gathering stitch that run parallel with the diagonal edges you have just created on your front and back skirt pieces.

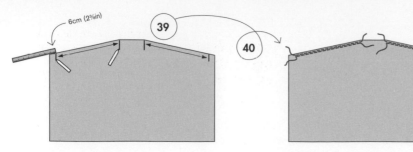

6cm (2⅜in)

(39)

(40)

Before you sew, measure 6cm (2⅜in) in from the edge of each piece and make a mark with chalk. This is where your gather stitching will begin. You are going to sew until your stitching is parallel with the point where the diagonal edge meets the straight edge at the top of your skirt piece. You can mark this point with chalk too, so it's easy to see. Set your machine to sew a long straight stitch – the longest your machine will allow.

Position your needle at the 6cm (2⅜in) mark and sew your first line of stitching 1.5cm (⅝in) inland from the sloping edge of your fabric. Don't run your stitches backwards at the start or end. Remove your fabric from your machine then snip the threads, leaving long thread tails. Reposition your fabric on the machine at the 6cm (2⅜in) mark, this time sewing your line 5mm (³⁄₁₆in) in from the sloping edge of the fabric. Again, don't run your stitches backwards at either end and leave long thread tails. Repeat this process along all four sloping edges.

Now you have two lines of stitching that run parallel with each of your diagonal edges. You are going to pull these stitches to create gathers.

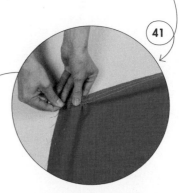

(41)

Take the two threads that sit on the same side of your fabric and gently tug them sideways, pushing crinkles into the fabric and then shifting the crinkles along the lines of thread.

(43)

(42)

Do the same thing with the two threads at the other end of your stitching too, pushing the gathers towards the centre.

Repeat this on the other side of your skirt piece, then compare the new width of the skirt piece to the bottom edge of your front bodice. Either add more gathers, or push out some of your gathers until the width of your skirt piece matches the width of your bodice piece.

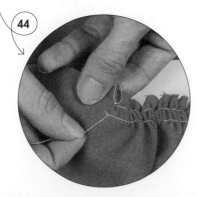

(44)

Once you have the right width, take one of the individual threads you have been pulling on and gently tug it. This will pull through a loop of thread from the other side of the fabric. Tease this loop through until both thread ends sit on the same side of the fabric, then tie them together with a few knots. Repeat with all of your thread ends, so your gathers don't slip out. Repeat this full process on your other skirt piece.

Attach your skirt pieces to the bodice of your dress.

Lay your bodice out flat, with one of your skirt pieces on top of it, right sides together. Match the gathered edge of the skirt with the bottom edge of the bodice piece.

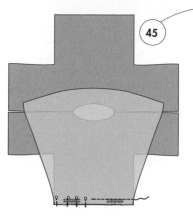

45

46

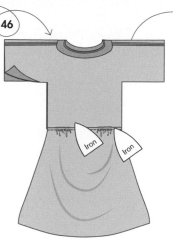

Pin then sew the two together, making sure the gathers are evenly distributed. Sew them together with a line of straight stitch that runs just below the lower line of your gathering stitch. This means both your lines of gathering stitch will be swallowed up by the seam allowance.

Repeat this with your second skirt piece. Press the seams you have made upwards, trying not to crush your gathers with the iron.

Now it's time to join the sides of your dress.

Lay the garment out so that the right sides are together, matching up your armpit points and the waist seams if possible. The bottom edges of the skirt pieces should sit on top of each other, but don't worry if they are mismatched.

Pin the front to the back of the dress, all the way under both sleeves and down both sides.

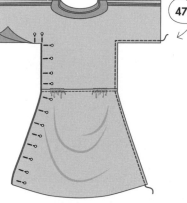

47

48

Sew the front to the back with a line of straight stitch. Your line will turn a corner at the armpit point. To make this corner sharp, sew up to the point where you need to turn then adjust your needle so it is in the down position, piercing the fabric. Lift your machine foot, twist your dress so it's facing the new direction you want to sew in, then put the foot down again and off you sew.

With both sides sewn, snip away small triangles of fabric at each armpit point. You can think of each triangle as an arrowhead, with the tip pointing towards your stitches right where they turn a corner.

49

These snips release the seams so you can open them out and press them.

All that's left to do is to hem the bottom edge of your dress and your sleeve ends. See page 77 of the Shirt Dress tutorial for instructions.

YOU HAVE MADE A DECO DRAPE DRESS!

Deco drape dress

1

Mairead's version of the dress is made in a light silk. It has full sleeves that do not have a split. The gathers at the front and back of the skirt are pushed into small sections that sit towards the sides of the dress. The neckline is finished with bias binding.

2

Linda wears a shorter version of the Deco Drape Dress, made in mint green lightweight synthetic charmeuse. The waistline sits slightly higher than the actual hip but remains loose. The skirt is cut asymetrically, with a deeper triangular section removed on the left side, causing it to rise up in more dramatic folds than on the right. The dress has split sleeves and a neckline finished with bias binding.

MATERIALS NEEDED

Fabric

Bias binding for neckline (can be bought, or made from the same fabric as the dress)

Small buttons (about 10)

Guide garment to mark out your sleeves. A dress or top made of woven, i.e non-stretchy, fabric will work perfectly. The garment should have sleeves

Newspaper to make template

SUITABLE FABRIC

This dress suits a thin or medium-weight cotton or similar fabric. It would work well as a day dress in a light denim or linen, or you could transform it into something more glamorous using a drapey fabric with a silky sheen.

BODY MEASUREMENTS NEEDED

Full bust

Full waist

Full hip

Nape to waist

Nape to under bust

MATHS TO DO

Full bust	**+**	10cm (4in) ease	**÷** 4	**=**	**QUARTER BUST**			

Full waist	**+**	8cm (3⅛in) ease	**÷** 4	**=**	**QUARTER WAIST**			

Full hip	**+**	16cm (6¼in) ease	**÷** 4	**=**		**+**	3cm (1⅛in) seam allowance	**=** **FRONT SKIRT WIDTH**

Under bust to waist	**=**	**TUCK LENGTH**

QUARTER BUST	**−**	**QUARTER WAIST**	**=**	**TUCK SPACE**

TUCK SPACE	**÷** 3	**=**	**÷** 2	**=** **TUCK DEPTH**

PIECES TO CUT

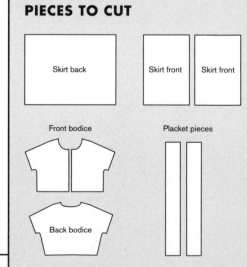

Skirt back

Skirt front   Skirt front

Front bodice   Placket pieces

Back bodice

SHIRT DRESS

This cute, versatile dress has a kimono-sleeved bodice that's shaped under the bust with tucks. The dress can be made with a scooped or V-shaped neck, which is finished with bias binding. Experiment with reducing ease at the waist for a more figure-hugging garment. Belt loops can be added so the dress can be drawn in at the waist. The length of the skirt is open for playing with!

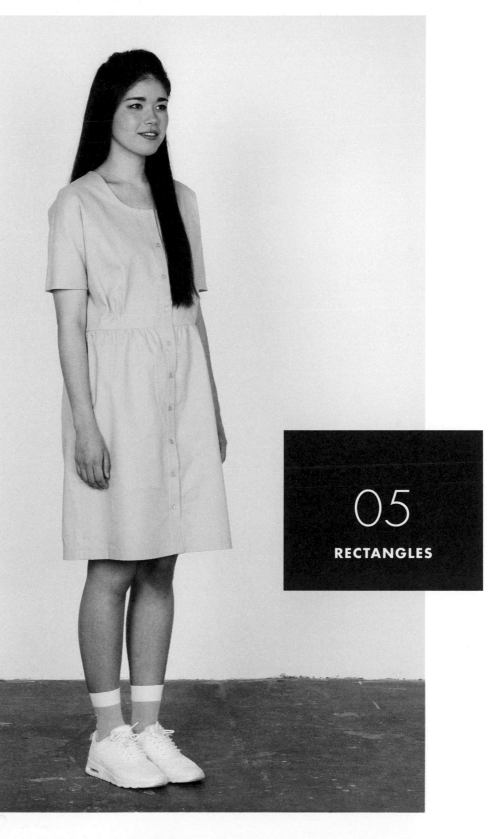

05

RECTANGLES

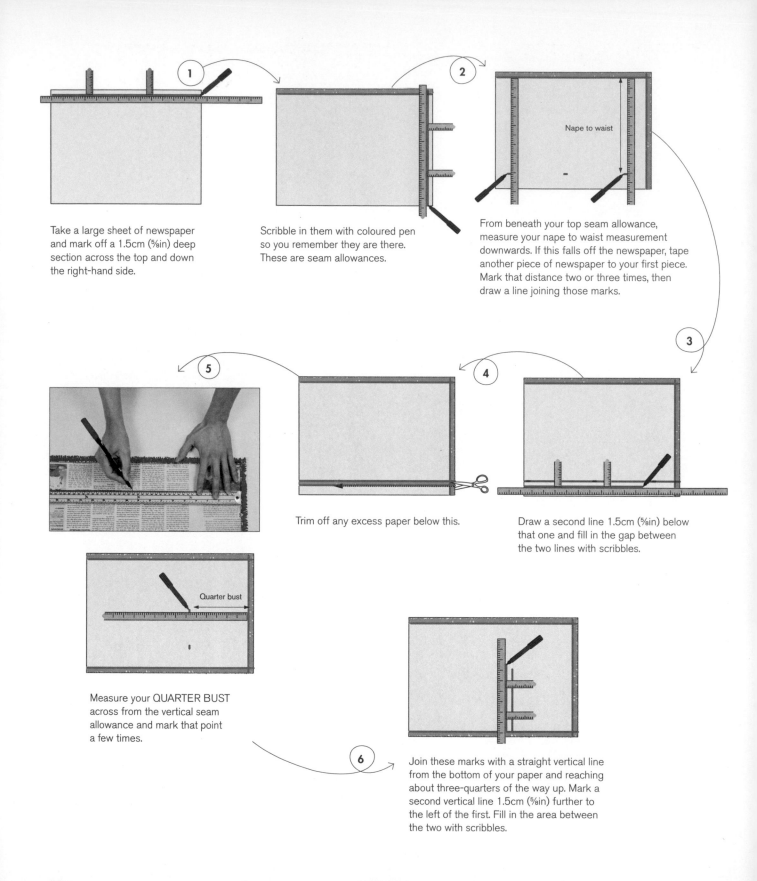

1 Take a large sheet of newspaper and mark off a 1.5cm (⅝in) deep section across the top and down the right-hand side.

2 Scribble in them with coloured pen so you remember they are there. These are seam allowances.

3 From beneath your top seam allowance, measure your nape to waist measurement downwards. If this falls off the newspaper, tape another piece of newspaper to your first piece. Mark that distance two or three times, then draw a line joining those marks.

Nape to waist

5 (image)

4 Trim off any excess paper below this.

Draw a second line 1.5cm (⅝in) below that one and fill in the gap between the two lines with scribbles.

Quarter bust

Measure your QUARTER BUST across from the vertical seam allowance and mark that point a few times.

6 Join these marks with a straight vertical line from the bottom of your paper and reaching about three-quarters of the way up. Mark a second vertical line 1.5cm (⅝in) further to the left of the first. Fill in the area between the two with scribbles.

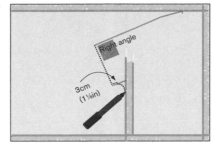

Lay your guide garment on top of your newspaper piece, lining up the centre of the garment with the inner edge of your vertical seam allowance strip. Draw a sloping shoulder edge onto your paper following your guide garment. This might change angle slightly at the shoulder point, so tip your ruler to reflect this. You can smooth out this point into a curve when you sew the front to the back later.

Mark the underside of the sleeve as well.

Remove your guide garment and draw a curve where the lower sleeve line meets the side seam. (See page 119 of the Ripple Wrap Blouse tutorial for a clever way of doing this.) Join the upper and lower sleeve lines with a line that sits at a right angle to them, 3cm (1⅛in) beyond the point where your curve meets the lower sleeve line.

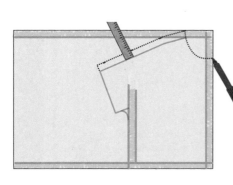

Add 1.5cm (⅝in) seam allowance above the shoulder line and fill in the gap with scribbles.

To make a V-shaped neck opening
Decide how low you want the point of your V to go, then draw a straight line from the shoulder point down that far, instead of sketching a scooped neckline.

Draw in a nice scooped neckline, using a curved object as a guide.

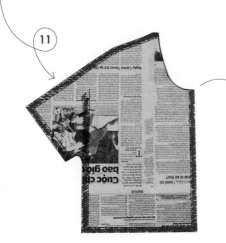

Cut out your shape.

Use the paper piece to cut two front pieces from your fabric.

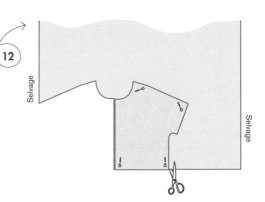

Pin your paper template to your fabric and cut around it, then unpin it, flip it over and cut a second piece that is a mirror image of your first.

You can mark and cut your skirt pieces now, too.

We added 16cm (6¼in) of ease to the full hip measurement to determine the FRONT SKIRT WIDTH. You can play with this measurement, making it wider to create a fuller skirt.

Decide how long you would like your dress to be. Measure down from your waist to wherever you would like your hem to hang, then add 4.5cm (1¾in) for seam and hem allowance. Write that number down here:

This is your SKIRT LENGTH.

⑬

To cut your back skirt piece, make a fold in your fabric and lay one of your front skirt pieces on top of it. Use it as a guide to cut your back piece, which is double the width of one of your front pieces.

Put your skirt pieces to one side for now.

⑭

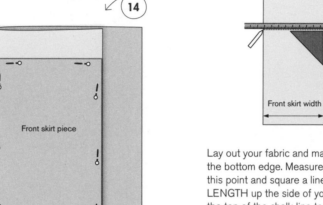

Lay out your fabric and mark your FRONT SKIRT WIDTH along the bottom edge. Measure your SKIRT LENGTH upwards from this point and square a line with chalk. Measure your SKIRT LENGTH up the side of your fabric, too, and join this point with the top of the chalk line to form a rectangle.

Cut out this piece and lay it out on your fabric, using it as a guide to cut a second rectangle exactly the same as your first.

It's time to sew the tucks into your front bodice pieces.

⑮

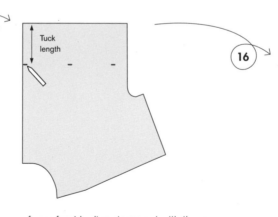

Lay one of your front bodice pieces out with the wrong side of the fabric facing up. You are working with the waist edge of the piece at the top and the shoulder edge at the bottom! Measure your TUCK LENGTH down from the top edge a few times and mark with chalk, then join the marks with a straight line of chalk.

⑯

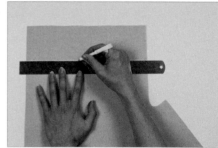

This shows you where you need to stop sewing when you make your tucks.

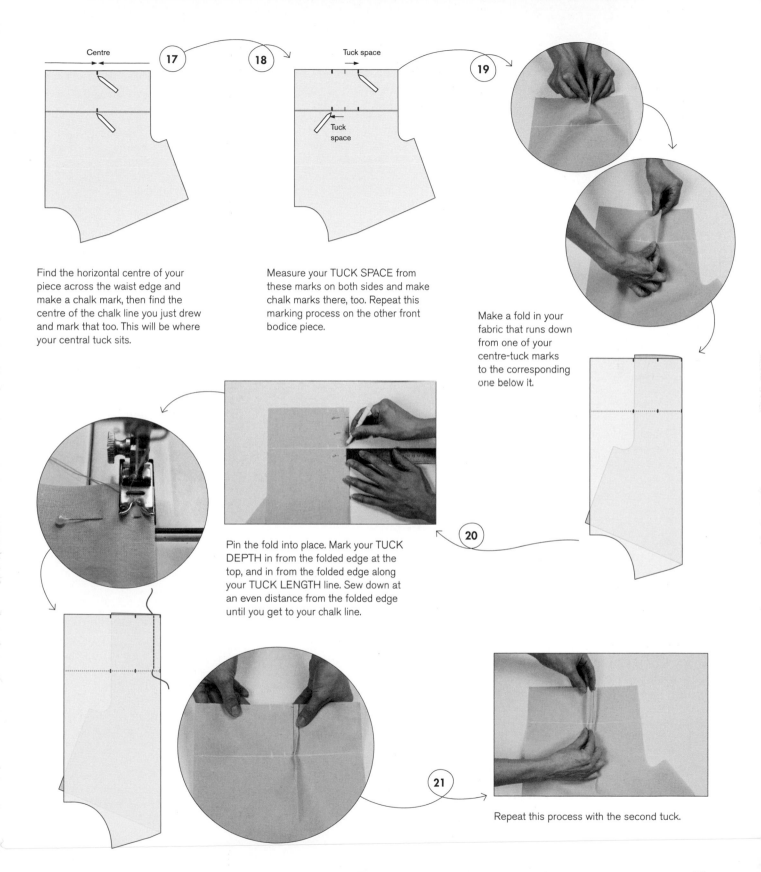

Find the horizontal centre of your piece across the waist edge and make a chalk mark, then find the centre of the chalk line you just drew and mark that too. This will be where your central tuck sits.

Measure your TUCK SPACE from these marks on both sides and make chalk marks there, too. Repeat this marking process on the other front bodice piece.

Make a fold in your fabric that runs down from one of your centre-tuck marks to the corresponding one below it.

Pin the fold into place. Mark your TUCK DEPTH in from the folded edge at the top, and in from the folded edge along your TUCK LENGTH line. Sew down at an even distance from the folded edge until you get to your chalk line.

Repeat this process with the second tuck.

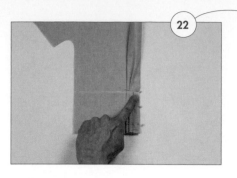

22 **23**

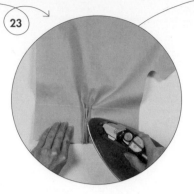

24

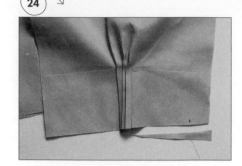

We flipped our front piece around to sew the third tuck, so the first two weren't creating lumps on the back of the fabric. This meant we sewed the tuck from the top to the bottom edge.

Once they are all sewn, press them all towards the straight edge that will be the centre front of your dress.

Repeat this full process with the other front piece. Adding tucks will have caused the bottom edge of your front piece to change shape, bending down under the sleeve. Trim off a skinny triangular slice of fabric to straighten it out.

Mark out a shallower neckline using chalk, then pin the piece down and cut around it, following the chalk neckline rather than the one on your front piece.

Sew your front bodice pieces to your back bodice piece.

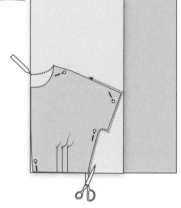

25

Use one of your front bodice pieces as a guide to cutting your back bodice piece.

Make a fold in your fabric as wide as your front bodice piece. Lay one of your front bodice pieces on top, with the centre front edge sitting right on top of the fold in your fabric.

26

Lay your back piece out and lay the two front pieces on top of it, right sides together. Match up the shoulder seams and pin them together. Sew along the pinned edges with straight stitch, running 1.5cm (⅝in) away from the edge.

27

Press the seams open.

28

Match the underarm and side seams and pin them together.

TUTORIAL

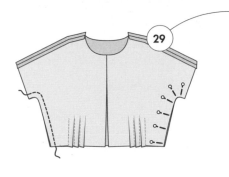

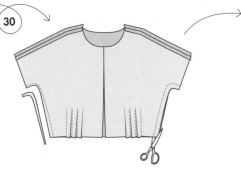

Sew them together with straight stitch.

Trim away some of the fabric at the curved underarm and snip into the seam to release tension, making sure you don't snip the stitches!

Press open the seams as much as you can, then zigzag all the raw edges including the shoulder seams, the side seams and the full bottom edge of the bodice.

Construct the skirt.

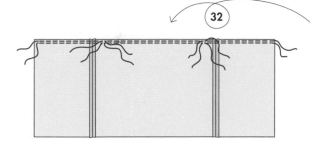

Gather the top edge of the whole skirt and attach it to your bodice.

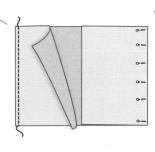

Set your machine to sew the longest straight stitch possible. You are going to sew two rows of stitches, but to make the gathering process easier, it's better to break up each long row into smaller sections. We sewed each line in three parts.

See page 48 in the Cape Sleeved Top and page 62 in the Deco Drape Dress instructions for further explanation of how to sew gathering stitch.

Lay the back piece of your skirt – the largest rectangle – out with the two front pieces on top of it, right sides together.

Pin the two smaller rectangles to the large one down each side. Sew them together with straight stitch. Press the seams open. Zigzag the raw edges of your seam allowances and also the full long edge across the top of your skirt.

Begin your first line 1.5cm (⅝in) from the edge of your front piece and sew until you have just passed the side seam. Trim your thread leaving a long tail, then begin again as close to where you left off as possible. When sewing your second row of stitches, try to break off and begin again right where you did so on the first line.

Pull the thread ends to create gathers, manoeuvring the gathers so that the side seams of the skirt match the side seams of the bodice. When the edge of each skirt piece is the same length as the corresponding section of the bodice, tie off your thread ends.

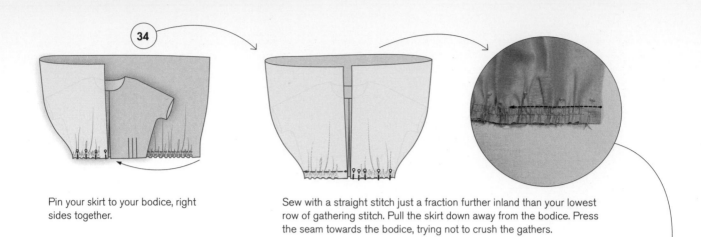

Pin your skirt to your bodice, right sides together.

Sew with a straight stitch just a fraction further inland than your lowest row of gathering stitch. Pull the skirt down away from the bodice. Press the seam towards the bodice, trying not to crush the gathers.

Each placket piece needs to be a very long rectangle of fabric, the same length as the centre front edge of your dress, so measure that edge now.

If you are making a V-shaped neckline
Make your placket piece 3cm (1⅛in) longer than the full length of the opening. You also need to finish the neck edge with bias binding now. You can use the method shown on page 76, so the binding is not visible from the outside, or the method shown on page 204 of the Triple Triangle Dress tutorial, where the binding creates a visible trim.

Now you're going to make a placket for each side of your dress.

Width of finished placket

The width of the rectangle needs to be double the depth you intend your fnished placket to appear, plus 2cm (¾in) for seam allowance. Our finished placket appears 3cm (1⅛in) wide, so we cut our rectangle 8cm (3in) wide. You can make your placket deeper than this if you like.

Iron

Cut out the first placket rectangle then lay it on your fabric and use it as a guide to cut a second one exactly the same.

Press a fold 1cm (⅜in) deep all the way along one of the long edges on both placket pieces.

Pin the unpressed side of your placket to the long front edge of your dress, with the right sides of the fabric together.

Sew the two together with a 1cm (⅜in) seam allowance.

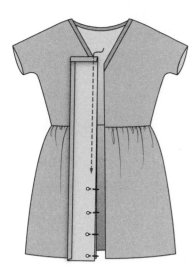

(39)

(40)

If you are making a V-shaped neckline
Press over the short edge at the top of your placket, too, before pinning it in place. Position the placket so the top, folded edge sits above the top corner at the front of your dress. Sew the two together starting at the exact point where the placket piece crosses over the sloping edge of your neckline.

Pull the placket away from the dress, then open up the front and press the entire seam allowance towards the placket.

(41)

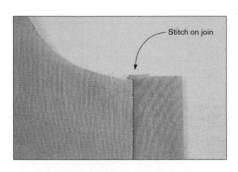

Flip your dress back over so you're looking at the right side and repin your placket from this side, removing your original pins from the back. Sew it down with your stitches running right on top of the join so they fall into it and practically disappear.

Stitch on join

(43)

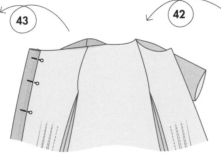

Press it down in this position then pin it in place with just a few pins.

(42)

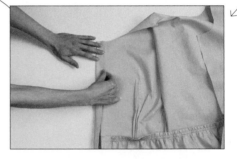

Now fold the pressed edge over towards the dress, folding the placket in half.

Position the pressed fold so it sits 2 or 3mm (⅛in) beyond the line of stitching that attaches the placket to the dress. The folded edge of the placket should completely hide this stitching from view.

(44)

Your stitches will be catching the other side of your placket on the back.

Repeat this full process with your second placket, on the other front edge of your dress.

**Finish the
neck edge of
the dress with
bias binding.**

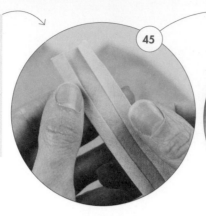

(45)

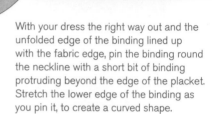

(46)

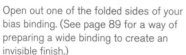

Open out one of the folded sides of your bias binding. (See page 89 for a way of preparing a wide binding to create an invisible finish.)

With your dress the right way out and the unfolded edge of the binding lined up with the fabric edge, pin the binding round the neckline with a short bit of binding protruding beyond the edge of the placket. Stretch the lower edge of the binding as you pin it, to create a curved shape.

Turn your dress inside out now, and press the binding down so it sits just below the neck edge of the dress. Tuck both ends under so they can't be seen from the front, then pin and sew the binding down close to the folded edge of the binding.

(48)

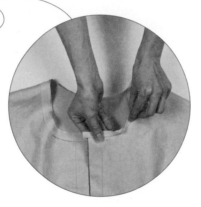

(47)

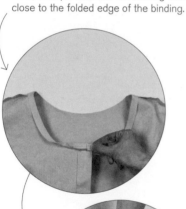

You are going to fold the binding to the inside of your dress.

Start sewing the binding to the dress at one of the front openings and sew it all the way round, with your stitches landing on the crease in the binding. Trim the seam allowance and snip into it, towards your stitches, to release tension.

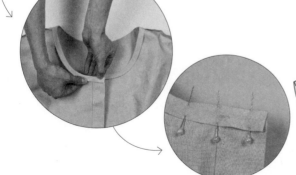

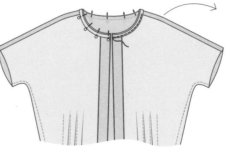

**Hem the bottom
edge and sleeve
ends of the dress.**

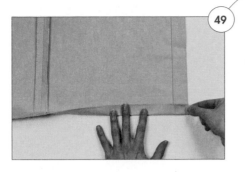

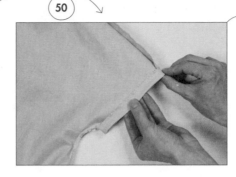

Create buttonholes in one of your plackets and add buttons to the other.

Neaten the bottom edge and raw edges of your sleeves with zigzag stitch. With your dress inside out, press up a fold 3cm (1⅛in) deep along the bottom edge. Pin the fold down and check that the dress is the same length at both front corners. Repress the fold until the length matches on both sides, then sew it down with one long line of straight stitch running close to the zigzagged edge.

Press a 1.5cm- (⅝in-) deep fold all the way around both sleeve ends and sew them down with straight stitch.

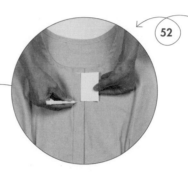

Your sewing machine should have an automatic buttonholing foot. Experiment with the foot on scrap fabric, then sew a buttonhole at each of your chalk marks.

We then used this as a guide to mark regular points down the placket at which to create buttonholes.

We positioned our buttons roughly where we wanted them, then cut out a rectangle of paper indicating the distance we wanted between each button.

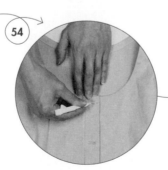

Open your buttonholes by poking your seam ripper into the fabric and carefully slicing a hole in the middle of your stitches.

Lay your dress out again with the plackets on top of one another and make a mark with chalk through each of the buttonholes. Sew a button to the placket on each of these chalk marks.

YOU HAVE MADE A SHIRT DRESS!

Shirt dress

1

Mairead's version of the dress is made in light silky fabric with a directional print. The skirt pieces have been cut with the selvage running horizontally across them, so the print contrasts with that on the bodice. The dress is cropped above the knee, has short cap sleeves and is fastened with cute white buttons.

Technical variations

2

Melody wears a more fitted version of the Shirt Dress, with less ease added to the initial measurements. Her version is made in custom-printed cotton and has a contrasting placket and a V-shaped neckline finished with visible bias binding. Belt loops have been added so the dress can be drawn in at the waist with a belt.

MAKE WITH CIRCLES

DRIP DRAPE SKIRT

This faux wrap skirt has a curved hemline that's deepest at the back, rising up at the front with both sides overlapping to create a tulip shape.

KEY SKILLS

Working with stretch fabric

Freestyle draping

Making a waistband

SEGMENT DRESS

This sleeveless swing dress is fitted at the top and flares outwards to create a full A-line shape. A ruffle can be added at the hem.

KEY SKILLS

Making a ruffle

Finishing a neckline and armholes with bias binding

Using a guide garment to create a paper template

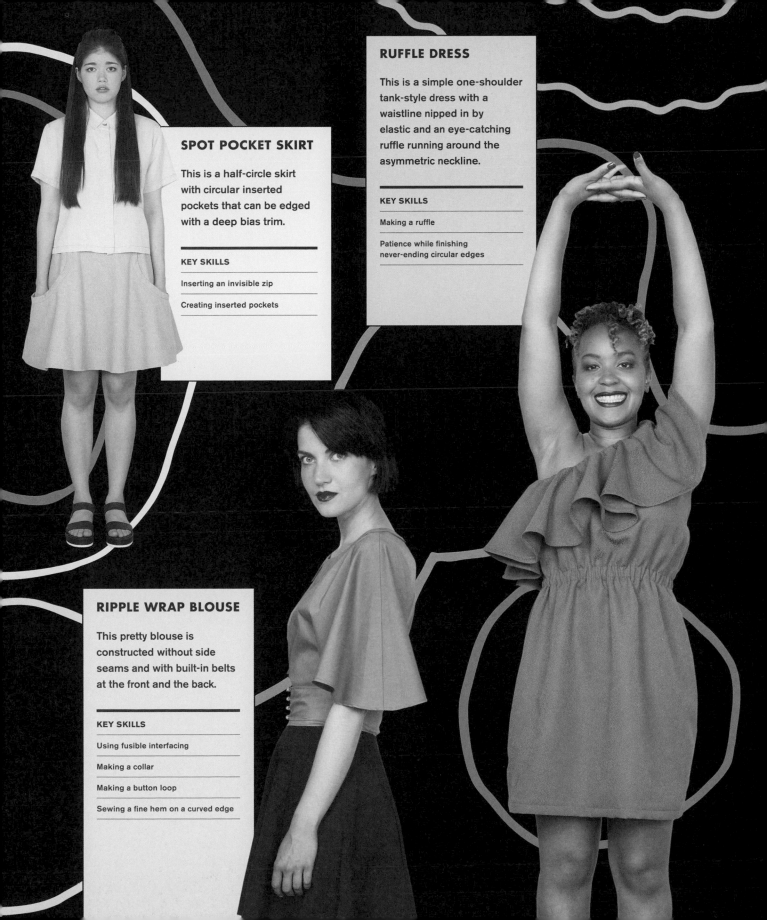

SPOT POCKET SKIRT

This is a half-circle skirt with circular inserted pockets that can be edged with a deep bias trim.

KEY SKILLS

Inserting an invisible zip

Creating inserted pockets

RUFFLE DRESS

This is a simple one-shoulder tank-style dress with a waistline nipped in by elastic and an eye-catching ruffle running around the asymmetric neckline.

KEY SKILLS

Making a ruffle

Patience while finishing never-ending circular edges

RIPPLE WRAP BLOUSE

This pretty blouse is constructed without side seams and with built-in belts at the front and the back.

KEY SKILLS

Using fusible interfacing

Making a collar

Making a button loop

Sewing a fine hem on a curved edge

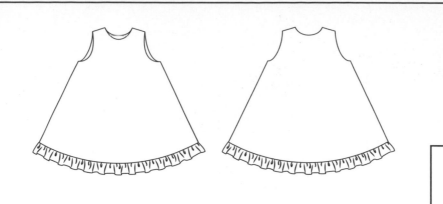

MATERIALS NEEDED

Fabric

Newspaper to make template

Bias binding

Guide garment, which should be sleeveless – a woven tank top or a sleeveless fitted dress would be perfect. You should like how it fits you at the shoulders and the neck

String

PIECES TO CUT

Front

Back

Ruffle

Ruffle

Ruffle

BODY MEASUREMENTS NEEDED

Desired dress length, which you will work out on page 86

MATHS TO DO

None!
There will be a little bit of maths to do along the way, but most of the marking out for this dress is based on your guide garment rather than on body measurements.

SUITABLE FABRIC

Stiff cottons from light- to medium-weight will work for this dress, giving it a defined shape. Drapey fabrics will let the dress hang more loosely in folds. You can use a contrasting fabric for the ruffle.

SEGMENT DRESS

This is a fun, free dress that requires no fastening. The addition of a shallow ruffle around the hem can create a girlish look, or shortening the main dress and adding a very deep ruffle can change the silhouette, creating the appearance of a dropped waistline. Leave the dress ruffle free for a clean, simple style.

01

CIRCLES

Start by taping two big sheets of newspaper together. Turn this rectangular sheet into a square by folding one corner across until the sides meet, then chop off the end.

You're going to turn this square into a quarter-circle segment, which will form a base template for your dress.

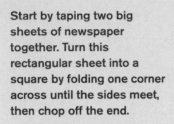

1

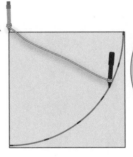

Measure one side of the square. Take your metre stick and position one end at one corner of the paper. Pivot the metre stick, measuring out and marking the length of the side of the square a few times.

2

3

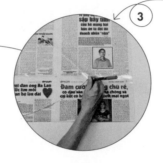

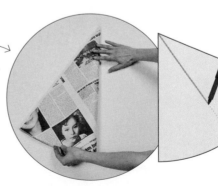

4

Cut along the pen line to create a quarter circle. Now fold your quarter circle in half firmly, creasing the fold.

Holding the pencil upright, swing your pen around on the string, drawing a curved line, which should hit the marks you made. See page 96 of the Drip Drape Skirt tutorial for an illustrated set of instructions.

Cut a piece of string that is a bit longer than the length you just measured. Tie one end of the string firmly to a pencil. This is going to be your pivot point. Tie the other end around a coloured pen until the string is the same length as one side of your square.

Unfold it, then fold one edge in towards the centre and make a crease.

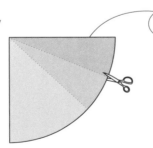

5

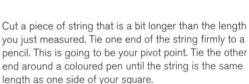

Open the fold out, then cut off the outer section.

Now fold what you have left in half. Open it up and mark that central crease with a pen to be sure you can see it.

84   **TUTORIAL**

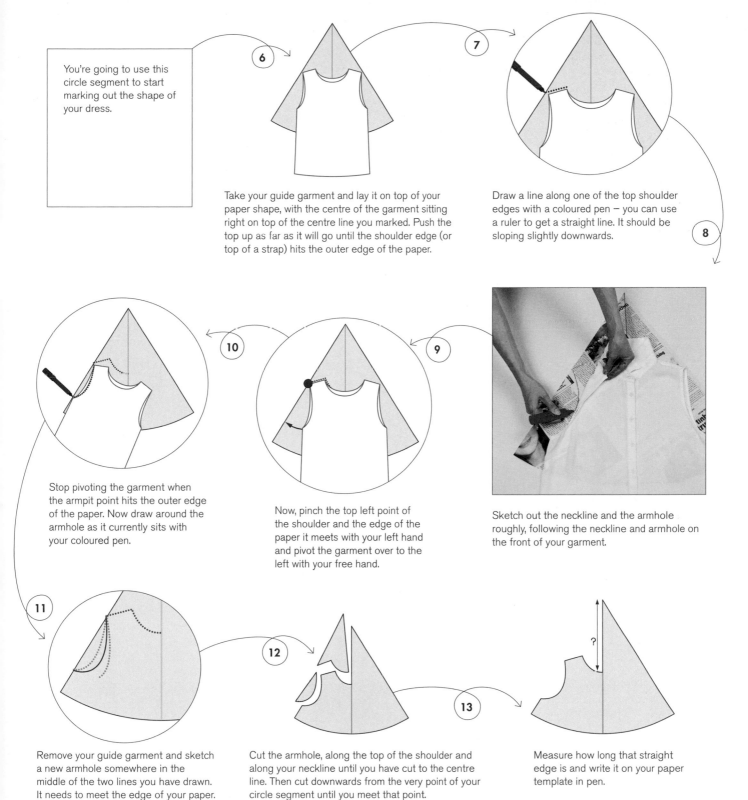

You're going to use this circle segment to start marking out the shape of your dress.

6 Take your guide garment and lay it on top of your paper shape, with the centre of the garment sitting right on top of the centre line you marked. Push the top up as far as it will go until the shoulder edge (or top of a strap) hits the outer edge of the paper.

7 Draw a line along one of the top shoulder edges with a coloured pen – you can use a ruler to get a straight line. It should be sloping slightly downwards.

10 Stop pivoting the garment when the armpit point hits the outer edge of the paper. Now draw around the armhole as it currently sits with your coloured pen.

9 Now, pinch the top left point of the shoulder and the edge of the paper it meets with your left hand and pivot the garment over to the left with your free hand.

8 Sketch out the neckline and the armhole roughly, following the neckline and armhole on the front of your garment.

11 Remove your guide garment and sketch a new armhole somewhere in the middle of the two lines you have drawn. It needs to meet the edge of your paper.

12 Cut the armhole, along the top of the shoulder and along your neckline until you have cut to the centre line. Then cut downwards from the very point of your circle segment until you meet that point.

13 Measure how long that straight edge is and write it on your paper template in pen.

Now you need to work out how long you are going to make your dress pieces.

Stand in front of a mirror and hold the paper template you have up in front of you, positioning it as it will roughly sit when made of fabric. You can make adjustments to the neckline at this point. We trimmed away our paper to make a much deeper neckline than the one on our guide garment. Remember, the neckhole needs to be big enough for your head to fit through!

With the paper held up in front of you or pinned to your clothing, use your metre stick to measure downwards from the centre bottom of the neckhole to wherever you want the bottom of your dress to hang (NB if you're adding a giant ruffle to the hem, this could be much higher than where the actual bottom of your dress will hang). This is your DESIRED DRESS LENGTH. Write that measurement down.

Add this measurement to the one written on your paper circle segment and write the result down. We'll call this your FABRIC REQUIREMENT.

It's time to cut your dress pieces from fabric.

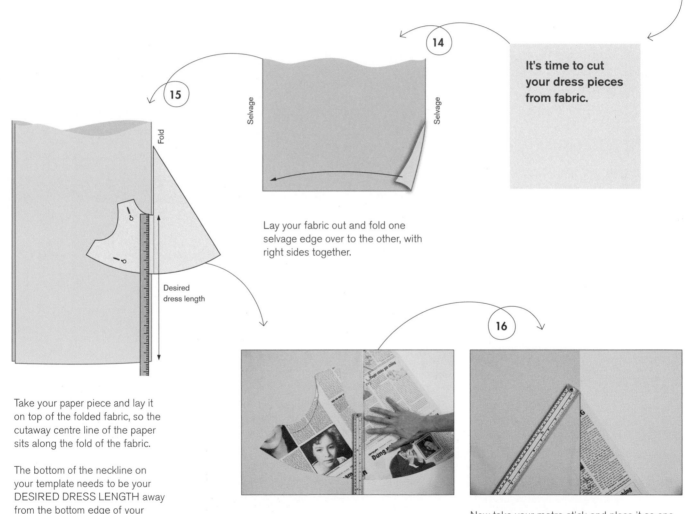

14

15

16

Lay your fabric out and fold one selvage edge over to the other, with right sides together.

Take your paper piece and lay it on top of the folded fabric, so the cutaway centre line of the paper sits along the fold of the fabric.

The bottom of the neckline on your template needs to be your DESIRED DRESS LENGTH away from the bottom edge of your fabric. Measure that distance with a metre stick.

Now take your metre stick and place it so one corner of it touches the point where the tip of your paper slice meets your fabric.

Run the stick downwards, parallel with the sloping side of your dress shape.

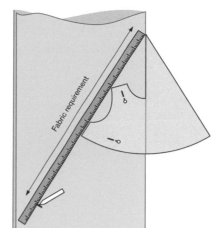

17

Measure your FABRIC REQUIREMENT along your metre stick from the top. If it lands somewhere on your fabric that's great! Make a mark.

If your fabric isn't wide enough, you can make the front of your dress in two halves. Unfold your fabric now. You can do the same with the back as well. Just add an extra 1.5cm (⅝in) at the centre front of each piece.

Draw a straight chalk line onto your fabric from the armpit point of your paper piece downwards along your ruler.

Pivot your metre stick from the top point, marking the FABRIC REQUIREMENT with chalk at multiple points.

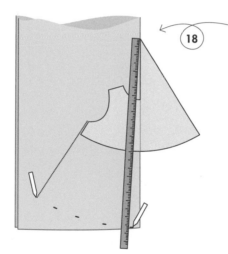

18

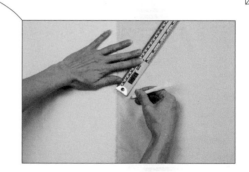

19

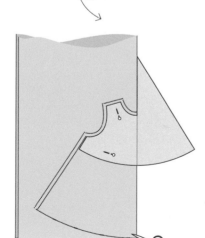

Join these points with chalk, drawing a smooth curved line, then cut along this line. Cut your side edge 1.5cm (⅝in) outside the chalk line you drew and 1.5cm (⅝in) away from the paper template.

If you are making your front and back from two pieces of fabric, join them together now.

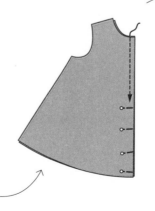

Use your front piece as a guide for cutting your back piece.

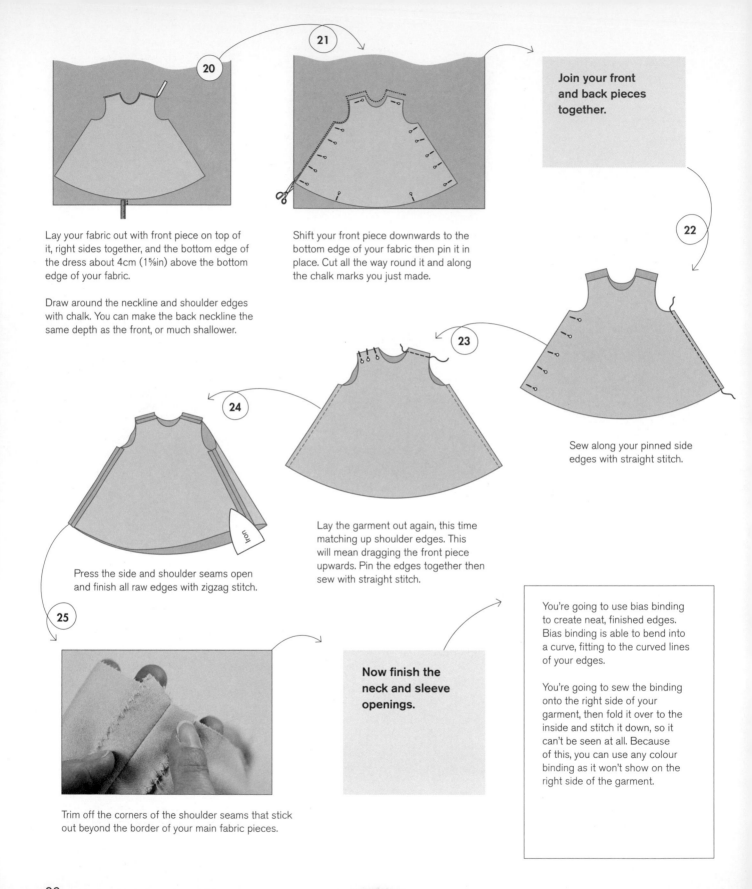

20

Lay your fabric out with front piece on top of it, right sides together, and the bottom edge of the dress about 4cm (1⅝in) above the bottom edge of your fabric.

Draw around the neckline and shoulder edges with chalk. You can make the back neckline the same depth as the front, or much shallower.

21

Shift your front piece downwards to the bottom edge of your fabric then pin it in place. Cut all the way round it and along the chalk marks you just made.

Join your front and back pieces together.

22

Sew along your pinned side edges with straight stitch.

23

Lay the garment out again, this time matching up shoulder edges. This will mean dragging the front piece upwards. Pin the edges together then sew with straight stitch.

24

Press the side and shoulder seams open and finish all raw edges with zigzag stitch.

25

Trim off the corners of the shoulder seams that stick out beyond the border of your main fabric pieces.

Now finish the neck and sleeve openings.

You're going to use bias binding to create neat, finished edges. Bias binding is able to bend into a curve, fitting to the curved lines of your edges.

You're going to sew the binding onto the right side of your garment, then fold it over to the inside and stitch it down, so it can't be seen at all. Because of this, you can use any colour binding as it won't show on the right side of the garment.

TUTORIAL

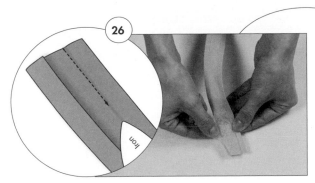

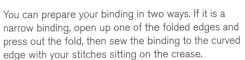

26

27

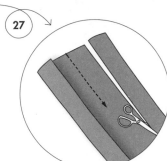

If it is a very broad binding, trim off one of the folded edges. You're going to match up the unfolded edge of the binding with the raw edge on your garment then sew the two together with a 1cm (⅜in) seam allowance. The depth of binding remaining on the left of your stitches (not including the fold) will be what is folded to the inside of your garment and stitched down.

You can prepare your binding in two ways. If it is a narrow binding, open up one of the folded edges and press out the fold, then sew the binding to the curved edge with your stitches sitting on the crease.

28

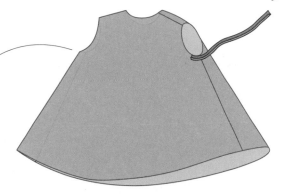

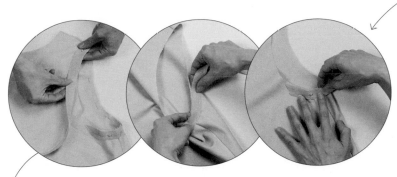

Pin it all the way around the armhole, stretching the folded edge of the binding bit by bit as you go so it becomes curved.

Cut a piece of binding a few centimetres (1in) longer than the edge you are applying it to. With your garment the right way out, begin pinning the unfolded edge of the binding to the right side of your dress somewhere near the armpit.

29

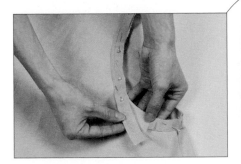

30

31

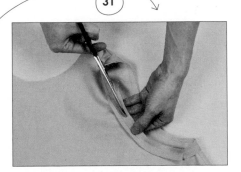

When you are almost back to where you started, fold back a small amount of the end of the binding you began with.

Lay the unpinned end on top of the folded end so they are overlapping and you can't see the fold, then pin them both down.

Sew the binding to the armhole all the way round, then trim away the seam so it is less deep than the binding on the other side of the stitches.

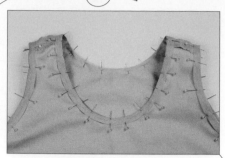

Snip into the trimmed seam all the way around to release tension, making sure you don't snip your stitches. Repeat this full process on the other armhole and the neckline.

With all three pieces of binding attached, trimmed and snipped, you are ready to turn your binding to the inside of your dress.

Turn your dress inside out and press the bindings so they sit just inside the garment edges. Pin them in place and sew them down with straight stitch, running close to the folded edge of the binding.

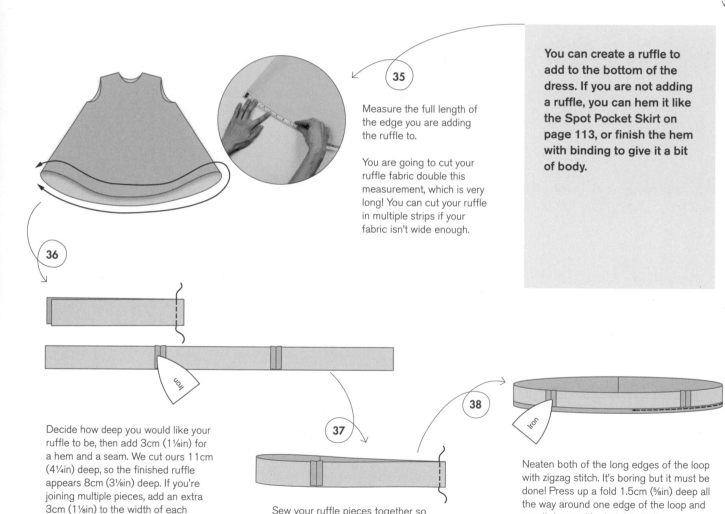

Measure the full length of the edge you are adding the ruffle to.

You are going to cut your ruffle fabric double this measurement, which is very long! You can cut your ruffle in multiple strips if your fabric isn't wide enough.

You can create a ruffle to add to the bottom of the dress. If you are not adding a ruffle, you can hem it like the Spot Pocket Skirt on page 113, or finish the hem with binding to give it a bit of body.

Decide how deep you would like your ruffle to be, then add 3cm (1⅛in) for a hem and a seam. We cut ours 11cm (4¼in) deep, so the finished ruffle appears 8cm (3⅛in) deep. If you're joining multiple pieces, add an extra 3cm (1⅛in) to the width of each piece, too.

Sew your ruffle pieces together so that they make a big loop.

Neaten both of the long edges of the loop with zigzag stitch. It's boring but it must be done! Press up a fold 1.5cm (⅝in) deep all the way around one edge of the loop and sew it down with straight stitch.

TUTORIAL

You're going to gather up the unhemmed edge of the loop. You need to sew two parallel lines of long straight stitches along this edge, but as you are gathering such a huge amount of fabric, you are going to break the lines up. Sew your first row 5mm (¼in) away from the edge. Count to ten as you begin sewing, then cut your threads and start sewing again as close to where you left off as you can, without overlapping your stitches. Keep doing this until you get back to where you started. You will probably have about six shorter lines of stitching, and a lot of dangling thread ends!

Sew your second row 1.5cm (⅝in) away from the edge. You need to sew your second row of stitches so that the sections start and finish exactly in line with the beginnings and ends of the stitches on your first row. As you sew, make sure you are not sewing over the dangling thread ends from your first row. You can hold them out to the right as you sew.

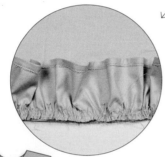

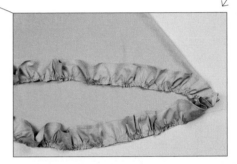

By gathering more or releasing different sections of the ruffle, adjust it until it fits the bottom edge of your dress exactly.

When you are happy with the fit, tie off all your thread ends and pin the ruffle to the dress, right sides together, all the way round.

Lay the ring of fabric out and carefully gather up all the individual sections, as shown on page 62 of the Deco Drape Dress tutorial. Keep gathering until the gathered edge looks roughly the same length as the bottom edge of your dress.

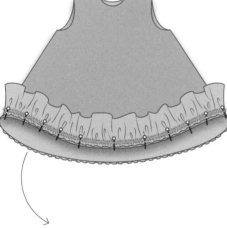

Sew the ruffle to the dress with a line of straight stitch, running fractionally below your lower row of gathering stitch, all the way round. Let the ruffle hang down and press it down, pressing the seam upwards.

YOU HAVE MADE A SEGMENT DRESS!

Segment dress

Kristina wears a simple version
of the dress, made in 100%
cotton with no additional ruffle.
The bottom edge is cleanly
finished with a hem.

2

Courtney's version of the Segment Dress is made in a fairly heavyweight scuba. The main part of the dress finishes just below the hip, but an extremely deep ruffle gives it additional length.

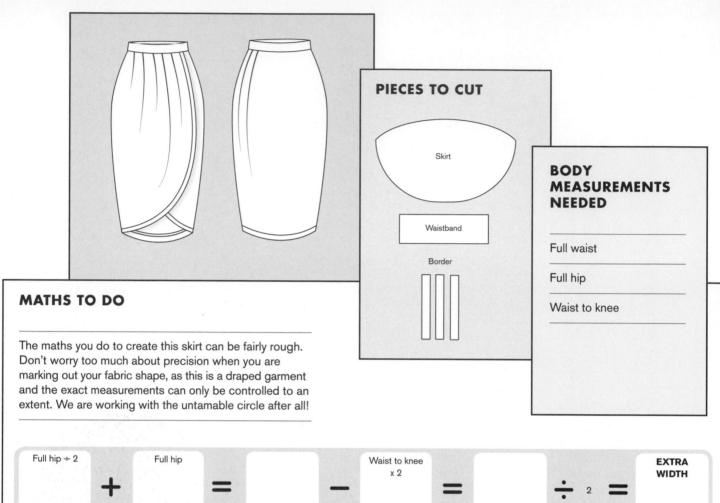

PIECES TO CUT

Skirt

Waistband

Border

BODY MEASUREMENTS NEEDED

Full waist

Full hip

Waist to knee

MATHS TO DO

The maths you do to create this skirt can be fairly rough. Don't worry too much about precision when you are marking out your fabric shape, as this is a draped garment and the exact measurements can only be controlled to an extent. We are working with the untamable circle after all!

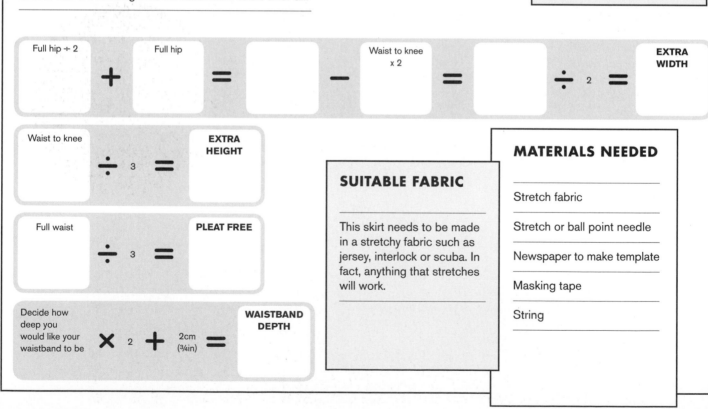

| Full hip ÷ 2 | **+** | Full hip | **=** | | **−** | Waist to knee x 2 | **=** | | **÷** 2 **=** | **EXTRA WIDTH** |

| Waist to knee | **÷** 3 **=** | **EXTRA HEIGHT** |

| Full waist | **÷** 3 **=** | **PLEAT FREE** |

| Decide how deep you would like your waistband to be | **✕** 2 **+** 2cm (¾in) **=** | **WAISTBAND DEPTH** |

SUITABLE FABRIC

This skirt needs to be made in a stretchy fabric such as jersey, interlock or scuba. In fact, anything that stretches will work.

MATERIALS NEEDED

Stretch fabric

Stretch or ball point needle

Newspaper to make template

Masking tape

String

DRIP DRAPE SKIRT

This comfortable faux-wrap skirt works well in any stretch fabric. Deep pleats across the front cause the fabric to hang in drapey folds. The long curved hem is finished with a narrow band of fabric. The skirt has a full, stretchy waistband, or it can be made as a true wrap skirt with an open waistband that fastens with a button or press stud. The skirt can be made shorter and tighter for a more figure-hugging look (see our version on page 102).

02

CIRCLES

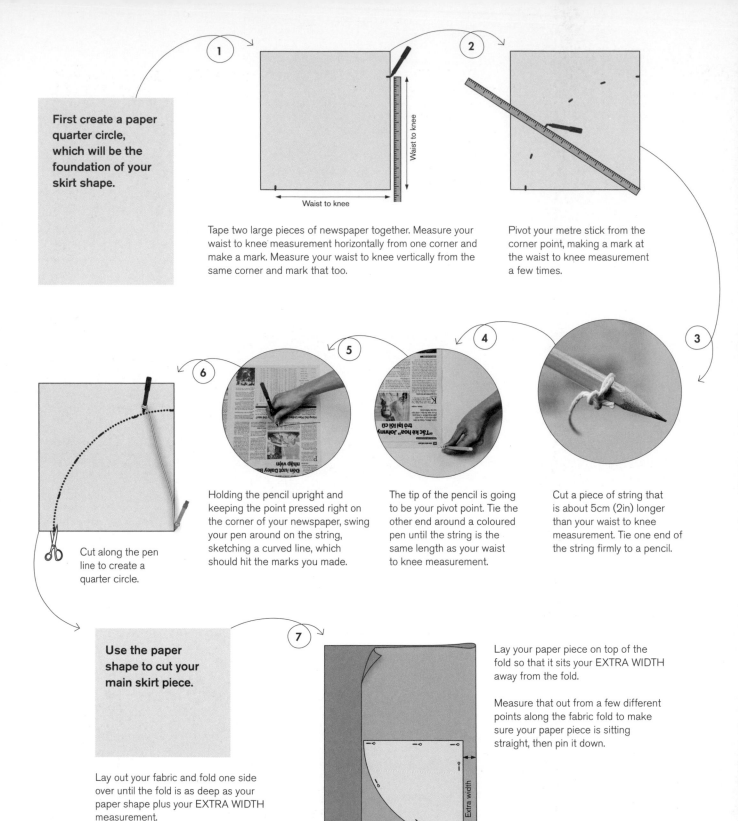

First create a paper quarter circle, which will be the foundation of your skirt shape.

1 Tape two large pieces of newspaper together. Measure your waist to knee measurement horizontally from one corner and make a mark. Measure your waist to knee vertically from the same corner and mark that too.

2 Pivot your metre stick from the corner point, making a mark at the waist to knee measurement a few times.

3 Cut a piece of string that is about 5cm (2in) longer than your waist to knee measurement. Tie one end of the string firmly to a pencil.

4 The tip of the pencil is going to be your pivot point. Tie the other end around a coloured pen until the string is the same length as your waist to knee measurement.

5 Holding the pencil upright and keeping the point pressed right on the corner of your newspaper, swing your pen around on the string, sketching a curved line, which should hit the marks you made.

6 Cut along the pen line to create a quarter circle.

Use the paper shape to cut your main skirt piece.

7 Lay out your fabric and fold one side over until the fold is as deep as your paper shape plus your EXTRA WIDTH measurement.

Lay your paper piece on top of the fold so that it sits your EXTRA WIDTH away from the fold.

Measure that out from a few different points along the fabric fold to make sure your paper piece is sitting straight, then pin it down.

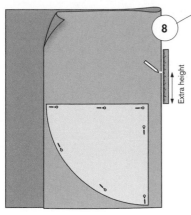

8

Measure your EXTRA HEIGHT upwards from a point on the fold that is roughly level with the top of your paper piece.

Mark that spot with a pin or chalk.

Extra height

9

Now comes a bit of freehand drawing. You need to sketch a curve that joins the point you have just marked with the far corner of your paper piece. You can sketch it with chalk, or if your fabric doesn't take chalk marks very well you can lay a piece of string on the fabric in roughly the shape you want, tape it to your fabric with masking tape and use that as a guide while you cut.

The curve should look something like the one shown here, but don't worry too much about the shape. As long as it is a gently sloping curve it will do the job.

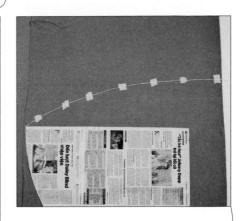

10

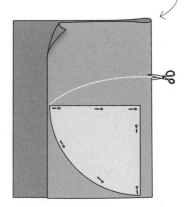

11

Cut out your skirt, cutting along the curve you just marked, all the way round the curve of the paper piece and straight along at the bottom to the folded edge.

While your piece is still folded, mark the centre with chalk or a pin.

Now pleat the gently curved edge to fit your waist.

12

You are going to add a number of fairly deep pleats along the top edge of your skirt, gathering the fabric so that it drapes in folds. You are going to leave a section of fabric at the centre back unpleated.

Pleat free

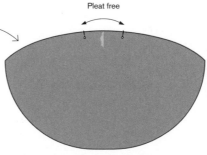

Unfold your skirt piece and lay it out with the right side facing up. Measure the PLEAT FREE measurement so that it is centred over the chalk mark you made.

Mark both ends of the PLEAT FREE measurement with pins.

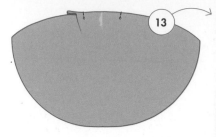

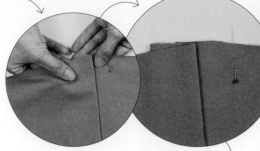

Start your first pleat beyond the marker pin. Fold the pleat so that the fold points towards the marker pin – you are dragging fabric towards the centre back of the skirt.

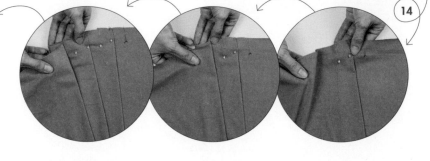

Pin each pleat securely with two pins pointing to the raw edge and one horizontally across the pleat.

Continue this process, adding more pleats to each side. Aim for rough symmetry but don't worry about precision, as this skirt is about random folds.

For now, make large pleats; you can adjust the size later on. Pin the first pleat into place, then make a corresponding pleat on the opposite side that is roughly the same depth.

Stop pleating when you have about 5cm (2in) of unpleated fabric left on each side.

Do a test fit for your skirt. The pleat-free stretch will sit on your back, and the pleated areas will wrap over your front, overlapping each other. The overlapping parts should not quite stretch fully over the front of your body.

Take the skirt off and adjust your pleats. If you want to reduce the length of the waistline you can add more pleats, or you can adjust the depth of all your pleats so they eat up more fabric. If you want to increase the waist edge, make your pleats shallower, releasing fabric.

We added five pleats on each side of the skirt. Our front pleats used up 7cm (2¾in) of fabric, so each pleat appears 3.5cm (1⅜in) deep. We made the pleats nearer the back of the skirt shallower. Those pleats use up 5cm (2in) of fabric each, so each pleat appears 2.5cm (1in) deep. Our variation on page 102 has much smaller pleats; the skirt on page 103 has extremely deep pleats.

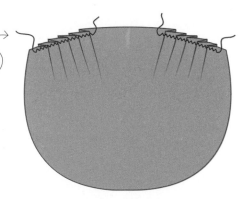

When you are happy with the positioning and size of all your pleats, sew along the pleated edge with a line of small zigzag stitch to hold them in place. Your stitches should sit about 1.5cm (⅝in) away from the top edge.

TUTORIAL

Finish the outer edge of your skirt.

You could leave the big, outer edge of your skirt raw as you are using stretchy fabric and it won't fray (though it may curl up).

You can finish the edge of the skirt in two ways. You can make a hem: sew a guide line of straight stitch all the way round the big curved edge, about 5mm (³⁄₁₆in) from the edge, then press the edge over so the stitching sits just on the inside and sew it down. See step 45 of the Spot Pocket Skirt on page 113 for a picture.

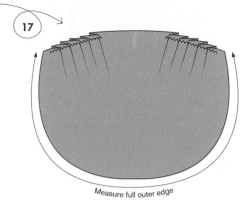

Measure full outer edge

Alternatively, you can finish the edge by attaching a border. You can make a paper template to mark it out. Measure the full raw edge of your skirt and write that down here:

We'll call this your BORDER LENGTH.

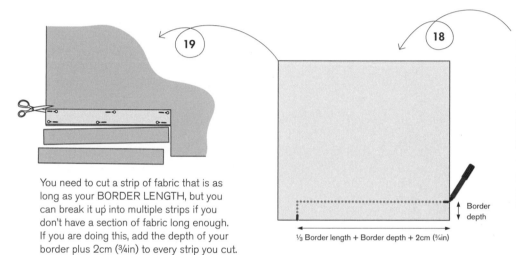

You need to cut a strip of fabric that is as long as your BORDER LENGTH, but you can break it up into multiple strips if you don't have a section of fabric long enough. If you are doing this, add the depth of your border plus 2cm (¾in) to every strip you cut.

Border depth

⅓ Border length + Border depth + 2cm (¾in)

Decide how deep you want the border to appear, then double it and add 2cm (¾in). This is your BORDER DEPTH. Write it down here:

The border on our skirt appears 2cm (¾in) deep on the finished garment, so our BORDER DEPTH is 6cm (2⅜in).

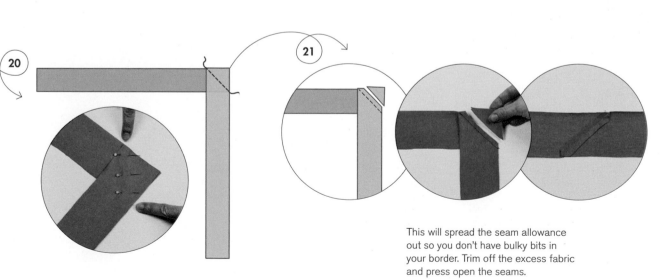

Sew your sections of fabric together like this, right sides together.

This will spread the seam allowance out so you don't have bulky bits in your border. Trim off the excess fabric and press open the seams.

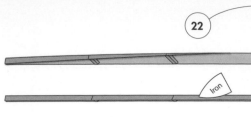

22

23

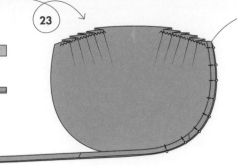

24

25

Now press your border piece in half lengthways, hiding the wrong side of the fabric (and the seams) on the inside. Give it lots of steam and pressure to ensure the crease stays put.

Pin your border strip to the right side of your skirt, matching up the two raw edges of the border piece with the raw edge of your skirt.

Try not to stretch the border piece as you pin.

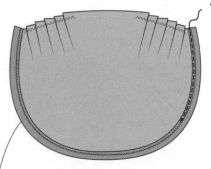

27

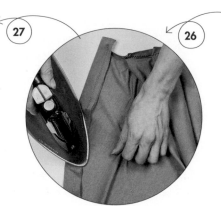

26

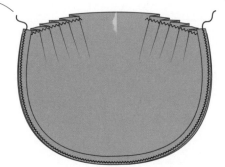

To stop the border from flipping upwards when you're wearing the skirt, sew the seam down to the main body of the skirt, with your stitches sitting about 3mm (⅛in) inland from the join. It will be easier to get a neater line of stitches if you sew while looking at the front of your skirt, but this illustration shows the position the stitches will be in viewed from the back.

Press the border away from the skirt, pressing the seam back towards the main body of the skirt.

Sew the border to the skirt with a small zigzag stitch, running 1cm (⅜in) away from the edge.

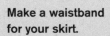

Make a waistband for your skirt.

28

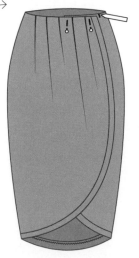

Wrap the skirt around you and make marks on the fabric where the top corner overlaps the layer beneath.

Take the skirt off and reconstruct it as worn, pinning the overlapping edges on top of each other.

Measure the distance around the waist edge, add 2cm (¾in) and write it down here:

We'll call this your WAISTBAND LENGTH. This should be roughly the same size as your full waist measurement, perhaps a little less if your skirt clings tightly to you, or more if it sits nearer your hips.

TUTORIAL

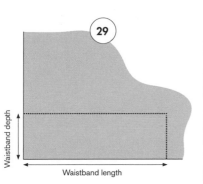

29

Waistband depth

Waistband length

Lay your fabric out and tug it with both hands to determine which direction it is most stretchy in. Measure your WAISTBAND LENGTH along the most stretchy edge. Measure your WAISTBAND DEPTH (see page 94) up along the less stretchy edge and cut a rectangle.

To make a wrap skirt with a waistband that opens
Cut a rectangle as in step 29. Fold it in half lengthwise, right sides together, and sew straight stitch across each short end. Turn right way out, then attach it to the waist edge of the skirt as described on page 191 (adding a border at the hem).

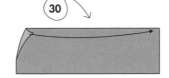

30

To make a full waistband, fold the strip of fabric in half, right sides together, so the short ends meet. Pin them together then sew with straight stitch 1cm (⅜in) from the edge. You have made a tube of fabric.

31

Press open the seam then fold the tube over on itself so the wrong side of the fabric is hidden on the inside.

32

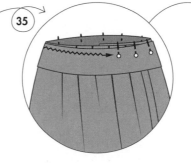

Pin the long edges together in this position.

33

Attach your waistband to your skirt.

Slide your waistband around your main skirt until the pinned edge is sitting over the pleated edge of your skirt. The folded edge will be pointing downwards.

34

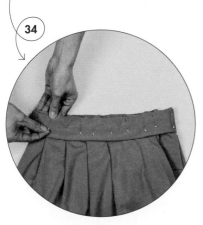

You're dealing with a lot of pins here, so be careful! Position the seam in your waistband at the centre back of your skirt. Unpin and repin your pins one at a time, so they are going through all the layers – both sides of your waistband and the skirt. Take out the pins that are holding the overlapping parts of your skirt together as you go.

35

Now sew your waistband to your skirt with a line of zigzag stitch. Fold the waistband upwards and press the seam allowance down.

YOU HAVE MADE A DRIP DRAPE SKIRT!

Drip drape skirt

1

Karishma wears a shorter, tighter version of the skirt, made in a lightweight silk jersey. Just a fifth of the waist to knee measurement was used to determine the EXTRA HEIGHT measurement. The skirt has six smaller pleats at each side and is finished with a small pressed hem rather than an additional band of fabric.

Kristina wears an almost
ankle-length version, which
is made in a heavy sweatshirt
jersey. The skirt has four deep
pleats on each side and is
finished with a wide border
made in a contrasting fabric.
The fabric was not stretchy
enough to make a full waistband,
so this skirt is really a wrap
skirt with an opening fastened
by a heavy-duty press stud.

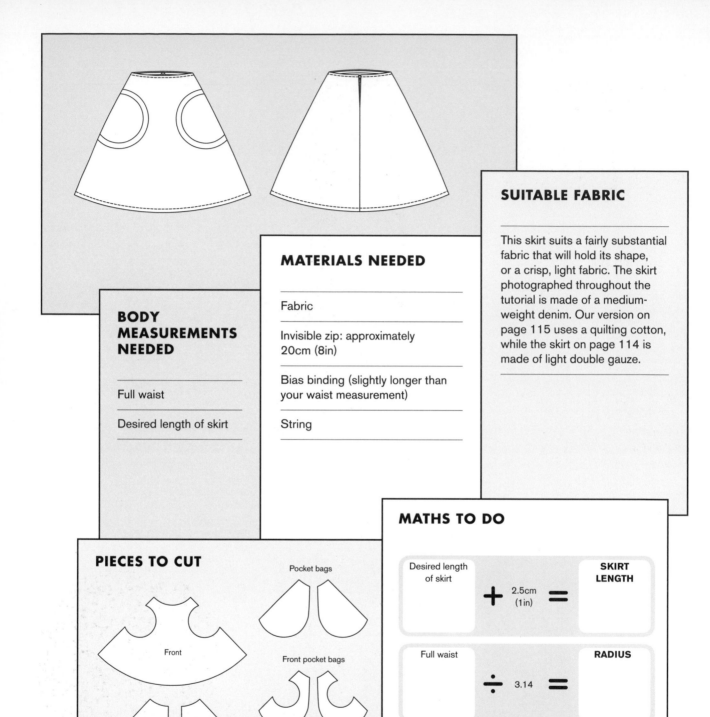

BODY MEASUREMENTS NEEDED

Full waist

Desired length of skirt

MATERIALS NEEDED

Fabric

Invisible zip: approximately 20cm (8in)

Bias binding (slightly longer than your waist measurement)

String

SUITABLE FABRIC

This skirt suits a fairly substantial fabric that will hold its shape, or a crisp, light fabric. The skirt photographed throughout the tutorial is made of a medium-weight denim. Our version on page 115 uses a quilting cotton, while the skirt on page 114 is made of light double gauze.

PIECES TO CUT

Front

Back

Back

Pocket bags

Front pocket bags

Bias binding

MATHS TO DO

| Desired length of skirt | **+** 2.5cm (1in) | **=** | **SKIRT LENGTH** |

| Full waist | **÷** 3.14 | **=** | **RADIUS** |

SPOT POCKET SKIRT

Taking its name from its bold, circular pockets, this comfy skirt invites a playful approach to fabrics. Use contrasting fabrics for the pocket backing and bias trim to make the design stand out! The waist edge is finished with bias binding and fastens at the centre back with an invisible zip.

03

CIRCLES

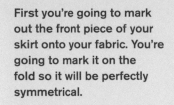

First you're going to mark out the front piece of your skirt onto your fabric. You're going to mark it on the fold so it will be perfectly symmetrical.

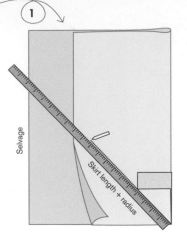

Add your SKIRT LENGTH and RADIUS together.

Make a big fold in your fabric. Position your cardboard set square (see page 10) so that it points to the folded corner of your fabric. Lay your metre stick so it runs along the sloping edge of the set square. Check that your SKIRT LENGTH + RADIUS fall onto the fold you have

made. Adjust the fold until it is big enough, then draw a line with chalk as long as your SKIRT LENGTH + RADIUS running parallel with the sloping edge of the square.

(You can also use a folded piece of paper to do this. See step 24 on page 161 for a photo.)

Position your pencil so the tip is pressing the very corner of your folded fabric. Hold the chalk at the end of your SKIRT LENGTH + RADIUS line and swing it around until reaches the mark on the fold, gently sketching a curved line as you go.

Cut a piece of string that's about 5cm (2in) longer than your SKIRT LENGTH + RADIUS. Tie it firmly near the point of a pencil at one end, and tie it to your tailor's chalk at the other. Check that it is exactly as long as your SKIRT LENGTH + RADIUS when the string is held taut.

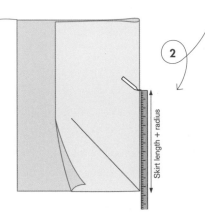

Put the paper to one side and measure your SKIRT LENGTH + RADIUS up the folded edge of your fabric, too, and make a mark there with chalk.

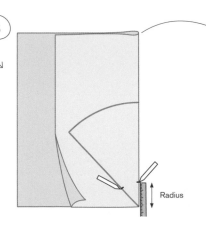

Now measure your RADIUS from the corner along your sloping chalk line and make a mark. Measure it down the folded edge, too, and make a mark there.

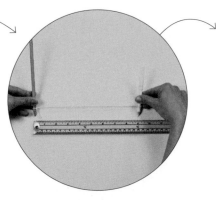

Cut down the string that's tied to your pencil, so that it is a bit longer than your RADIUS, then retie the cut end to your fabric chalk, so that the string is as long as your RADIUS when held taut.

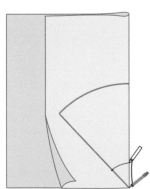

With the pencil on the very tip of the folded corner again, swing your chalk round, marking out a curved waistline.

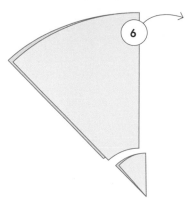

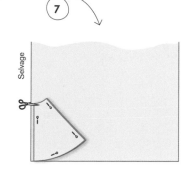

Now use the front piece as a guide to cut out your two back pieces.

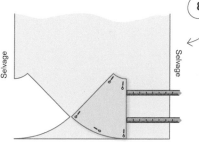

With the front piece remaining folded, lay it on your fabric with the folded edge running parallel with the straight selvage edge of your fabric, but sitting 1.5cm (⅝in) away from it. Pin it down to hold it in place and cut around it, leaving that extra strip of 1.5cm (⅝in). This is one of the back pieces of your skirt.

Cut along your chalk lines. This is the front piece of your skirt. Save the little quarter-circle segment that you cut away.

Mark and cut your circular pocket holes.

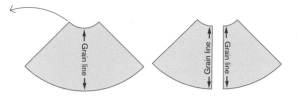

You now have a front piece and two back pieces, all cut on the straight grain.

Flip the newly cut back piece over so you are looking at the right side and lay it out on your fabric, making sure the long straight edge is sitting parallel to the other selvage edge of your fabric. You can measure in from the selvage edge a couple of times to check the straight line is an even distance away from it. Pin it down and cut around it.

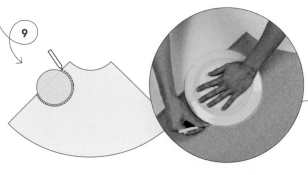

Lay out your front skirt piece and take a circular object that is the size you want your pocket openings to be. We used a plate that measures 23cm (9in) across the widest part. Lay it over one of the sides of your skirt, about 5cm (2in) below the waistline, bearing in mind the waistline will become lower when finished later. The top of our plate sits 7cm (2¾in) below the waistline here. We laid much more than half of our plate over the fabric of the skirt, with only a little bit hanging over the side edge. Draw around the object with chalk.

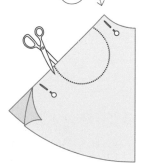

Fold your skirt piece in half so you can still see the chalk, then cut along the chalk line, cutting through both sides of your skirt at once.

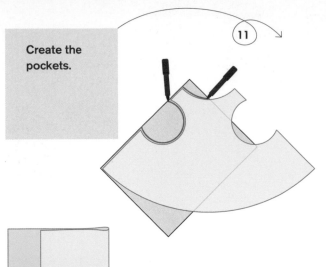

Create the pockets.

(11)

You need to cut four pieces of fabric to create the pocket bags for your skirt – two for each side. All four pieces begin with the same shape.

To make a deep pocket

Draft a shape on a piece of newspaper. Lay your front piece onto the newspaper with the sloping side edge along one side of the newspaper. Draw around the waist edge and around the pocket hole.

(12)

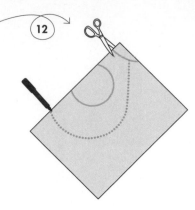

Remove the skirt and draw your pocket bag.

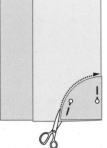

(14)

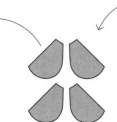

(13)

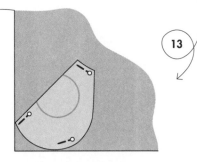

To make a shallow pocket

You could also use the little quarter-circle segment you cut out in step 6 as a guide to make your pocket bag pieces, which is what we did. This will make fairly shallow pockets, but your skirt will be made totally from circles!

Make a fold in your fabric that's wider than the segment, lay the segment on top of it and cut around it. Check it is bigger than the hole you have cut in your skirt! Then cut three more identical pieces.

Cut out this shape, then use the newspaper piece to cut out four pieces this shape from your fabric. Make sure you cut two pieces the same, and two that are mirror images.

Attach the pocket bag pieces.

With the right side of your skirt piece facing up, take two of your pocket bag pieces and lay one on each side under the pocket holes.

If you are adding bias binding to the edge of the holes, you need to be looking at the wrong side of the pocket bag fabric.

If you are not adding binding, you should be looking at the right side of the pocket bag fabric.

(15)

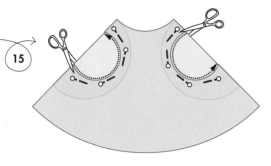

Pin the pocket bags into place then cut out the circular hole shapes.

TUTORIAL

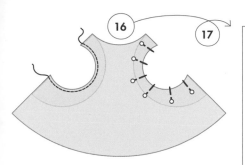

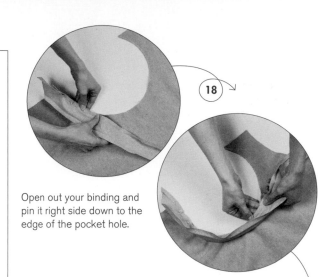

If you are adding binding, leave your pocket pieces pinned on the wrong side of the skirt and sew them to the skirt with your stitches running 5mm (³⁄₁₆in) away from the raw edge. If you are not adding binding, skip to step 23.

For a quick method of binding application, fold a piece of bias binding in half down the middle and sandwich the curved edge of your pocket between the two halves of the binding (as in step 57 of the Triple Triangle Dress tutorial on page 204).

If you want no stitching to appear on the outside of your skirt you can choose a slightly longer process, shown in the following steps.

Open out your binding and pin it right side down to the edge of the pocket hole.

If you choose this method, make sure you stretch out this edge of the binding as much as possible as you pin. This will cause the unpinned edge of the binding to curl up. That's fine.

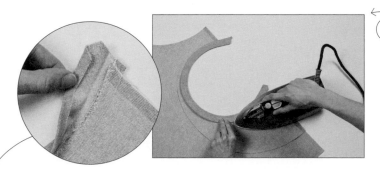

Fold the binding down to the back of the skirt piece. Stretch out the unjoined folded edge then, pulling small sections of it with your fingers, arrange it so the binding sits flat. Make the binding slightly deeper on this side of the skirt than on the front. It should cover the stitches that join the binding to the skirt. Press the binding down in this position.

Sew the pinned edge down along the pressed crease, then lift the binding up towards the pocket hole. Turn the whole piece over and press the seam you have made towards the binding.

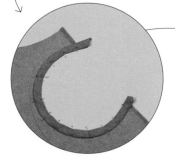

Pin the binding down with the pin heads sticking out into the pocket hole.

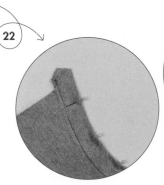

Flip the piece over so you are looking at the right side of the skirt and sew around the binding, with your stitches falling right on top of the seam that joins the binding to the skirt. They should fall into this crease and look invisible, but should catch the deeper binding on the other side.

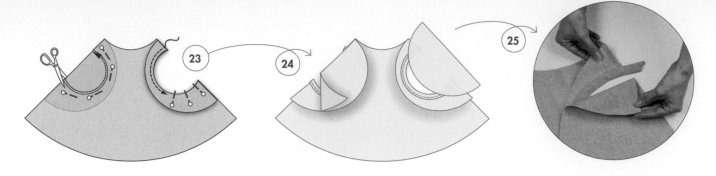

If you are not adding binding, unpin the pocket bag pieces and lift them onto the front of your skirt. The *wrong* side of the pocket bag will be touching the *right* side of the skirt. Sew them into place here. Make snips at various places around the seam allowance, right up to the stitches, then flip the pocket bag pieces over to the wrong side of the skirt and press them neatly into place.

For both versions of the skirt, lay out your front skirt piece so you're looking at the wrong side, i.e. you can see the pocket bag pieces you have already attached.

Lay your second pocket bag pieces right side down on top of these.

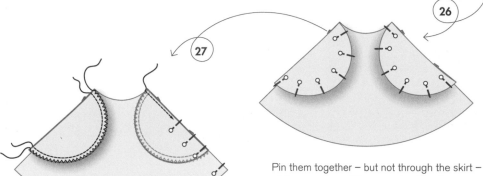

Sew the two pocket bag pieces together with straight stitch then zigzag all the way round the big curved edge as well, sealing the two pieces together.

Arrange the pocket bags so they are sitting flat against the skirt piece, pin them in place and sew a line of straight stitch 5mm (³⁄₁₆in) away from the edge all the way down each side of the skirt, joining both pocket bag pieces to the skirt.

Pin them together – but not through the skirt – all the way around the curved outer edge.

Sew an invisible zip to your skirt at the centre back.

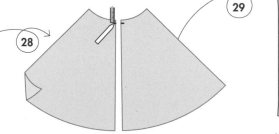

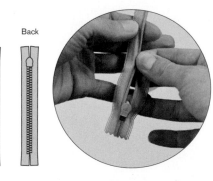

Neaten the straight edge on each of your back pieces with zigzag stitch. Lay the pieces next to each other, with the right side of the fabric facing up, and make a mark 1cm (³⁄₈in) below the waistline on both pieces. This is where the top of your zip teeth will sit.

Front   Back

Unzip your zip. This will make the teeth of the zip curl back towards the zip tape. You want to get rid of this curling effect!

With the zip facing down, press the teeth away from the tape with your iron, forcing them to sit flat.

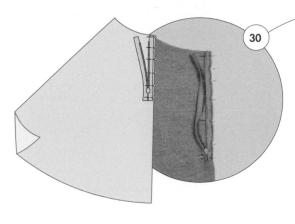

30 Lay your zip face down on top of your left back piece. The right side of the zip should be touching the right side of your fabric. Pin it down with the zip teeth sitting 1.5cm (⅝in) away from the straight edge of your skirt, all the way down. Use your pins to help prevent the teeth from curling back.

31

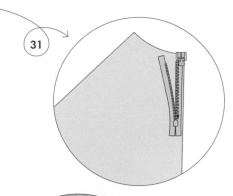

32 Attach a zipper foot to your machine so the main body of the foot sits on the right, away from the zip teeth. Sew your zip to your skirt with straight stitch, positioning your needle as close to the teeth as you can get.

Sew all the way from the top of the zip down to just above the zip pull, removing pins as you go. If you think you can sew closer to the teeth now your pins have gone, sew a second line of stitching. You don't need to unpick the first line! Measure how far away the end of your line of stitching is from the top of your zip pull and write that down here:

33

34 Press your zip away from the skirt.

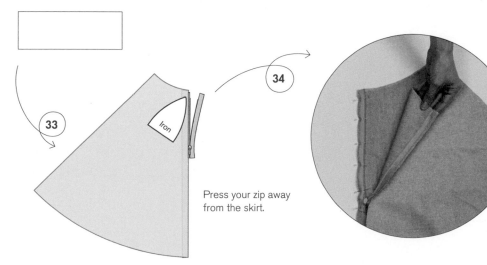

Lay the other side of your skirt out with the right side of the fabric facing up. Lay your piece with the zip attached on top of it, right side down. Take the free side of the zipper tape and pin it face down to the right side of the skirt piece, making sure the teeth sit 1.5cm (⅝in) from the straight edge of the skirt all the way down.

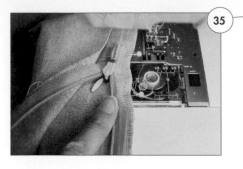

35

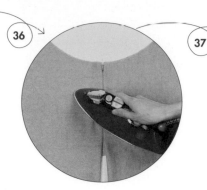

36

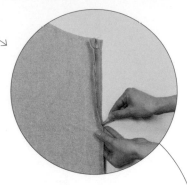

37

Sew this side of the zip to the skirt, this time sewing from the zip pull towards the waist edge of the skirt. Make sure you start your line of stitching the same distance away from the zip pull as your first line of stitching.

Again, if you think you can sew even closer to the zip teeth after you've sewn your zip once, sew a second line of stitching.

Open out your skirt pieces and close your zip. Press the skirt flat on top of the zip.

Now fold your skirt pieces back together with right sides together. You need to sew them together below the zip. Fold the tail of the zip up, away from the skirt, and pin the edges of the skirt together, pinning the tail out of the way.

38

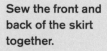

Sew the front and back of the skirt together.

39

Sew down from here to the bottom of your skirt. Open your skirt out and press this seam flat, lifting the tail of the zip and pressing up as far as your iron will go.

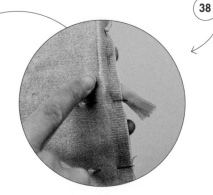

With your zipper foot still on your machine and the main body of the foot sitting over to the left, begin a line of straight stitch right on top of the stitches that join your zip to the skirt.

40

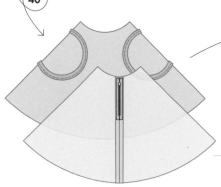

Lay your skirt front out with the back piece on top of it, right sides together.

41

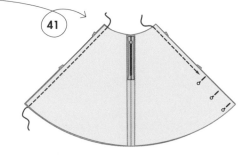

Pin them together along the sloping side edges. Sew down each edge with straight stitch, running 1.5cm (⅝in) away from the edge.

TUTORIAL

Press open the side seams and finish each of the four raw edges with zigzag stitch. Check the skirt fits! Try it on inside out. If it is too big, sew deeper side seams, unpick the first ones and press open the new seam.

Finish the waist edge of your skirt with bias binding.

42

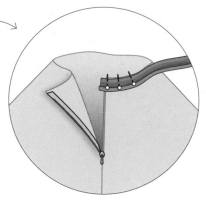

Cut a piece of bias binding that is 2 or 3cm (¾ or 1⅛in) longer than the full waist edge of your skirt. Open out one side of the binding and press it open. With your skirt right way out, pin the open edge of the binding to the waist edge, with a little bit of binding protruding beyond the zip opening at both sides.

44

43

Turn the skirt inside out and bring the binding over to sit on the wrong side of the skirt. Press it so it sits just below the waist edge, tucking the protruding ends under so they sit behind the zip teeth. Pin it in this position and sew it down.

Sew the binding to the skirt, all the way round. Trim the seam down so it is smaller than the depth of the binding.

45

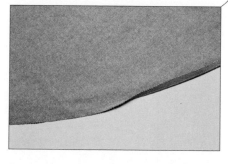

Finish the bottom edge of the skirt.

YOU HAVE MADE A SPOT POCKET SKIRT!

Sew a line of straight stitch all the way around your skirt, 1cm (⅜in) from the raw edge. This stitching will act as a guide when you press the edge up. Neaten the raw edge with zigzag stitch. With your skirt inside out, press up the raw edge so your straight stitching sits just over on the inside of the skirt. Pin the pressed fold into place and stitch it down with straight stitch all the way around the skirt.

Spot pocket skirt

1

Courtney wears a shorter
version of the skirt, made in
a delicate double gauze. The
pockets are finished cleanly,
with no bias binding.

Technical variations

2

Melody's version of the skirt is made in a boldly printed quilting cotton, with contrasting plain fabrics used for the pocket trim and pocket backing. This is a full, sweeping skirt that finishes below the knee.

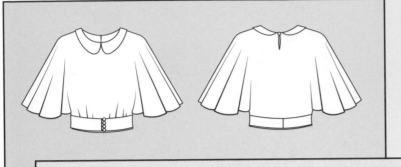

SUITABLE FABRIC

This blouse has sleeves that drape from the shoulders so it suits a fluid fabric that will hang in folds, such as a silk-like fabric, rayon challis or crepe. It can also be made in something slightly crisper, such as a thin cotton or polycotton. This will create a smart-looking garment with slightly fuller-bodied sleeves.

PIECES TO CUT

Front collar and lining   Back collar and lining

Front

Back facing   Front facing

Back

||||| Button loops

Belt facing

Belt facing

MATERIALS NEEDED

Fabric

Small buttons x 5

Skirt/trouser flat fasteners

Fusible interfacing

Guide garment to help draft a sloping shoulder seam – any garment with sleeves will work

String

Newspaper to make template

MATHS TO DO

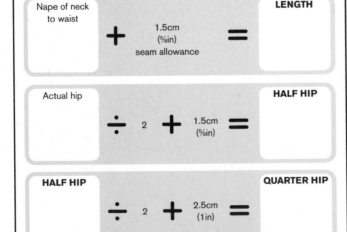

| Nape of neck to waist | **+** 1.5cm (⅝in) seam allowance | **=** | **LENGTH** |

| Actual hip | **÷** 2 **+** 1.5cm (⅝in) | **=** | **HALF HIP** |

| **HALF HIP** | **÷** 2 **+** 2.5cm (1in) | **=** | **QUARTER HIP** |

BODY MEASUREMENTS NEEDED

Actual hip

Nape of neck to waist

Nape of neck to elbow

RIPPLE WRAP BLOUSE

This blouse has fluted, rippling sleeves, and is worn apron-style, with the front belt wrapping around and fastening at the back, and the back belt wrapping around and fastening at the front to create a cinched waist. The belt can be fastened at the front with buttons or a belt buckle, or the two ends can be tied together in a knot. The blouse has a Peter Pan collar and a split at the centre back neckline that fastens with a button and loop.

04

CIRCLES

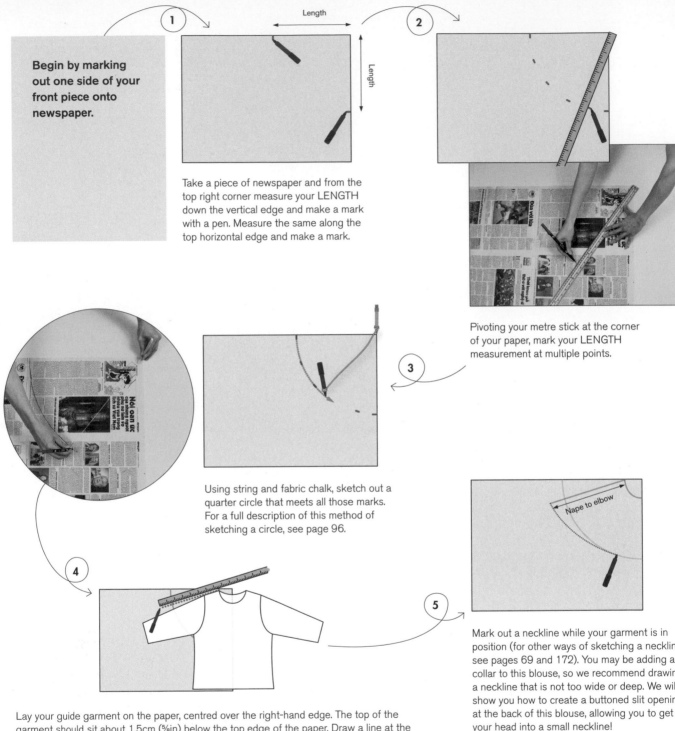

Begin by marking out one side of your front piece onto newspaper.

1

Take a piece of newspaper and from the top right corner measure your LENGTH down the vertical edge and make a mark with a pen. Measure the same along the top horizontal edge and make a mark.

2

Pivoting your metre stick at the corner of your paper, mark your LENGTH measurement at multiple points.

3

Using string and fabric chalk, sketch out a quarter circle that meets all those marks. For a full description of this method of sketching a circle, see page 96.

4

Lay your guide garment on the paper, centred over the right-hand edge. The top of the garment should sit about 1.5cm (⅝in) below the top edge of the paper. Draw a line at the same angle as the slope of the shoulder of your guide garment.

This size circle means your sleeves will end about halfway between your shoulder and your elbow. You can resketch the circle to add additional length to your sleeve. To do so, extend the sloping line beyond the circle, so it is as long as your nape to elbow measurement.

5

Mark out a neckline while your garment is in position (for other ways of sketching a neckline, see pages 69 and 172). You may be adding a collar to this blouse, so we recommend drawing a neckline that is not too wide or deep. We will show you how to create a buttoned slit opening at the back of this blouse, allowing you to get your head into a small neckline!

Sketch a new curve stretching from the end of your sloping nape to elbow line to meet the bottom of your circle, using your initial circle as a visual reference to create a nice smooth arc.

TUTORIAL

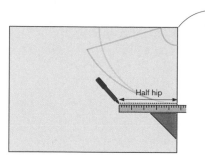

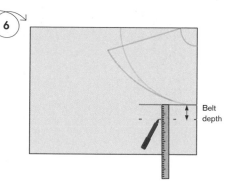

6

Square a line as long as your HALF HIP outwards from the bottom of the circle where it meets the edge of your paper.

Belt depth

This is the upper edge of the belt part of your blouse. You need to decide how deep you would like your belt to be. Our version has a belt 6.5cm (2½in) deep. Once you have decided how deep your belt will be, add 2cm (¾in) to this and write it down here.

We'll call this your BELT DEPTH.

Measure this down from the initial line you have drawn, a few times, then join your marks with a line as long as your HALF HIP. Draw a short vertical line joining the ends of those two lines.

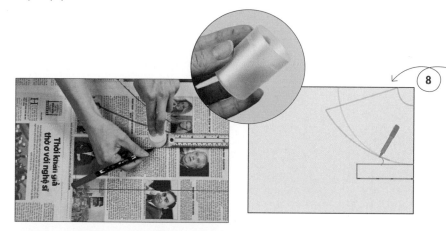

8

7

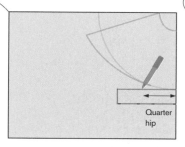

Quarter hip

From this point, sketch a curve that joins the belt part of your top to the main circle. You can sketch this freehand or use a small circular object to help you. We used the lid of a hair product to get a nice smooth curve.

Measure your QUARTER HIP from the edge of your paper along the upper line and make a mark.

9

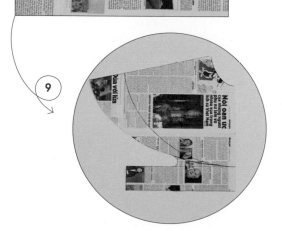

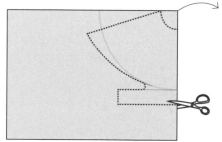

Cut out your paper shape.
(Cut around the original circle if you are not lengthening the sleeves.)

Next you will use your paper piece to cut the front piece of your blouse.

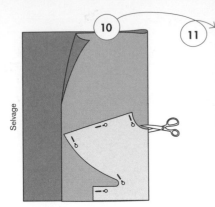

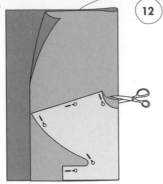

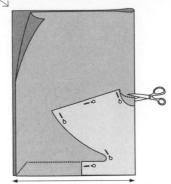

To make a blouse that fastens with a belt buckle or a knot
You need to extend the belt part of your back piece. Make a fold in your fabric that is as wide as your HALF HIP plus about 20cm (8in) and cut the belt part of your top this wide.

Half hip + 20cm (8in)

Make a fold in your fabric that is as wide as your paper piece. Lay the vertical edge of your paper piece on top of the fold in your fabric, pin it down so it doesn't move and cut around it.

Use your paper shape to cut a back piece the same but with a shallower neckline.

Use your front piece to mark out a facing piece for the front of your blouse, marking out the neckline then removing the paper and marking various points 6cm (2⅜in) deeper than the neck edge. See page 59 of the Deco Drape Dress tutorial for a more detailed explanation of making a facing.

Make facings for the front and back of your blouse, allowing for a slit opening at the back.

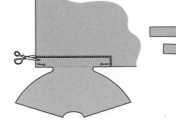

Use your first fabric piece to cut two strips of fabric the same depth and width as the belt part. If you extended the length of the belt on your back piece, use your back piece as a guide to cut one of these strips instead.

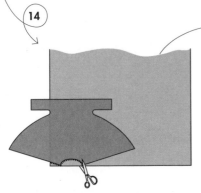

On your back facing, you need to create an extension to allow for a slit opening. Use your back piece as a guide to cut the neck edge.

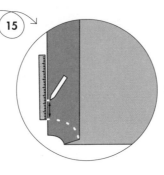

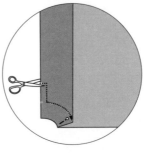

Decide how long you want your slit to be. We cut ours 8cm (3⅛in) deep. Fold the neckline shape you have cut in half. Mark out the lower edge of your facing then measure the slit depth + 4cm (1⅝in) down the folded edge of the fabric. Cut an extension about 3cm (1⅛in) wide. This will double when you open out the folded piece. You now have a front facing and a back facing piece.

TUTORIAL

Use your facing pieces to help sketch your Peter Pan collar pieces.

Each side of your collar is going to be made of four small pieces of fabric. One front piece and one back piece will form the outer part of the collar and then two more will form a lining. This means you'll be cutting eight little pieces of fabric. Bear with the instructions and you will get there! It helps to interface the lining pieces of the collar, simply to help distinguish between the lining and the outer parts of the collar.

16

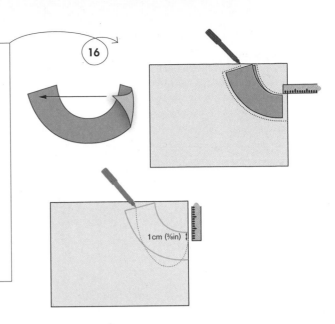

1cm (⅜in)

17

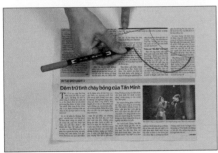

Fold your front facing piece in half and lay it on a piece of newspaper, 1cm (⅜in) in from the edge.

Draw around the facing then remove it. Sketch out a curved collar shape that reduces the width of the shoulder edge at the top.

Repeat this with the back facing piece, but lay it right at the edge of your newspaper.

Draw around the piece and mark the shoulder edge the same width as on the front collar piece.

Draw a curve that tapers towards the centre back edge.

18

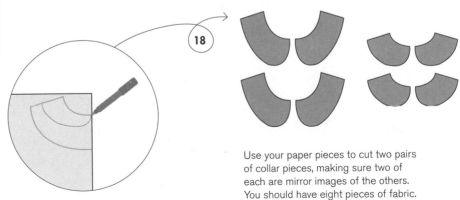

Use your paper pieces to cut two pairs of collar pieces, making sure two of each are mirror images of the others. You should have eight pieces of fabric.

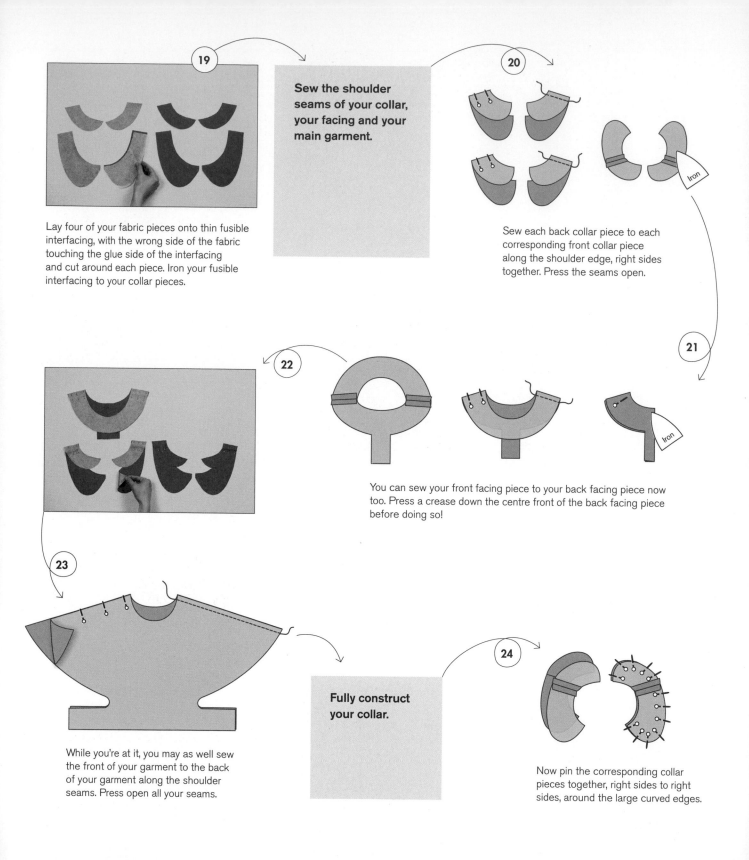

19

Lay four of your fabric pieces onto thin fusible interfacing, with the wrong side of the fabric touching the glue side of the interfacing and cut around each piece. Iron your fusible interfacing to your collar pieces.

Sew the shoulder seams of your collar, your facing and your main garment.

20

Iron

Sew each back collar piece to each corresponding front collar piece along the shoulder edge, right sides together. Press the seams open.

21

22

Iron

You can sew your front facing piece to your back facing piece now too. Press a crease down the centre front of the back facing piece before doing so!

23

While you're at it, you may as well sew the front of your garment to the back of your garment along the shoulder seams. Press open all your seams.

Fully construct your collar.

24

Now pin the corresponding collar pieces together, right sides to right sides, around the large curved edges.

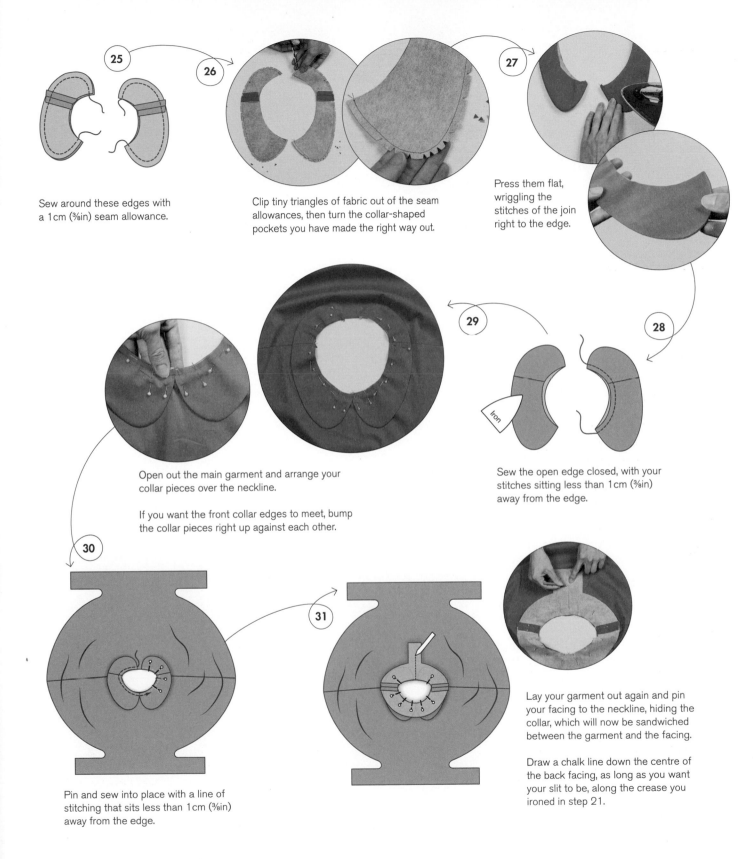

25

Sew around these edges with a 1cm (⅜in) seam allowance.

26

Clip tiny triangles of fabric out of the seam allowances, then turn the collar-shaped pockets you have made the right way out.

27

Press them flat, wriggling the stitches of the join right to the edge.

29

Open out the main garment and arrange your collar pieces over the neckline.

If you want the front collar edges to meet, bump the collar pieces right up against each other.

28

Sew the open edge closed, with your stitches sitting less than 1cm (⅜in) away from the edge.

30

Pin and sew into place with a line of stitching that sits less than 1cm (⅜in) away from the edge.

31

Lay your garment out again and pin your facing to the neckline, hiding the collar, which will now be sandwiched between the garment and the facing.

Draw a chalk line down the centre of the back facing, as long as you want your slit to be, along the crease you ironed in step 21.

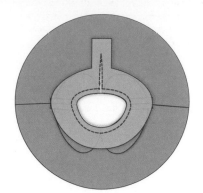

32 **33**

Sew the facing to the blouse with straight stitch, 1cm (⅜in) away from the edge. Start stitching just outside your chalk line, sewing around the neckline until you get back to the chalk line. Pause just before it with your needle in the down position, pivot your fabric, then sew towards the bottom of the chalk line, just outside it, angling your line so that it hits the point of the chalk line.

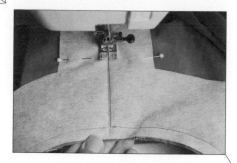

Then pivot again, sewing up the other side of the line until you get back to the stitches at the neckline where you began.

34

Before you cut into the slit, you're going to make some button loops.

Make one button loop for the neck opening and four for the waistband. Each loop needs to be able to fit around whatever buttons you are using and have a little bit of extra length on top of that. You can make all the loops together by cutting one long strip of fabric. The fabric should be roughly four times the depth of the final button loop. Our button loops are 4mm (⅛in) deep, so our initial strip of fabric was 1.6cm (½in) deep. Press each long side of the strip in to the centre, then fold the strip in half lengthwise and sew all the way along it with straight stitch. Snip the long strip you have made into sections to create your individual button loops.

Finish your neckline and add the button loop.

35

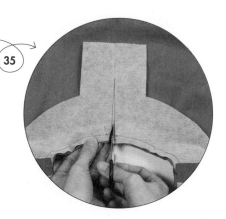

Cut along the chalk line to create your slit.

TUTORIAL

(36) Unpick a few stitches on one side of the slit, at the top near the neckline, and push one of your button loops into the opening you have made. Push the folded end of the loop in under the facing and leave the tails just protruding from the slit.

Sew over the area of stitching you unpicked, sewing over the ends of the button loop.

Turn your garment inside out and lift your facing over so it sits on the wrong side. Press it into place, making sure the collar remains on the outside of your garment.

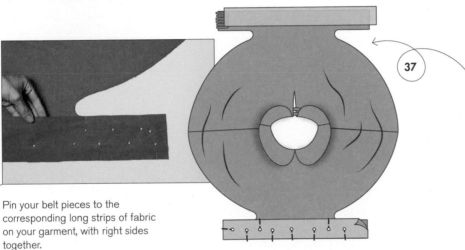

(37)

Create neatly finished edges.

(38) Pin your belt pieces to the corresponding long strips of fabric on your garment, with right sides together.

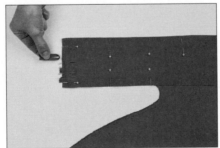

Position your three button loops on one side of the belt at the *back* of your blouse. This will wrap around your body and end up sitting at the front of your garment.

Use pins to help space your loops evenly. You'll be sewing all the way around this rectangle, so make sure the loops don't sit in the seam allowance at the top and bottom of the belt.

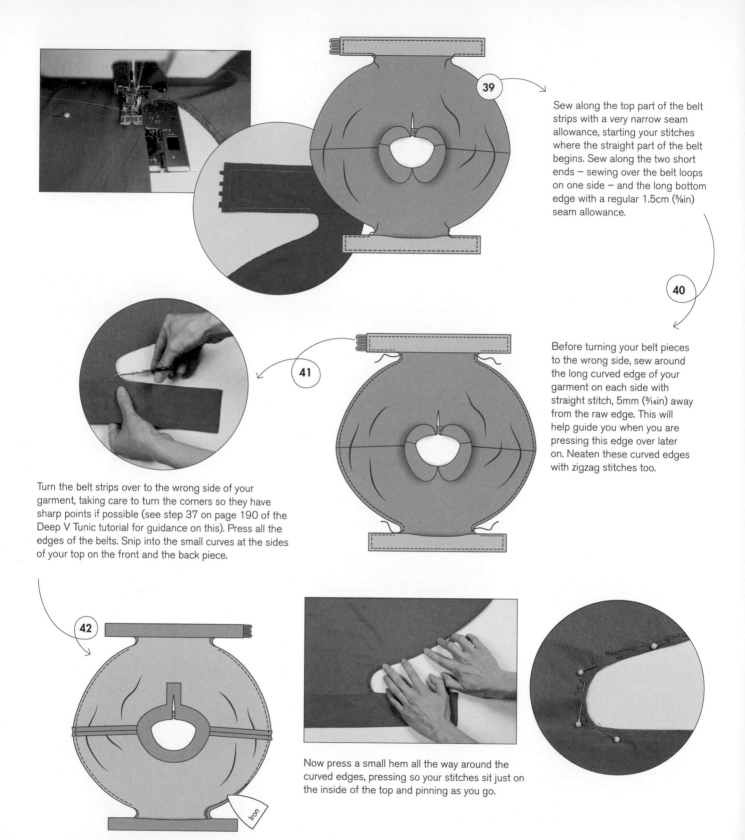

Sew along the top part of the belt strips with a very narrow seam allowance, starting your stitches where the straight part of the belt begins. Sew along the two short ends – sewing over the belt loops on one side – and the long bottom edge with a regular 1.5cm (⅝in) seam allowance.

Before turning your belt pieces to the wrong side, sew around the long curved edge of your garment on each side with straight stitch, 5mm (³⁄₁₆in) away from the raw edge. This will help guide you when you are pressing this edge over later on. Neaten these curved edges with zigzag stitches too.

Turn the belt strips over to the wrong side of your garment, taking care to turn the corners so they have sharp points if possible (see step 37 on page 190 of the Deep V Tunic tutorial for guidance on this). Press all the edges of the belts. Snip into the small curves at the sides of your top on the front and the back piece.

Now press a small hem all the way around the curved edges, pressing so your stitches sit just on the inside of the top and pinning as you go.

TUTORIAL

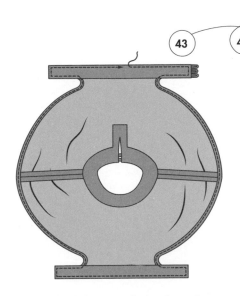

(43) (44)

Stitch the pressed edge down all the way round, continuing your stitches around the edges of both belt sections.

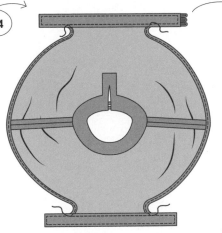

Sew along the tops of the belt rectangles to close the openings there.

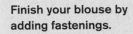

Finish your blouse by adding fastenings.

(45)

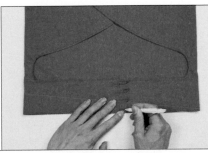

Lay out your blouse with the back belt ends folding to the front and overlapping, making sure the belt will fit around your body. Make chalk marks where your buttons will sit. Mark the neck closure in the same way. Hand sew buttons into place on the back neck and the back belt, which will sit at the centre front. Hand sew flat fasteners to the front belt, which will wrap around and sit at your centre back.

YOU HAVE MADE A RIPPLE WRAP BLOUSE!

Ripple wrap blouse

1

Melody's version of the
Ripple Wrap Blouse is made
in an extremely drapey
lightweight crepe. The top has
a contrasting collar made in
semi-sheer chiffon and has a
long waistband fastening at the
front, with a belt buckle.

Technical variations

2

Karishma wears a collarless version of the blouse, made in a thick silk. The neckline is wide and deep, meaning there is no need for a split opening at the back. The waistband on this version fastens with buttons at the front.

MATERIALS NEEDED

Fabric

Elastic for neck and waist

Bias binding

A guide garment with armholes that are not too deep; a sleeveless dress or top would be ideal

SUITABLE FABRIC

This dress will work well in almost any fabric. Use light and crisp fabric, or something weightier and slightly stiff to create a dramatic dress with a full-bodied, voluminous ruffle. Choose a drapier fabric to create a flowing dress with soft folds.

PIECES TO CUT

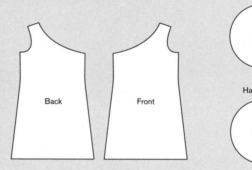

Back

Front

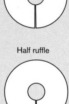

Half ruffle

Half ruffle

BODY MEASUREMENTS NEEDED

Full waist

Full hip

MATHS TO DO

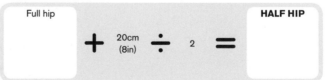

Measure from the nape of your neck to where you would like your hem to fall

$+$ 6cm (2⅜in) $=$ **DRESS LENGTH**

Full hip $+$ 20cm (8in) $\div$ 2 $=$ **HALF HIP**

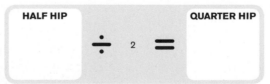

HALF HIP $\div$ 2 $=$ **QUARTER HIP**

RUFFLE DRESS

This dress can be a dramatic sculptural piece when made with stiff fabric, or feminine and floaty when made with a more delicate, drapey fabric. The neckline is gently gathered with elastic, giving the ruffle extra body. The ruffle is finished with bias binding, which can be pressed to the under side so that it is hidden, or used as a trim in a contrasting colour. Add an extra ruffle to create even more waves and ripples. The dress can be as long or as short as you like.

05
CIRCLES

Mark out and cut the front and back pieces of your dress.

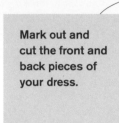

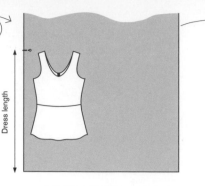

1 Measure your DRESS LENGTH up the selvage edge of your fabric and put a pin in to mark that spot. If your guide garment doesn't have a distinct waistline, put it on and put a pin in at the level of your waist to mark it, then take the garment off. Lay your guide garment on your fabric with the shoulder edge sitting just below the level of your DRESS LENGTH marker pin.

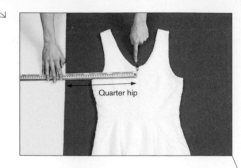

2 Measure your QUARTER HIP horizontally from the selvage edge and shift your guide garment so its centre sits roughly at your QUARTER HIP point.

3 Sketch around your guide garment with tailor's chalk, drawing your lines about 1.5cm (⅝in) outside the garment. Start at one armpit, draw up around the armhole and along the shoulder edge, then roughly sketch the first part of the neckline.

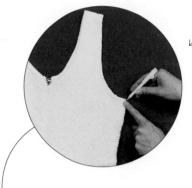

4 Mark the other armpit point with a dot of chalk too.

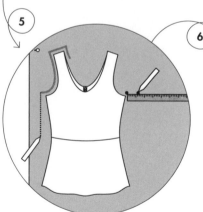

5 If your guide garment fits you closely, measure about 8cm (3⅛in) outwards from this armpit point and make a mark there. If your guide garment is a fairly baggy garment (it doesn't cling to you under the armpits) then you can skip this step.

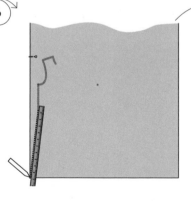

6 On the left, draw a line straight down from the armpit point until you are level with the waist of your garment. This is marked by the pin you put in while wearing it (or on our guide garment by the waist seam). Remove your guide garment. Draw a straight line sloping from the waist point out to the bottom corner of your fabric.

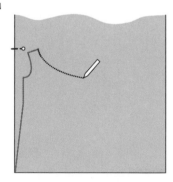

7 Sketch a scooped neck edge. This can start by following the part of the neckline you already drew and should slope down towards the armpit point (or the additional mark you made if your guide garment is tight fitting).

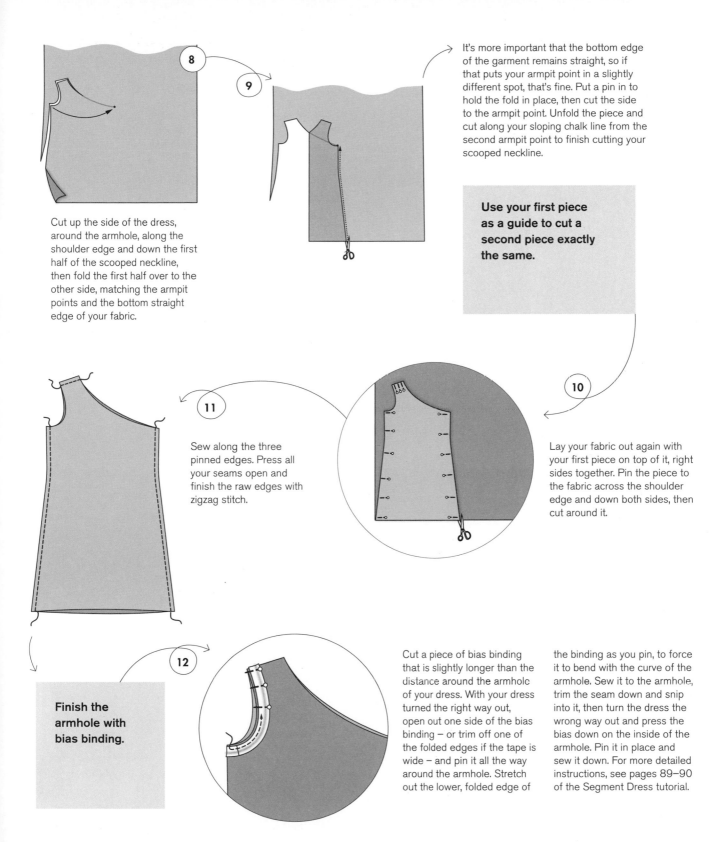

8

9

Cut up the side of the dress, around the armhole, along the shoulder edge and down the first half of the scooped neckline, then fold the first half over to the other side, matching the armpit points and the bottom straight edge of your fabric.

It's more important that the bottom edge of the garment remains straight, so if that puts your armpit point in a slightly different spot, that's fine. Put a pin in to hold the fold in place, then cut the side to the armpit point. Unfold the piece and cut along your sloping chalk line from the second armpit point to finish cutting your scooped neckline.

Use your first piece as a guide to cut a second piece exactly the same.

11

Sew along the three pinned edges. Press all your seams open and finish the raw edges with zigzag stitch.

10

Lay your fabric out again with your first piece on top of it, right sides together. Pin the piece to the fabric across the shoulder edge and down both sides, then cut around it.

12

Finish the armhole with bias binding.

Cut a piece of bias binding that is slightly longer than the distance around the armhole of your dress. With your dress turned the right way out, open out one side of the bias binding – or trim off one of the folded edges if the tape is wide – and pin it all the way around the armhole. Stretch out the lower, folded edge of the binding as you pin, to force it to bend with the curve of the armhole. Sew it to the armhole, trim the seam down and snip into it, then turn the dress the wrong way out and press the bias down on the inside of the armhole. Pin it in place and sew it down. For more detailed instructions, see pages 89–90 of the Segment Dress tutorial.

Now it's time to create your ruffle.

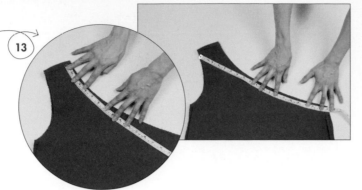

(13)

Lay your garment out and measure along the neck edge at either the front or back with your tape measure, curving the tape measure to match the curve of the neckline as much as possible. Double it, then write that number down here:

We'll call this your INNER CIRCLES measurement.

(14)

We made our ruffle out of three smaller rings of fabric to get some fairly dramatic folds, so we divided our INNER CIRCLES measurement by 3, added 3cm (1⅛in) to that and found a round object with a circumference that was pretty similar to that measurement. You might be lucky and find a bowl or plate that has exactly the right circumference, but if not just find something that has a slightly bigger circumference. You can chop the excess fabric off later.

Inner circle

Your ruffle is going to be made of a number of pieces of fabric that are the shape of ring doughnuts. If you were to make your ruffle out of one big ring, the distance around the edge of the hole in the middle of the doughnut would need to be your INNER CIRCLES measurement plus 3cm (1⅛in). You can make your ruffle out of one big ring, but this would create a fairly undramatic ruffle – more of a gentle wave. The tighter the central ring of your doughnut is, the more ruffles you will create.

(15)

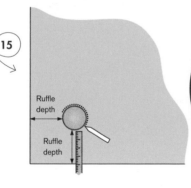

Ruffle depth

Ruffle depth

Creating a ruffle out of three rings means we have a seam in the ruffle at the centre front and centre back of the dress. Our two variations of the dress each used two rings to create the ruffles, meaning the joining seam sits neatly at the shoulder.

Decide how deep you want your ruffle to be, add 2cm (¾in) and write that down here. We'll call this the RUFFLE DEPTH.

Ours is 23cm (9in) deep. Position your round object – in our case a bowl – so that its edges sit at the RUFFLE DEPTH inland from two edges of your fabric.

Draw around your object with tailor's chalk.

(16)

Using your ruler, make marks all the way around it at your RUFFLE DEPTH. Cut a circle following these marks.

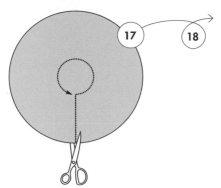

(17) **(18)**

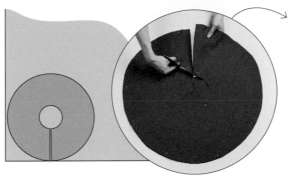

Cut a straight line into your circle from the edge, then cut out the inner ring to create your doughnut shape.

Use this first ruffle piece as a guide to cut the other pieces you need.

Join your rings of fabric together to create a continuous ruffle piece.

(19)

Now join your ruffle to your dress.

Lay out two of your rings, right sides together. Match up two of the straight edges and pin them together. Sew the two together with a line of straight stitch. If you are adding a third ring, open up the joined rings and lay them out right side up. Lay the third ring on top of one of them, right sides together, then pin the straight edges and sew with straight stitch.

Press open your seams and finish the raw edges with zigzag stitch.

(20) **(21)**

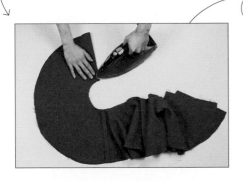

Find the centre of the inner edge of your ruffle. If it is made of two pieces, it will be the seam that joins the two parts. If it is made of three, fold it in half and mark that centre spot by pressing a small crease in it with your iron.

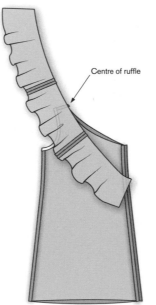

Centre of ruffle

With your dress inside out and the wrong side of the ruffle facing you, line up the centre of the ruffle with the shoulder seam of your dress. Pin the ruffle to the dress here.

Continue pinning the ruffle to the dress. Put your pins in about 1cm (⅜in) away from the edges of the fabric. This is where you'll be sewing, and pinning at this depth will help you avoid sewing pinches of fabric into your ruffle.

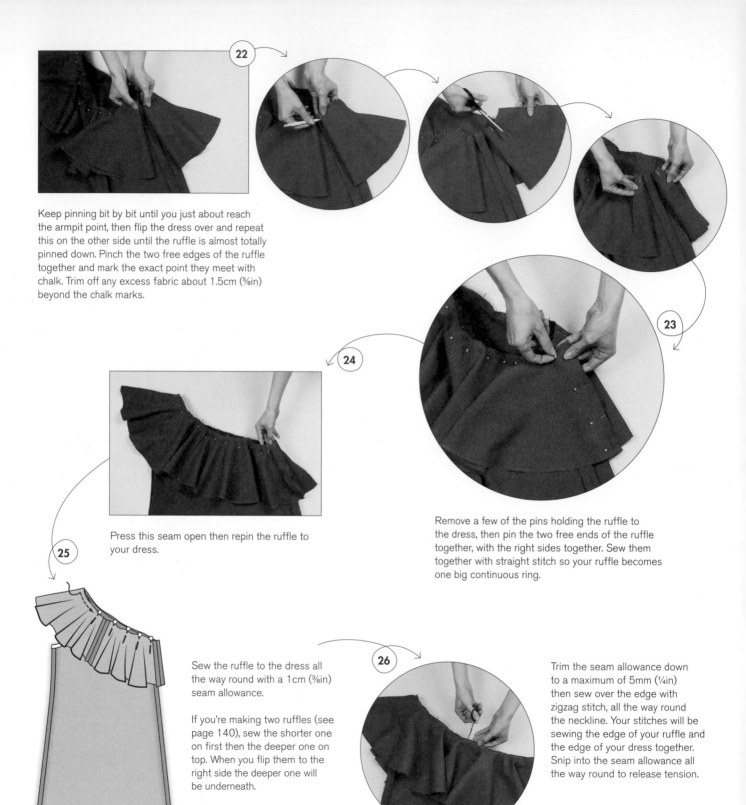

Keep pinning bit by bit until you just about reach the armpit point, then flip the dress over and repeat this on the other side until the ruffle is almost totally pinned down. Pinch the two free edges of the ruffle together and mark the exact point they meet with chalk. Trim off any excess fabric about 1.5cm (⅝in) beyond the chalk marks.

Press this seam open then repin the ruffle to your dress.

Remove a few of the pins holding the ruffle to the dress, then pin the two free ends of the ruffle together, with the right sides together. Sew them together with straight stitch so your ruffle becomes one big continuous ring.

Sew the ruffle to the dress all the way round with a 1cm (⅜in) seam allowance.

If you're making two ruffles (see page 140), sew the shorter one on first then the deeper one on top. When you flip them to the right side the deeper one will be underneath.

Trim the seam allowance down to a maximum of 5mm (¼in) then sew over the edge with zigzag stitch, all the way round the neckline. Your stitches will be sewing the edge of your ruffle and the edge of your dress together. Snip into the seam allowance all the way round to release tension.

TUTORIAL

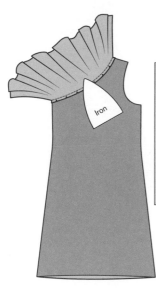

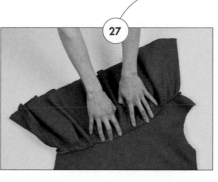

27

Use the tip of your iron to press the trimmed seam allowance down towards the dress. You will find this easiest if you pull your dress over the end of your ironing board.

Create a channel at the neck edge to thread elastic through.

You are going to apply a piece of bias binding to your dress where it is joined to your ruffle, all the way round the neck edge. It will technically be on the right side of your dress, but the ruffle will hide it. The binding will form a channel through which you can thread a piece of elastic. The bias binding can be any colour as it won't show on the outside of the dress. A silky binding will work best as it will help the elastic to slip through easily. The binding needs to be wider than the elastic you will be threading through. Our bias binding is 1.5cm (⅝in) deep and our elastic is 7mm (¼in) wide.

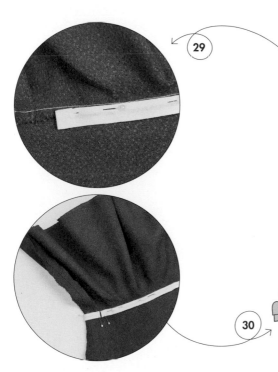

29

Cut a piece of binding that is a few centimetres (1–2in) longer than your INNER CIRCLES measurement (see step 13).

Fold one of the short ends of the binding under and start pinning it to the dress over the seam you pressed down. The top edge of the binding should run right under the line of stitching that joins the ruffle to the dress.

28

Pin the binding all the way round, then tuck the short end of the binding under so that the two ends of binding just about touch each other.

30

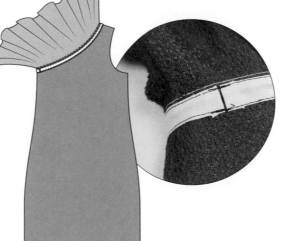

Sew the binding to the dress all the way round, with your stitches running just below the top edge of the binding. Then run a second line of stitching all the way round the lower edge of the binding. You have made your channel!

31

Add a channel for elastic at the waist of your dress.

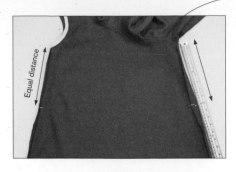

Try your dress on inside out and put a pin in on one side where you would like the dress to pinch the waist. Take the dress off and measure down from the armpit to the marker pin. Measure this same distance down the other side of the dress from the armpit and make a mark with chalk.

32

Draw a chalk line across the front of your dress between these two points. Flip the dress over and draw one on the back, too.

You can use a wide piece of silky bias binding to create your waistband channel, or you can use a strip of fabric. If you are using fabric, cut a strip that is 3cm (1⅛in) deeper than the elastic you will be using, then press 1cm (⅜in) over along both of the long raw edges. You don't need to cut this on the bias.

33

Thread elastic through both of your channels.

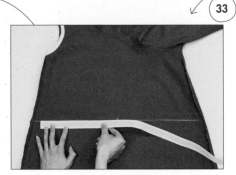

Pin your binding or fabric strip to your dress with the top edge sitting right along the chalk line you have drawn, and folding under the ends of the binding, as for the previous elastic channel. Sew along the top and bottom of your binding. It will be easiest to insert the bottom of the dress over the end of your machine to sew these lines.

34

Cut a piece of elastic as long as your full waist measurement and, with your dress remaining inside out, thread it through the waist channel using a large safety pin. When the safety pin emerges, pin the two ends together for now.

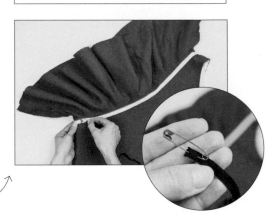

35

Turn the dress the right way out and thread a piece of elastic through the channel that runs around your neck edge. Determining the length of this takes a bit of trial and error. Cut a piece that is about 10cm (4in) shorter than your INNER CIRCLES measurement, but be prepared to make it tighter when you try your dress on.

138

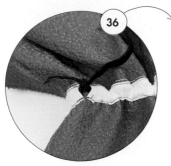

36

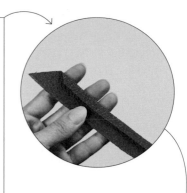

Finish the edge of your ruffle.

Tie the ends together in a knot. Try your dress on and adjust the elastic at the waist and neck until you are happy with the tension and fit. Trim the elastic and sew the ends together.

You are going to finish the edge of your ruffle with bias binding. You can bind the edge so that it clearly shows, like in our version on page 140 (see page 204 in the Triple Triangle Dress for instructions), or you can hide your tape by pressing it to the inside as we have done here. The tape may still show in places, so it is best to use a similar colour or to make your tape from the same fabric as the ruffle.

37

38

If your bias binding is thick or stiff, it will help maintain structured, undulating folds. If you are using a softer, drapier fabric, like our palm tree crepe version on page 141, you may want to choose (or make) a binding from soft fabric too, so the natural properties of the binding don't argue with the properties of the fabric you have chosen.

To create a hidden binding, pin the tape to the edge of the ruffle on the right side, trim it to the correct length then sew it into place.

Trim the seam allowance down then flip your binding to the wrong side of the ruffle, pressing it so it sits just inside the edge.

39

Hem the bottom edge.

Pin it in position here and sew it down, all the way round.

Zigzag all the way round the raw edge at the bottom of the dress, then press it up. You may find you are pressing up a deeper hem at the sides of your dress because of the sloping angle of the side seams. Try to make sure you press up the same amount on either side of your dress so the hem appears even when viewed from the front or back. Pin the hem in place then sew it down with your stitches sitting the same distance from the folded edge of the dress all the way round.

YOU HAVE MADE A RUFFLE DRESS!

Ruffle dress

1

Linda's version of the Ruffle Dress is made in thick polished cotton that holds its shape. The dress has two ruffles at the neckline, each finished with a visible bias trim. The trim itself is crisp, forcing the ruffles to hang in wide, undulating folds. The dress is cropped just above the knee and has a deep waistband.

2

Melody wears a version of
the dress made in a drapey
crepe, which gives the dress
a soft, flowing feel. Instead of
a channel at the waistline, a
single piece of narrow elastic
was sewn directly to the dress
with zigzag stitch. There is
technically no difference
between the front and back of
this dress, so you can wear it
sweeping over either shoulder!

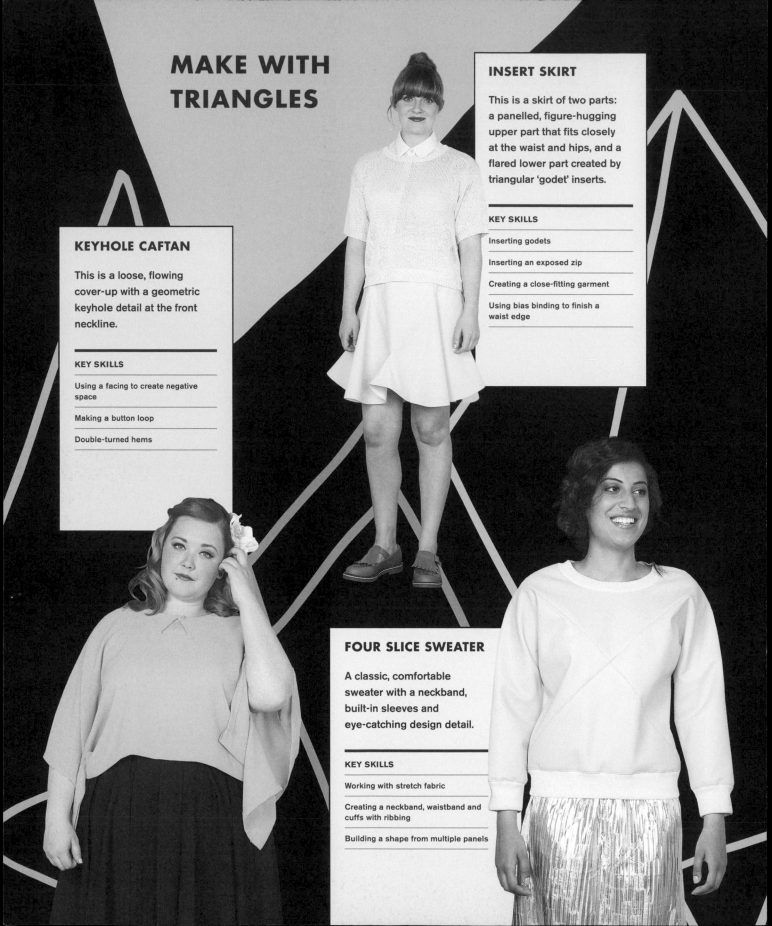

MAKE WITH TRIANGLES

INSERT SKIRT

This is a skirt of two parts: a panelled, figure-hugging upper part that fits closely at the waist and hips, and a flared lower part created by triangular 'godet' inserts.

KEY SKILLS

Inserting godets

Inserting an exposed zip

Creating a close-fitting garment

Using bias binding to finish a waist edge

KEYHOLE CAFTAN

This is a loose, flowing cover-up with a geometric keyhole detail at the front neckline.

KEY SKILLS

Using a facing to create negative space

Making a button loop

Double-turned hems

FOUR SLICE SWEATER

A classic, comfortable sweater with a neckband, built-in sleeves and eye-catching design detail.

KEY SKILLS

Working with stretch fabric

Creating a neckband, waistband and cuffs with ribbing

Building a shape from multiple panels

TRIPLE TRIANGLE DRESS

This sleeveless sheath dress has a fitted skirt and shaped bodice made of two angular halves that overlap to create a V-shaped neckline and a triangle of negative space at the waistline.

KEY SKILLS

Marking and sewing darts

Inserting an invisible zip

Using body measurements to create a paper template

Creating a close-fitting garment

DEEP V TUNIC

An elegant tunic with graphic sleeve caps and a deep V-shaped placket that creates a plunging triangular neck opening.

KEY SKILLS

Inserting a placket

Adding sleeve caps

MATERIALS NEEDED

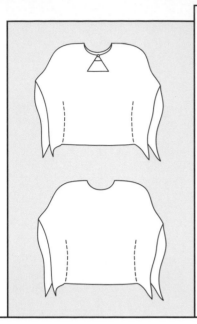

Fabric

Fusible interfacing

Small button or hook and eye

Ribbon to tie fronts or create button loop (optional)

Guide garment with sleeves and a round, shallow neckline

Scrap paper

BODY MEASUREMENTS NEEDED

Full hip or full bust (whichever is bigger)

Shoulder peak to shoulder peak

From shoulder peak to desired length of sleeve

Nape of neck to desired length of garment

MATHS TO DO

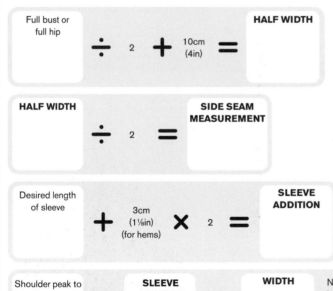

| Full bust or full hip | ÷ 2 | + 10cm (4in) | = | HALF WIDTH |

| HALF WIDTH | ÷ 2 | = | SIDE SEAM MEASUREMENT |

| Desired length of sleeve | + 3cm (1⅛in) (for hems) | × 2 | = | SLEEVE ADDITION |

| Shoulder peak to shoulder peak | + | SLEEVE ADDITION | = | WIDTH |

NB! The WIDTH should be at least 20cm (8in) bigger than your HALF WIDTH. If not, use your HALF WIDTH + 20cm (8in) as your WIDTH (you'll just have slightly longer sleeves than you planned). You can of course add even more than 20cm (8in) to this measurement if you want.

| Nape of neck to desired length of garment | + 6cm (2⅜in) | = | LENGTH |

SUITABLE FABRIC

The Keyhole Caftan is ideally suited to thin, drapey woven fabric. We used a medium-weight crepe for this tutorial, which was only just thin enough to avoid bulkiness in the double-turned hems. This top would work very well in light, fluid fabric such as rayon challis, or any fabric that hangs in loose folds when left to its own devices.

PIECES TO CUT

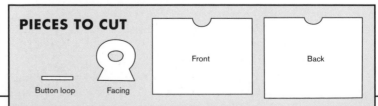

Button loop

Facing

Front

Back

KEYHOLE CAFTAN

This caftan can be worn as a top or made longer and worn as a dress. Lines of shirring can be sewn at the waist to create shape. The top of the keyhole fastens with a button and loop, with thin ribbons tied in a bow or with a hook and eye hidden at the back. The caftan has double-turned hems to finish all four edges neatly.

01
TRIANGLES

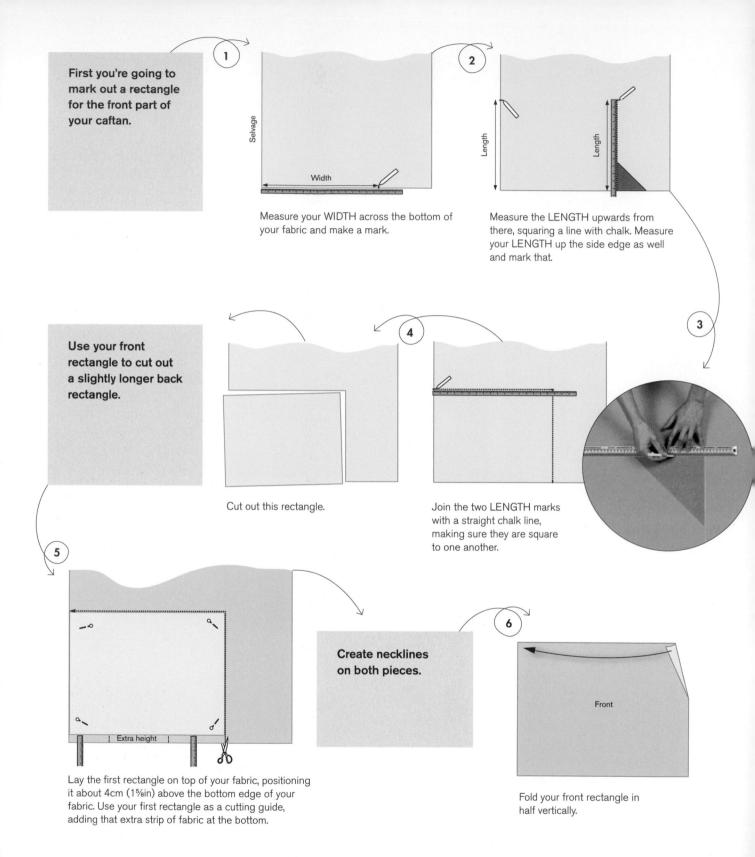

First you're going to mark out a rectangle for the front part of your caftan.

Selvage

Width

Measure your WIDTH across the bottom of your fabric and make a mark.

Length

Length

Measure the LENGTH upwards from there, squaring a line with chalk. Measure your LENGTH up the side edge as well and mark that.

Use your front rectangle to cut out a slightly longer back rectangle.

Cut out this rectangle.

Join the two LENGTH marks with a straight chalk line, making sure they are square to one another.

Extra height

Lay the first rectangle on top of your fabric, positioning it about 4cm (1⅝in) above the bottom edge of your fabric. Use your first rectangle as a cutting guide, adding that extra strip of fabric at the bottom.

Create necklines on both pieces.

Front

Fold your front rectangle in half vertically.

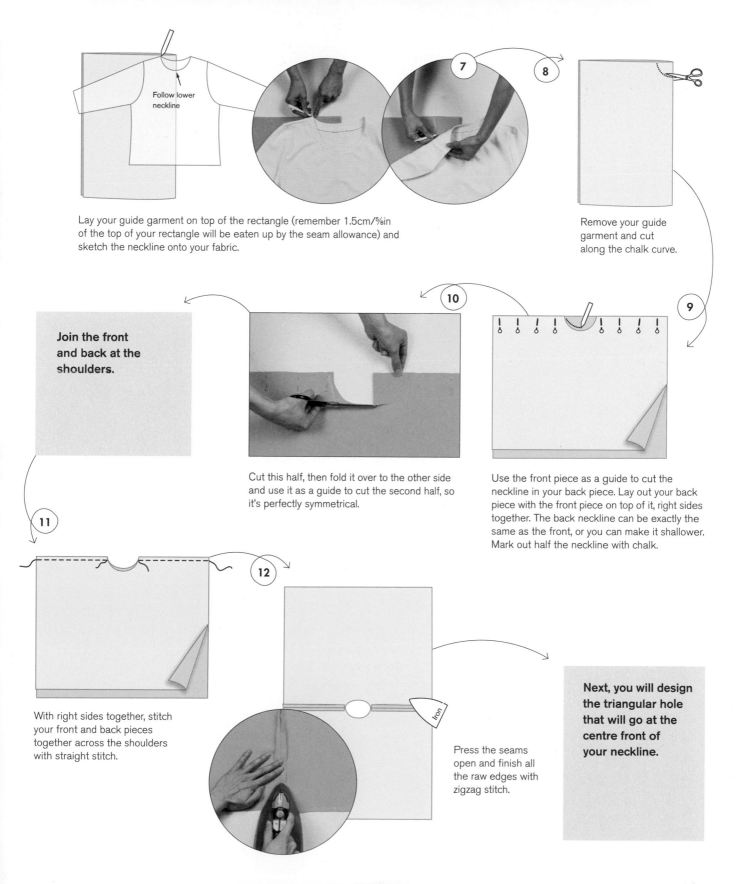

Follow lower neckline

7

8

Lay your guide garment on top of the rectangle (remember 1.5cm/⅝in of the top of your rectangle will be eaten up by the seam allowance) and sketch the neckline onto your fabric.

Remove your guide garment and cut along the chalk curve.

9

10

Join the front and back at the shoulders.

Cut this half, then fold it over to the other side and use it as a guide to cut the second half, so it's perfectly symmetrical.

Use the front piece as a guide to cut the neckline in your back piece. Lay out your back piece with the front piece on top of it, right sides together. The back neckline can be exactly the same as the front, or you can make it shallower. Mark out half the neckline with chalk.

11

12

With right sides together, stitch your front and back pieces together across the shoulders with straight stitch.

Iron

Press the seams open and finish all the raw edges with zigzag stitch.

Next, you will design the triangular hole that will go at the centre front of your neckline.

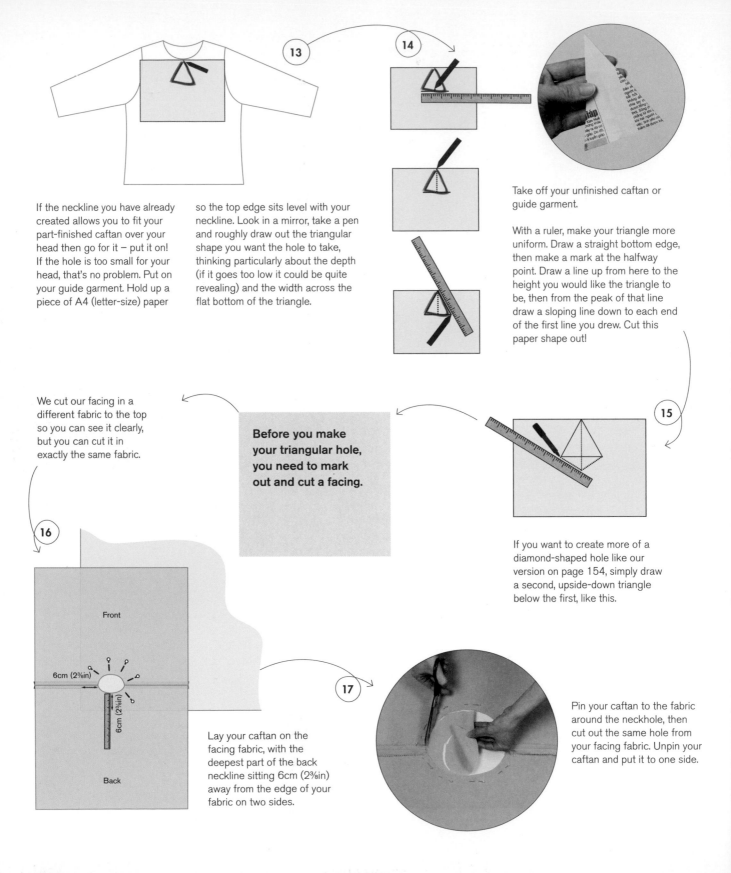

If the neckline you have already created allows you to fit your part-finished caftan over your head then go for it – put it on! If the hole is too small for your head, that's no problem. Put on your guide garment. Hold up a piece of A4 (letter-size) paper so the top edge sits level with your neckline. Look in a mirror, take a pen and roughly draw out the triangular shape you want the hole to take, thinking particularly about the depth (if it goes too low it could be quite revealing) and the width across the flat bottom of the triangle.

Take off your unfinished caftan or guide garment.

With a ruler, make your triangle more uniform. Draw a straight bottom edge, then make a mark at the halfway point. Draw a line up from here to the height you would like the triangle to be, then from the peak of that line draw a sloping line down to each end of the first line you drew. Cut this paper shape out!

We cut our facing in a different fabric to the top so you can see it clearly, but you can cut it in exactly the same fabric.

Before you make your triangular hole, you need to mark out and cut a facing.

If you want to create more of a diamond-shaped hole like our version on page 154, simply draw a second, upside-down triangle below the first, like this.

Front

6cm (2⅜in)

6cm (2⅜in)

Back

Lay your caftan on the facing fabric, with the deepest part of the back neckline sitting 6cm (2⅜in) away from the edge of your fabric on two sides.

Pin your caftan to the fabric around the neckhole, then cut out the same hole from your facing fabric. Unpin your caftan and put it to one side.

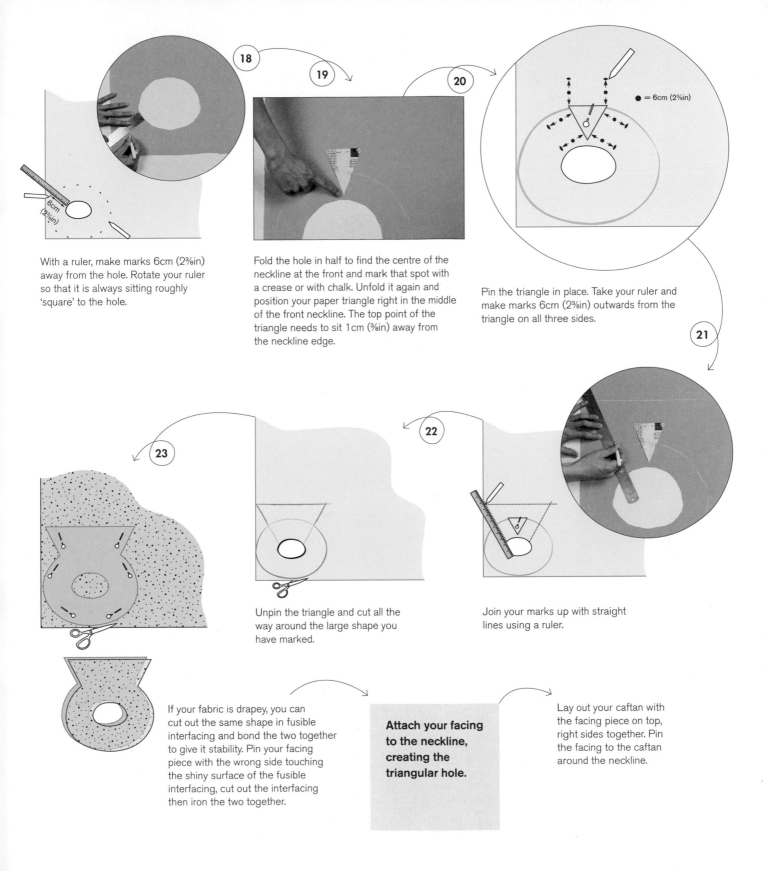

18 **19** **20**

With a ruler, make marks 6cm (2⅜in) away from the hole. Rotate your ruler so that it is always sitting roughly 'square' to the hole.

Fold the hole in half to find the centre of the neckline at the front and mark that spot with a crease or with chalk. Unfold it again and position your paper triangle right in the middle of the front neckline. The top point of the triangle needs to sit 1cm (⅜in) away from the neckline edge.

Pin the triangle in place. Take your ruler and make marks 6cm (2⅜in) outwards from the triangle on all three sides.

21

● = 6cm (2⅜in)

22 **23**

Unpin the triangle and cut all the way around the large shape you have marked.

Join your marks up with straight lines using a ruler.

If your fabric is drapey, you can cut out the same shape in fusible interfacing and bond the two together to give it stability. Pin your facing piece with the wrong side touching the shiny surface of the fusible interfacing, cut out the interfacing then iron the two together.

Attach your facing to the neckline, creating the triangular hole.

Lay out your caftan with the facing piece on top, right sides together. Pin the facing to the caftan around the neckline.

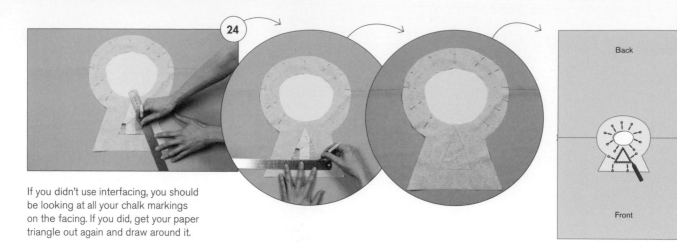

If you didn't use interfacing, you should be looking at all your chalk markings on the facing. If you did, get your paper triangle out again and draw around it.

The front of your caftan should be to your left. The expanse of the neckhole will be to the right of the machine needle and the entire back piece of your caftan sitting on your right, awkwardly bunched up in the crook of the machine!

From this point, sew all the way around the curved neckline until you are almost back to where you started.

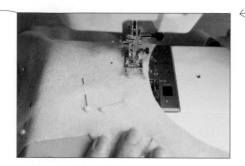

To sew the facing to the caftan, position your needle at the centre front of your neckhole, with your needle sitting just outside the chalk marks of your triangle.

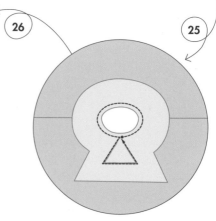

Stop your stitching 2 or 3mm (⅛in) away from where you started. You need to leave a gap so that you can snip down into it and still have a teeny seam allowance on the inside of each stitching line. With the needle in the down position, lift the presser foot and pivot your fabric to make it turn a sharp corner.

Put the presser foot back down and sew down to the bottom corner of your triangle, sewing just outside your chalk marks. At the bottom corner of your triangle, pivot your caftan again so you can sew a straight line across the bottom of your triangle.

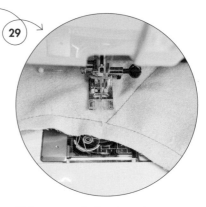

At the corner, pivot again and sew up the last side until you are back to where you began your stitching.

TUTORIAL

30

Snip down into the tiny gap you left until you have snipped into the middle of your triangle. Then snip around your shape, cutting about 5mm (³⁄₁₆in) away from your stitching. Snip into the bottom corners of the shape, almost until you touch the stitching but not quite (see the photos below). This seems scary, but the closer you get to the stitching, the flatter the facing will sit when it is turned through to the other side.

If you are adding a button loop to the top of the triangular hole, now is the time to do so.

You can choose to add ribbons to tie the triangle together at the top, like our version on page 155. We made our ribbons out of the main fabric of the dress. We did this in exactly the same way as we created a button loop, by cutting strips of fabric and folding the edges in on themselves. You can choose to buy ribbon if you like. The triangle will keep its shape best if the ribbon is narrow.

For a completely invisible fastening, like in our version on page 154, you don't need to do anything now as you will be sewing a hook and eye to your caftan right at the end.

31

33

32

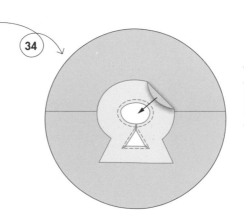

Carefully unpick some stitches to slip it in there. Push the loop as far up towards the top of the triangle as you can and pin it in place, then sew over it, sewing up the area you unpicked.

The loop is going to sit between the main fabric of your garment and the facing.

Create a button loop by cutting a strip of fabric four times as wide as you want the finished loop to be. Ours is about 2cm (³⁄₄in) wide. Cut the strip quite a bit longer than you intend the finished loop to be. Press both raw edges of the strip in to the centre, then press the whole strip in half, completely encasing the raw edges. Sew a line of straight stitch along this skinny strip of fabric to secure it.

Snip off the corners of the seam allowance at the front of the neckline and trim the whole curved seam until it's about 5mm (³⁄₁₆in) deep. Snip into it to release tension (see step 31 of the Deco Drape Dress tutorial on page 60 for photos of this).

34

Turn the facing through to the wrong side of your garment. Pulling at your button loop will help turn out a nice pointy corner on that side.

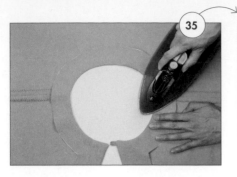

(35)

Press the facing so it sits neatly on the inside. Put in a couple of hand stitches to attach it to the garment at the seams. See step 34 of the Deco Drape Dress tutorial on page 61 for a photograph of this.

Hem the straight edges of your caftan.

You're going to make double-turned hems along all four edges of your caftan.

If you want to try mitring the corners of your caftan instead of the simpler method chosen here, press double-turned hems along all four edges of your garment then use the instructions for the Asymmetric Mini Skirt on page 35. Mitring would be a good technique to use if your fabric is fairly thick.

(36)

Create 'sleeves' in your caftan.

(37)

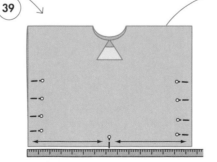

Repeat this process with the horizontal front and back edges, completely hiding all raw edges.

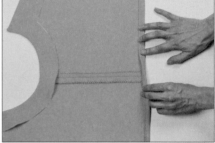

With your caftan wrong side up, press a 1.5cm- (⅝in-) deep fold along each of the side edges. On each side, turn the first fold over on itself again, completely hiding the raw edge.

Press this fold and pin it down. Sew the fold down, with your stitches running close to the inner edge of the fold.

(38)

 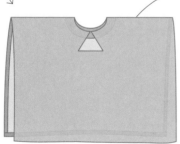

Lay your caftan out so that the bottom edges are aligned. Make sure you are looking at the right side of your garment (the neck facing should be hidden on the inside).

(39)

Pin the front to the back up the side edges. Find the centre of your garment across the bottom and mark the central point with a pin.

(40)

Side seam measurement

On both sides, measure your SIDE SEAM MEASUREMENT from the central pin and mark that spot.

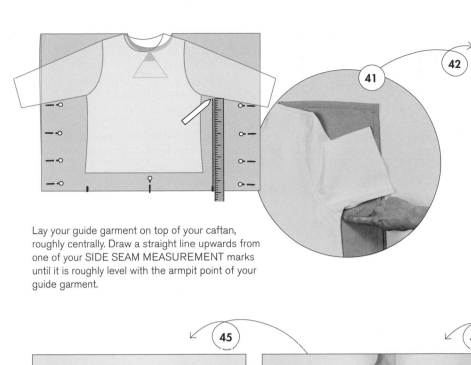

Lay your guide garment on top of your caftan, roughly centrally. Draw a straight line upwards from one of your SIDE SEAM MEASUREMENT marks until it is roughly level with the armpit point of your guide garment.

41

42

Remove the guide garment. Measure how long this chalk line is, then mark the same length line upwards from the other SIDE SEAM MEASUREMENT mark.

43

45

44

If you are adding a hook and eye, hand sew them on the inside of the garment so your stitches go through the facing and just catch the main fabric.

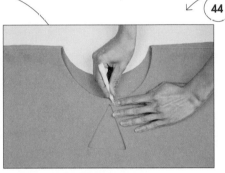

Finally, mark the spot on the front of your caftan where you need to sew your button. Hand sew your button onto that spot.

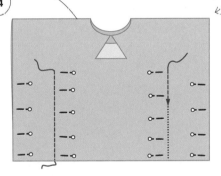

Place more pins into your garment, then sew a line of straight stitch running along each chalk line.

46

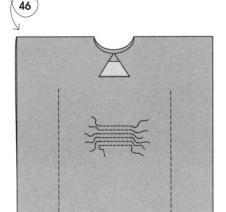

To add shirring
Hand wind shirring elastic onto your bobbin. Try your Keyhole Caftan on and slip a pin into the fabric a little way under your bust. Take the garment off and sew your first line of shirring at that level. The shirring should cover about a third of the full distance between the side seams, and be centred between them. Sew a second line about 1cm (⅜in) below, and continue until you have created a block of shirring.

YOU HAVE MADE A KEYHOLE CAFTAN!

Keyhole caftan

1

Courtney's version of the Keyhole Caftan is made using a medium-weight, drapey polyester. The top has a fairly small neck opening and the keyhole detail has been adapted into a diamond shape. The opening fastens with a hook and eye sewn on the inside so there is no visible fastening.

Technical variations

Karishma wears a dress-length version of the caftan, made in an extremely drapey voile-like cotton fabric. The triangular keyhole shape is tall and narrow and fastens at the top with ties rather than a button. Five lines of shirring sewn in a rectangular shape at the front draw in the dress at the waistline.

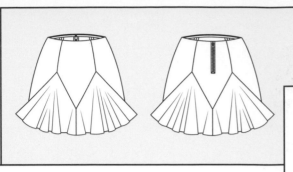

PIECES TO CUT

Main panels

Bottom inserts

SUITABLE FABRIC

For the main body of the skirt use a fabric that isn't too flimsy – a crisp cotton, denim or even a light wool. You can use the same fabric for the flared panels or you can choose something different. For a full, structured look use fairly stiff or thick fabric. For a more delicate, flowing look pick something drapey or lightweight.

MATHS TO DO

Full hip	÷ 4 =	QUARTER HIP

QUARTER HIP	+ 4cm (1⅝in)	3cm (1⅛in) of that is for seam allowance (each panel will be seamed on both vertical sides) and 1cm (⅜in) adds a bit of ease.	=	PANEL WIDTH

Your inserts are going to extend beyond the main panels of the skirt, lengthening it. Decide how long you want them to extend by and write it here:	EXTENSION

Desired length of skirt	−	EXTENSION	=	PANEL LENGTH

Full waist	÷ 4 =		+	3cm (1⅛in)	=	QUARTER WAIST

PANEL WIDTH	−	QUARTER WAIST	=		÷ 2 =	PANEL REDUCTION

Waist to full hip or actual hip (see page 158)	+	3cm (1⅛in)	=	PANEL SLOPE

MATERIALS NEEDED

Fabric for panels

Fabric for inserts (can be different)

Small square of fusible interfacing

Bias binding

Chunky zip (roughly the same length as your waist to hip measurement)

Sheet of paper, A4 or letter size

String

BODY MEASUREMENTS NEEDED

Full waist

Full hip or actual hip (you can use either or somewhere in between, depending on how you would like your skirt to appear. See page 158 to decide)

Waist to hip (full or actual hip, as above)

Desired length of skirt

INSERT SKIRT

The upper and lower parts of this geometrically inspired skirt can be made in contrasting fabric to accentuate the spiked angles where the two parts meet. The inserts can be made from stiff or springy fabric to create rolling waves and give the skirt a full, structured shape, or from a drapey fabric so that they hang down against the body in loose folds. The skirt fastens at the centre back with an exposed zip.

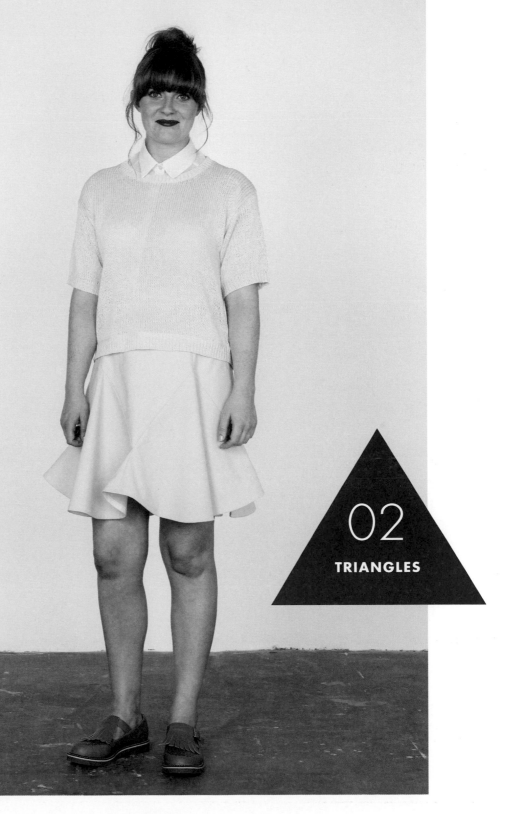

02

TRIANGLES

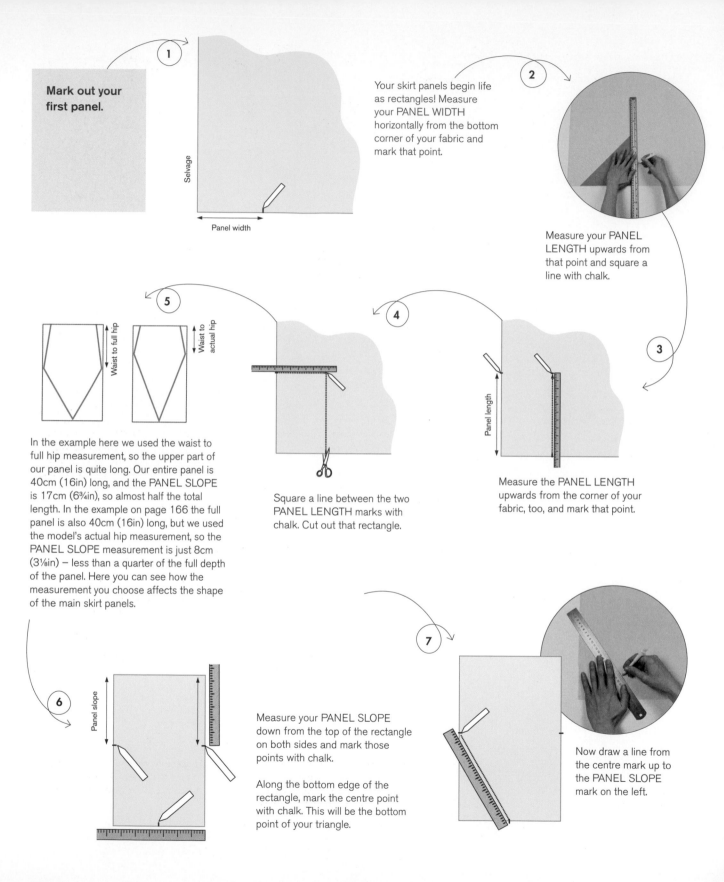

Mark out your first panel.

1

Selvage

Panel width

2 Your skirt panels begin life as rectangles! Measure your PANEL WIDTH horizontally from the bottom corner of your fabric and mark that point.

Measure your PANEL LENGTH upwards from that point and square a line with chalk.

3

4 Measure the PANEL LENGTH upwards from the corner of your fabric, too, and mark that point.

Panel length

5 Square a line between the two PANEL LENGTH marks with chalk. Cut out that rectangle.

Waist to full hip

Waist to actual hip

In the example here we used the waist to full hip measurement, so the upper part of our panel is quite long. Our entire panel is 40cm (16in) long, and the PANEL SLOPE is 17cm (6¾in), so almost half the total length. In the example on page 166 the full panel is also 40cm (16in) long, but we used the model's actual hip measurement, so the PANEL SLOPE measurement is just 8cm (3⅛in) – less than a quarter of the full depth of the panel. Here you can see how the measurement you choose affects the shape of the main skirt panels.

6 Panel slope

Measure your PANEL SLOPE down from the top of the rectangle on both sides and mark those points with chalk.

Along the bottom edge of the rectangle, mark the centre point with chalk. This will be the bottom point of your triangle.

7 Now draw a line from the centre mark up to the PANEL SLOPE mark on the left.

TUTORIAL

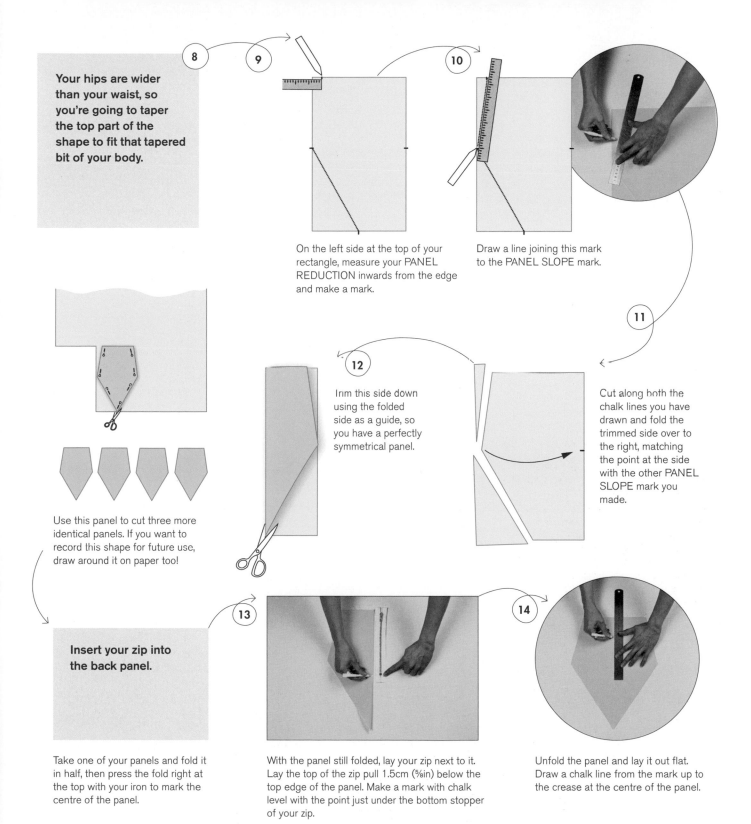

8 **9** **10**

Your hips are wider than your waist, so you're going to taper the top part of the shape to fit that tapered bit of your body.

On the left side at the top of your rectangle, measure your PANEL REDUCTION inwards from the edge and make a mark.

Draw a line joining this mark to the PANEL SLOPE mark.

11

Cut along both the chalk lines you have drawn and fold the trimmed side over to the right, matching the point at the side with the other PANEL SLOPE mark you made.

12

Trim this side down using the folded side as a guide, so you have a perfectly symmetrical panel.

Use this panel to cut three more identical panels. If you want to record this shape for future use, draw around it on paper too!

Insert your zip into the back panel.

13

Take one of your panels and fold it in half, then press the fold right at the top with your iron to mark the centre of the panel.

With the panel still folded, lay your zip next to it. Lay the top of the zip pull 1.5cm (⅝in) below the top edge of the panel. Make a mark with chalk level with the point just under the bottom stopper of your zip.

14

Unfold the panel and lay it out flat. Draw a chalk line from the mark up to the crease at the centre of the panel.

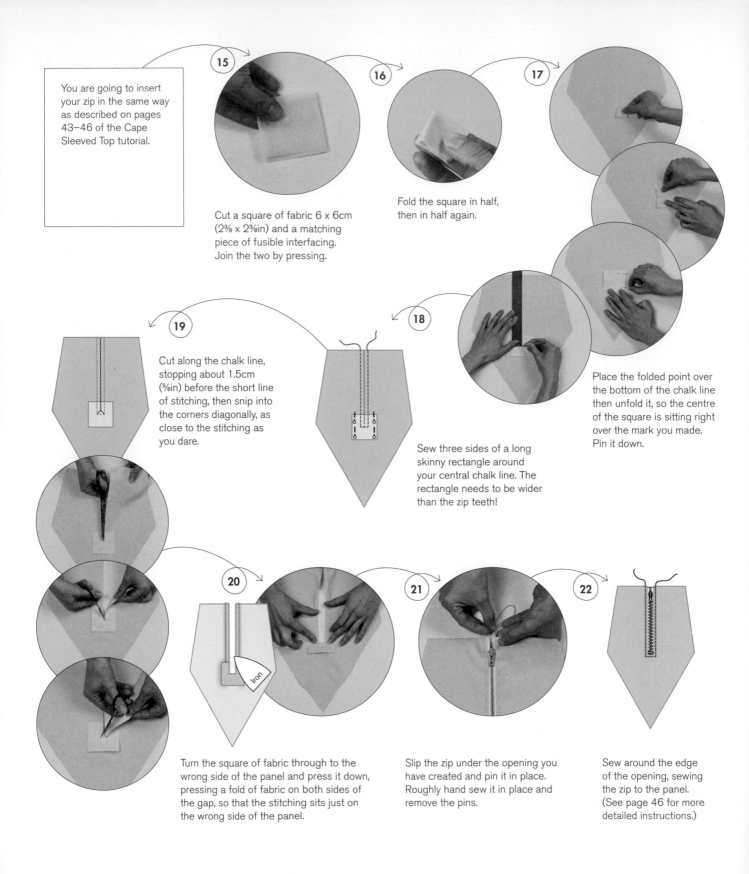

You are going to insert your zip in the same way as described on pages 43–46 of the Cape Sleeved Top tutorial.

15

Cut a square of fabric 6 x 6cm (2⅜ x 2⅜in) and a matching piece of fusible interfacing. Join the two by pressing.

16

Fold the square in half, then in half again.

17

Place the folded point over the bottom of the chalk line then unfold it, so the centre of the square is sitting right over the mark you made. Pin it down.

18

Sew three sides of a long skinny rectangle around your central chalk line. The rectangle needs to be wider than the zip teeth!

19

Cut along the chalk line, stopping about 1.5cm (⅝in) before the short line of stitching, then snip into the corners diagonally, as close to the stitching as you dare.

20

Turn the square of fabric through to the wrong side of the panel and press it down, pressing a fold of fabric on both sides of the gap, so that the stitching sits just on the wrong side of the panel.

21

Slip the zip under the opening you have created and pin it in place. Roughly hand sew it in place and remove the pins.

22

Sew around the edge of the opening, sewing the zip to the panel. (See page 46 for more detailed instructions.)

23 Measure the length of one of the lower diagonal edges of your skirt panels. Add your EXTENSION measurement plus an additional 3cm (1⅛in). Write the total down here.

This will be the length of each sloping side of your insert. We'll call it your INSERT LENGTH.

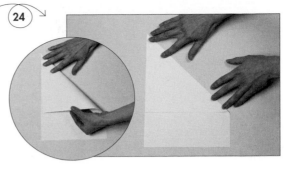

Now it's time to create your flared inserts.

24

Take a piece of A4 (letter-size) paper and carefully fold one corner fully over until it meets the other side.

Lay two of your panel pieces next to each other. The insert is going to be a triangle of fabric sewn into the triangle of emptiness between the two panels. To create an insert that folds/flares, the triangle needs to be bigger than the space it is filling.

To help mark it out, take your paper square and position it in the triangular gap between your two skirt panels with the fold line running down the centre. If it fits perfectly like ours does, you need to add width to your insert in order to create volume.

We added an extra 6cm (2⅜in) at each side. We'll call this the EXTRA WIDTH measurement. Decide how much extra width you want and write that down here.

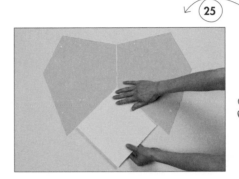

25

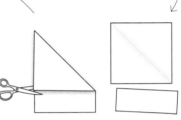

Cut off the excess paper. You now have a square with a fold in it.

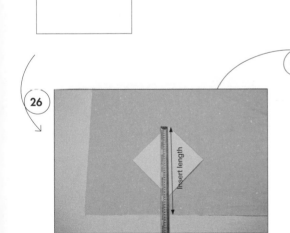

26 Lay the paper square on top of your fabric so the fold is running parallel with the selvage edge of your fabric.

You need to shuffle the paper piece around until the *top* point is your INSERT LENGTH away from the bottom edge of your fabric as well as your INSERT LENGTH away from the side of the fabric. It helps to use your metre stick and your ruler at the same time.

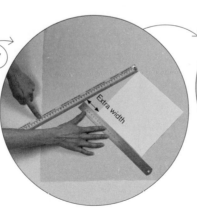

27

With your ruler, measure your EXTRA WIDTH upwards from the corner of your paper diamond and let your metre stick rest at that height, as shown.

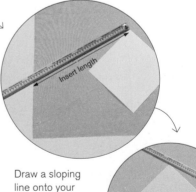

Draw a sloping line onto your fabric with chalk.

Then repeat this on the other side.

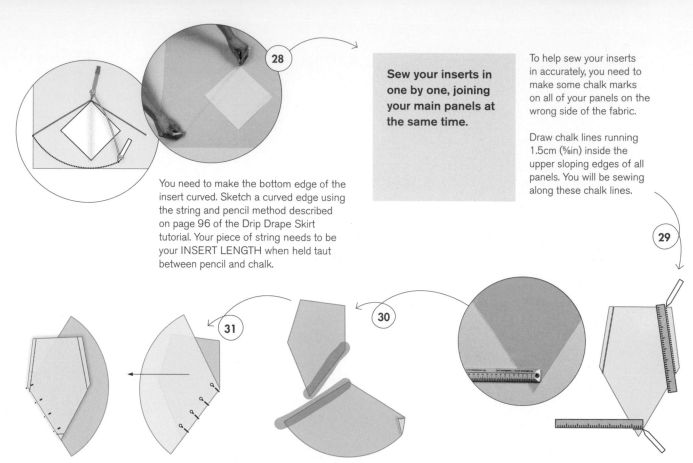

28

You need to make the bottom edge of the insert curved. Sketch a curved edge using the string and pencil method described on page 96 of the Drip Drape Skirt tutorial. Your piece of string needs to be your INSERT LENGTH when held taut between pencil and chalk.

Sew your inserts in one by one, joining your main panels at the same time.

To help sew your inserts in accurately, you need to make some chalk marks on all of your panels on the wrong side of the fabric.

Draw chalk lines running 1.5cm (⅝in) inside the upper sloping edges of all panels. You will be sewing along these chalk lines.

29

31

30

Flip the insert up on top of the panel. Match the point at the peak of the insert with the point in your skirt panel. Pin the edges together then flip the whole thing over so you are looking at the side that was just sitting at the back!

Lay one panel out with the right side of the fabric facing up (so you won't be able to see the chalk marks you just made). Lay one insert, right side up, roughly in the space it's going to fit.

Find the point where the tip of the triangle at the bottom of your panel is exactly 3cm (1⅛in) across and draw a line in chalk at this level. This line tells you where you need to stop or start sewing.

32

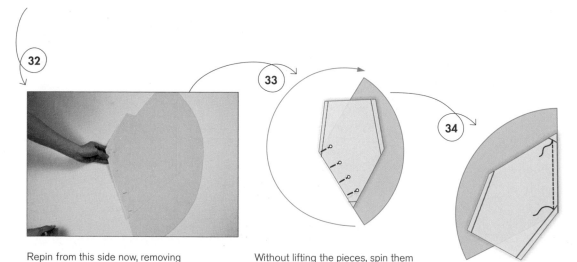

33

34

Repin from this side now, removing the first lot of pins.

Without lifting the pieces, spin them around clockwise so the pinned stretch of fabric is on your right.

Sew your pinned edge, beginning on the chalk line across the tip of the panel. Your needle should be sitting right in the middle of this line. Finish your line of stitches right on the chalk line that indicates the 1.5cm (⅝in) seam allowance.

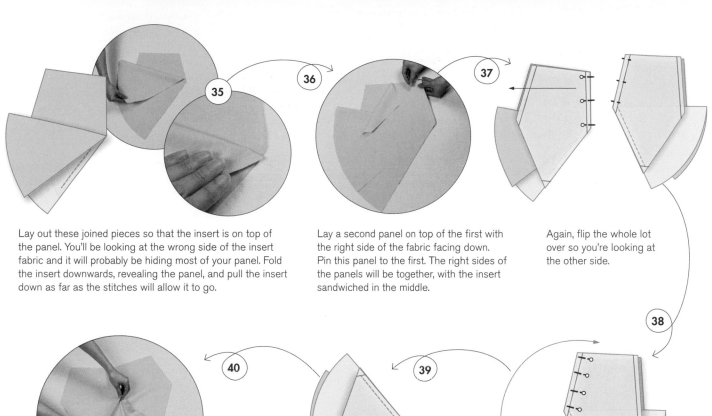

Lay out these joined pieces so that the insert is on top of the panel. You'll be looking at the wrong side of the insert fabric and it will probably be hiding most of your panel. Fold the insert downwards, revealing the panel, and pull the insert down as far as the stitches will allow it to go.

Lay a second panel on top of the first with the right side of the fabric facing down. Pin this panel to the first. The right sides of the panels will be together, with the insert sandwiched in the middle.

Again, flip the whole lot over so you're looking at the other side.

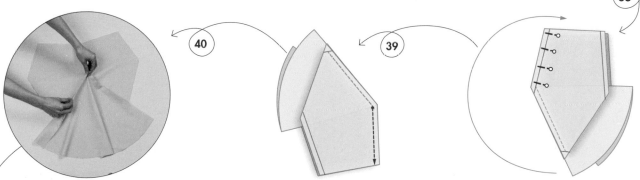

Open up the whole lot and lay it out with the wrong side facing up. Bring the unattached sides of the panel and the insert together, with the right sides of the fabric touching.

Sew the panels together, with your needle starting exactly where the last row of stitches ends, and sew to the waist edge of the fabric.

Repin from this side, removing the pins on the back, then spin the piece around clockwise so your pins are sitting on your right.

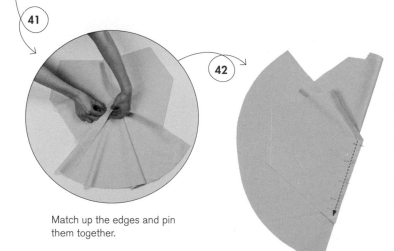

Match up the edges and pin them together.

Sew them together, beginning your stitching with your needle right where the upper line of stitching stops, and making sure the first panel is lifted up and out of the way.

Stop sewing when you hit the chalk line that marks off the tip of the panel.

You have sewn your first insert! Sewing the rest will be a piece of cake.

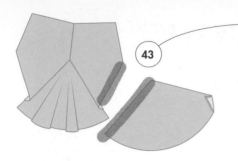

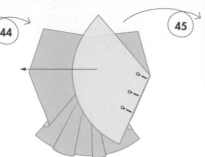

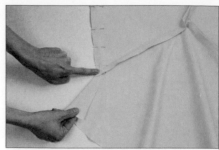

To attach your second insert, lay out both the insert and the pieces you have just joined together, right sides facing up.

Flip the insert up on top of the other pieces and pin it to the panel. You are attaching this one in exactly the same way as the first.

Flip it over so you're looking at the back, then repin. Spin it round so the pins are on your right. When you start this line of stitching, you'll be starting with your needle right where another line of stitching ends.

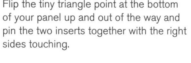

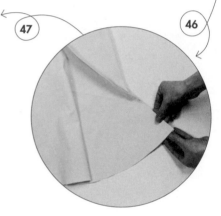

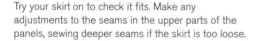

Flip the tiny triangle point at the bottom of your panel up and out of the way and pin the two inserts together with the right sides touching.

Sew along this edge, starting with your needle right on the end of the stitching you can see, and sewing to the bottom.

When the second insert is attached, you need to join it to the first one.

Repeat this full process until you have attached all your inserts and sewn the last two panels and inserts together.

Try your skirt on to check it fits. Make any adjustments to the seams in the upper parts of the panels, sewing deeper seams if the skirt is too loose.

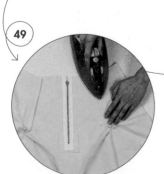

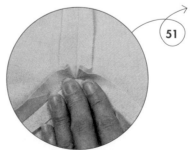

Press open the seams that join all the upper panels together.

Make little folds to flatten out the excess fabric on the sides of the seams that are made of panel fabric.

Snip into the sides of the seams that are made of your insert fabric. Make two snips, one either side of the triangle point.

TUTORIAL

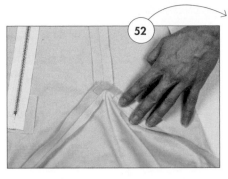

This will allow you to press this side of the seam down so it lies flat against your insert or godet.

Zigzag stitch along all the raw edges.

Finish the top edge of your skirt.

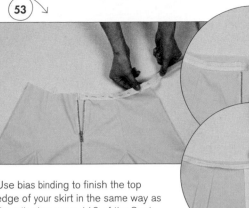

Use bias binding to finish the top edge of your skirt in the same way as described on page 113 of the Spot Pocket Skirt tutorial.

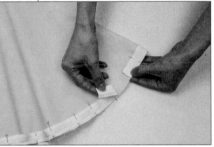

Sew the bias binding to the skirt.

Pin your bias binding to the right side of your skirt, all the way around, snipping it so you have a couple of centimetres (1–2in) overlap. Fold one of the ends back on itself and lay the other end on top of that.

The bottom edge of your skirt is curved.

You could choose to finish your skirt in the same way as the Spot Pocket Skirt (see page 113, step 45) by ironing up a hem and sewing it down. We finished ours with bias binding.

Finish the bottom edge of your skirt.

Trim the skirt and the bias binding together so they are less deep than the bias binding that remains on the other side of the stitching. Turn your skirt inside out and press the bias binding to the inside.

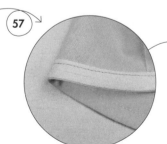

Pin it in place and sew it down close to the folded edge of the bias binding.

YOU HAVE MADE AN INSERT SKIRT!

Insert skirt

Linda wears a knee-length version of the skirt, the extra length being created by the inserts, which are made from drapey rayon challis. The skirt is finished with a delicate rolled hem. The starkly contrasting upper panels have a very short PANEL SLOPE, creating the appearance of a shallow band of solid black around the hips and elongated triangles pointing downwards. These panels are made from a medium-weight cotton twill.

2

Courtney wears a short, fitted
version of the Insert Skirt. The
upper panels are made from a
thick, hairy wool and the lower
inserts from a springy scuba.
The skirt fastens with
a contrasting gold zip.

MATHS TO DO

This maths needs to be done once you have taken measurements from your guide garment. Follow the measurement process explained on page 170, then fill in the boxes here so you can refer to them as you go.

NECK WIDTH

WIDTH

HALF WIDTH

SLEEVE DEPTH

NARROW SLEEVE DEPTH

LENGTH

EXTRA LENGTH

SMALL TRIANGLE HEIGHT

SMALL TRIANGLE WIDTH

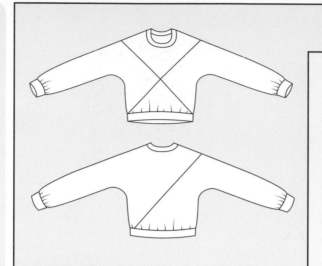

MATERIALS NEEDED

Stretch fabric

Stretch or ball point needle

Ribbing (optional)

Guide garment – a sweater or knitted jumper you like the shape of

Newspaper to make template

Masking tape

SUITABLE FABRIC

You can make this sweater out of any fabric that has a bit of stretch in it. The version photographed throughout the tutorial is made of faux leather, which has a very small amount of stretch. The sweater can be made using scuba, interlock or any kind of stable jersey, sweatshirt fleece, ponte di roma and even stretch lace. You can also experiment with the design by using different fabrics for each of the four front sections of the sweater.

PIECES TO CUT

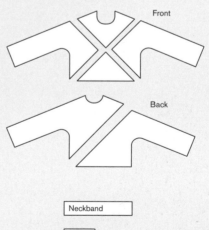

Front

Back

Neckband

Cuff

Cuff

Waistband

FOUR SLICE SWEATER

The front of this sweater is divided into four triangular slices whose points meet in the middle. Make all four slices out of the same fabric or play with contrasting colour combinations. A waistband and cuffs can be added to pinch in the sleeve ends and waistline and create a fuller shape, or they can simply be hemmed for a clean, straight finish.

03
TRIANGLES

Begin by taking a number of measurements from your guide garment. Write these down in the 'Maths to do' section on page 168.

Try on a sweater you like the general fit of. It's important that you like the width, as you can alter the length of your sweater more easily than the width. While you are wearing it, look to see if you are happy with the length too.

①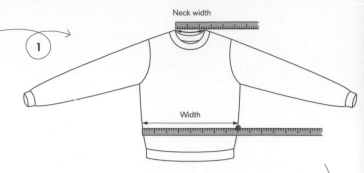

Take the sweater off and lay it out flat.

Measure across the gap created by the neckhole in your guide garment. Add 3cm (1⅛in) to this. This is your NECK WIDTH.

②

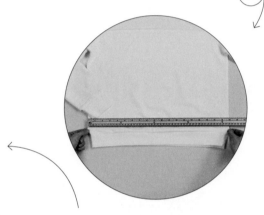

Measure the guide garment across the widest part. If the bottom is pinched in by a waistband, stretch it out to its full width and measure that.

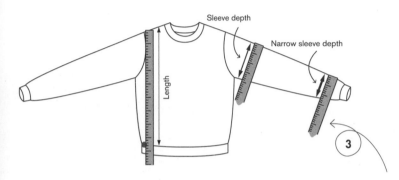

③

Measure the depth of the sleeve of your garment. The Four Slice Sweater photographed throughout our tutorial has a sleeve that is an even depth all the way down. This means the sleeve is fairly wide at the wrist but is gathered in by a band of ribbing. To create a sleeve of even depth, measure across the sleeve of your guide garment somewhere near the top where it meets the main body part. Add 3cm (1⅛in) to that and write it down. We'll call this the SLEEVE DEPTH.

You can choose to create a tapered sleeve. To do this, measure your sleeve depth across the narrowest part of the sleeve as well, near the wrist of your guide garment. Add 3cm (1⅛in) to this measurement and write it down. We'll call this the NARROW SLEEVE DEPTH.

Measure the length of your guide garment vertically down from the shoulder point to the bottom edge of your garment (or if it has a waistband, to the top of the waistband). Add 3cm (1⅛in). We'll call this your LENGTH.

Add 3cm (1⅛in) to this then write that measurement down. We'll call this your WIDTH. Divide that by two. This is your HALF WIDTH.

Your WIDTH will also determine the length of the sweater you are making, because our four triangles make a square!

If you want your sweater to be longer than your WIDTH, you can add length by attaching a deep waistband at the bottom, or you can lengthen the lower panel at the front of your sweater.

Compare your WIDTH to your LENGTH. If you like the length of your guide garment and it is longer than your WIDTH, subtract the WIDTH from the LENGTH and write that down. We'll call this your EXTRA LENGTH. See step 18 for a visual of this.

You're going to build the front of your sweater first. It is made of four pieces of fabric. Each piece is based on a large triangle template. Start by marking your template triangle on paper.

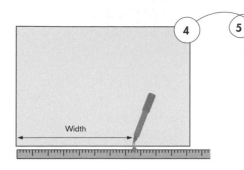

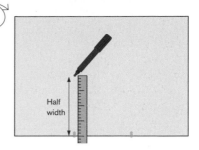

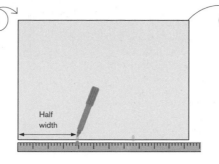

Take a sheet of newspaper and measure your WIDTH across the longest straight edge. Mark that point with a pen.

Measure the HALF WIDTH along the same edge and mark that point too.

Now square a line as long as your HALF WIDTH upwards from the mark you just made and make a dot.

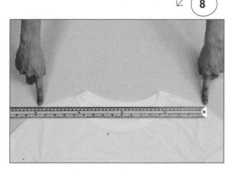

Create smaller paper triangles to add a sloping rise at the shoulders of your sweater.

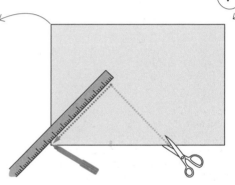

Lay your guide garment out flat again. Rest your metre stick across the garment so it sits just below the shoulder points.

Draw two sloping lines that join this dot to the corner of your newspaper and to the WIDTH mark you made. You have drawn a big triangle. Cut it out. This is your main template for the sweater.

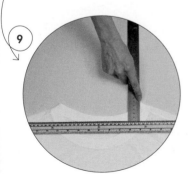

With your metre stick remaining in place, take your ruler and measure vertically from the top edge of your guide garment down to the metre stick. Record this measurement on page 168. We'll call this your SMALL TRIANGLE HEIGHT.

Now subtract your NECK WIDTH from your WIDTH. Halve the result. We'll call this your SMALL TRIANGLE WIDTH.

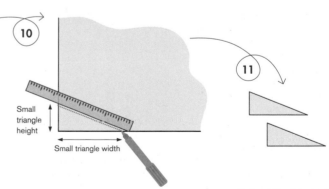

Use these two measurements to mark out a triangle like this on a piece of newspaper.

Cut out the triangle! Repeat this so you have two of the same triangle.

It is time to mark and cut the fabric pieces for the front of your sweater. We will start with the piece at the top of the sweater, the one that has the neckhole in it.

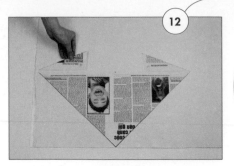

Lay your fabric out with the wrong side facing up. Place your big paper triangle on top, with the point downwards. Your triangle needs to be sitting a couple of centimetres (1–2in) inland from the side of the fabric. Pin the triangle in place.

Take your two little paper triangles and pin them flush to the big triangle, as shown.

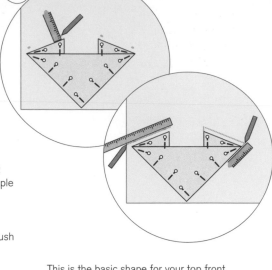

This is the basic shape for your top front piece, but you need to add some extra seam allowance across the top. With your ruler at a right angle to the top sloping edge of the small triangles, measure 1.5cm (⅝in) upwards at a couple of intervals on each side and mark those points with chalk. Join the marks together. Draw short lines either end of your chalk lines to meet the paper pieces.

Cut around this shape. Unpin the paper pieces and store the two little triangles for another time.

You need to finish this piece by cutting a curved neck shape into it.

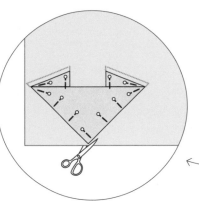

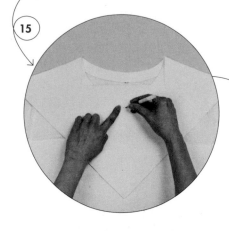

Take your guide garment and lay the piece you have just cut on top of it, wrong side facing up. Feel through the fabric to where the neckline sits on your template garment and make a mark with chalk at this point.

Lift your fabric piece up and fold it in half, so you can still see the chalk mark you just made, matching the corners of the square neckhole you currently have. Pin the two halves together roughly then draw a curve that joins this chalk mark to the corner of the square hole. Cut along that line. See step 17 on page 58 of the Deco Drape Dress tutorial for guidance on using a round object to draw a curve.

Now use your big paper triangle to mark and cut the bottom piece of your sweater.

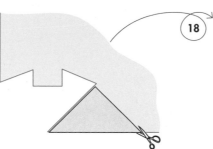

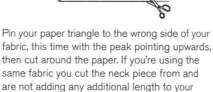

(17)

Pin your paper triangle to the wrong side of your fabric, this time with the peak pointing upwards, then cut around the paper. If you're using the same fabric you cut the neck piece from and are not adding any additional length to your sweater, it should fit nicely onto your fabric.

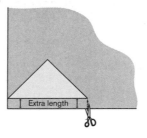

(18)

Extra length

If you would like to add length to your sweater, position your paper triangle above the bottom edge of your fabric. Pin it in place and cut around the shape, adding your EXTRA LENGTH at the bottom.

Now use your big paper triangle to mark out the final pieces of your sweater – the side pieces.

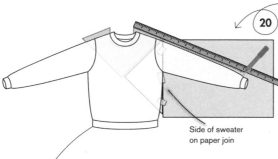

(20)

Side of sweater on paper join

Take your guide garment and lay it on top of the paper triangle. The armpit point of the sweater should be sitting in line with the paper join you have just taped. Rest your metre stick along the sloping shoulder line of your first garment piece, extending towards the cuff of your guide garment. Draw a straight line with pen, running from the point of the paper triangle down to the cuff of your sweater.

Remove the guide garment.

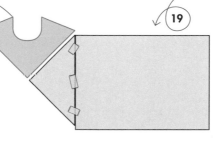

(19)

Take a fresh sheet of newspaper and tape it to the long edge of your big triangle with masking tape.

Take the first fabric piece you cut – the piece with the neckhole – and lay it above your paper triangle.

(21)

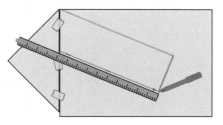

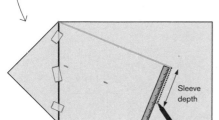

Sleeve depth

Measure your SLEEVE DEPTH downwards from the sloping pen line in two or three places. Join these marks together with one long straight line using your metre stick. At the tip of your first line draw a short line down at a right angle to mark the end of the sleeve.

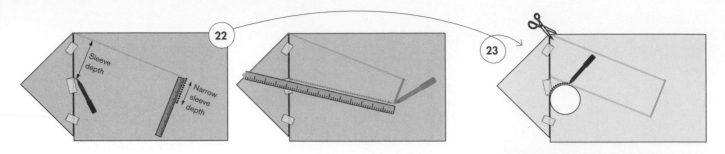

If you are making a tapered sleeve

Measure your SLEEVE DEPTH down from the sloping line at the paper triangle end, and the NARROW SLEEVE DEPTH at the other end. Draw a short line down at a right angle to mark the sleeve end. Join the points with your metre stick.

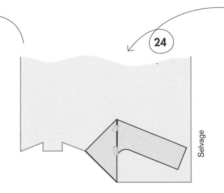

The line marking the lower sleeve edge will meet your paper triangle at a sharp angle. You need to smooth this angle off into a curve. Take a suitable round object (we used a roll of tape) and use it as a guide to draw a nice smooth curve that joins the under sleeve to the paper triangle.

Cut out your sleeve shape!

Unpin your paper shape and flip it over so the sleeve is now on the left. Pin it to your fabric like this and cut around it. You might be using a different fabric for this side of the sweater.

You have cut all your front pieces and can start joining them together.

Pin it to the wrong side of your fabric, making sure the join between the two pieces of paper is running parallel with the selvage edge of your fabric. Cut around your paper shape.

You are going to join your pieces together in pairs. Lay them all out with the right sides of the fabric facing up. You can see how this puzzle is going to fit together!

Flip the top piece with the neckhole in it down and to the left.

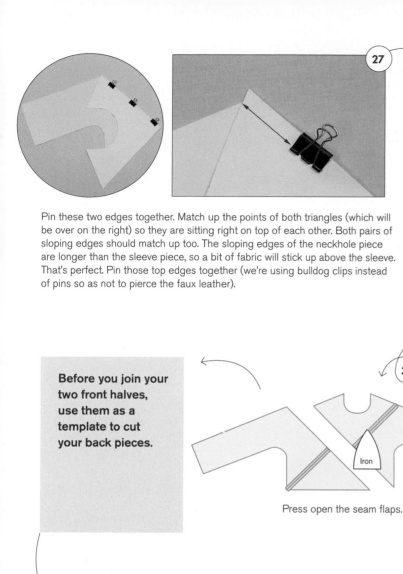

Pin these two edges together. Match up the points of both triangles (which will be over on the right) so they are sitting right on top of each other. Both pairs of sloping edges should match up too. The sloping edges of the neckhole piece are longer than the sleeve piece, so a bit of fabric will stick up above the sleeve. That's perfect. Pin those top edges together (we're using bulldog clips instead of pins so as not to pierce the faux leather).

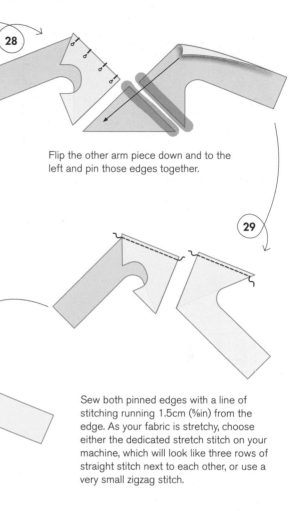

27 **28**

Flip the other arm piece down and to the left and pin those edges together.

29

30

Sew both pinned edges with a line of stitching running 1.5cm (⅝in) from the edge. As your fabric is stretchy, choose either the dedicated stretch stitch on your machine, which will look like three rows of straight stitch next to each other, or use a very small zigzag stitch.

Before you join your two front halves, use them as a template to cut your back pieces.

Press open the seam flaps.

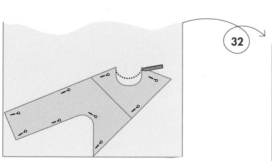

31

Lay your top front piece out on the fabric you are using to make the back, wrong sides together. Put a few pins in to hold your front piece in place. Using chalk, mark a shallower neckline for the back.

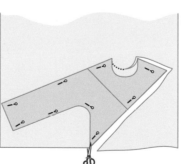

32

Cut the piece out, cutting up the diagonally sloping edge, along the short shoulder edge and around just half of the neckhole.

Cut around the sleeve and along the shoulder edge. Unpin and remove your front piece.

Fold the right side of the back piece over to the left, matching up the shoulder points. Use the half of the neckline you've cut as a guide to cut the second half so they are identical.

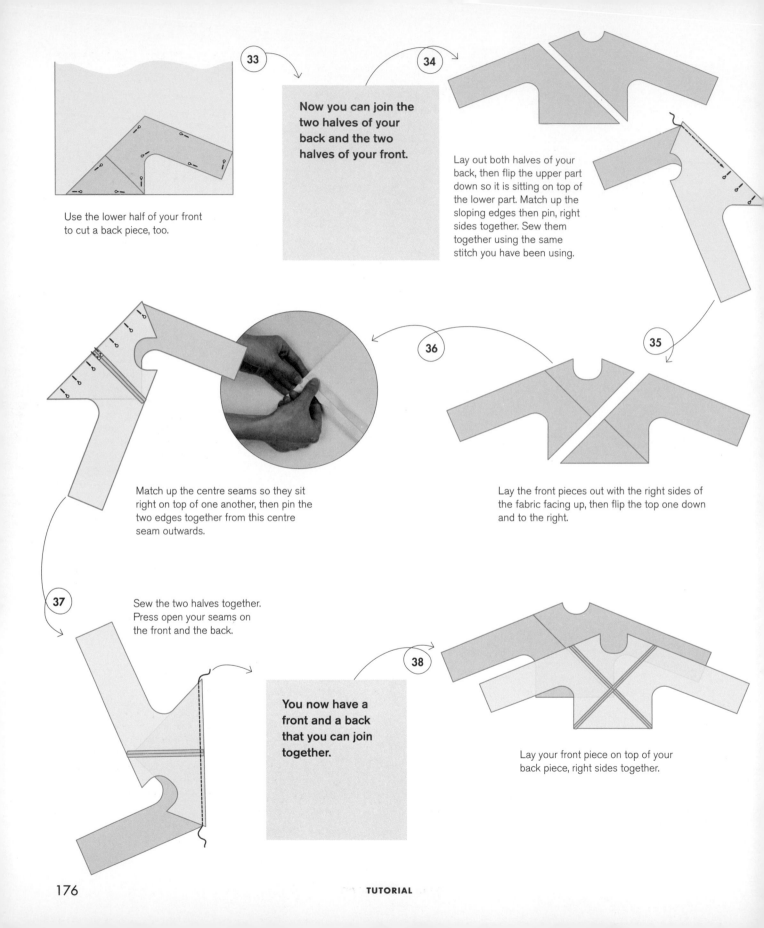

Use the lower half of your front to cut a back piece, too.

(33)

Now you can join the two halves of your back and the two halves of your front.

(34)

Lay out both halves of your back, then flip the upper part down so it is sitting on top of the lower part. Match up the sloping edges then pin, right sides together. Sew them together using the same stitch you have been using.

(35)

Match up the centre seams so they sit right on top of one another, then pin the two edges together from this centre seam outwards.

(36)

Lay the front pieces out with the right sides of the fabric facing up, then flip the top one down and to the right.

(37)

Sew the two halves together. Press open your seams on the front and the back.

You now have a front and a back that you can join together.

(38)

Lay your front piece on top of your back piece, right sides together.

TUTORIAL

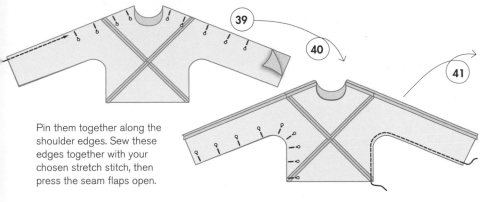

39

Pin them together along the shoulder edges. Sew these edges together with your chosen stretch stitch, then press the seam flaps open.

40

Lay the pieces out again. This time match up and pin the underarm and side edges. Sew them with your stretch stitch.

41

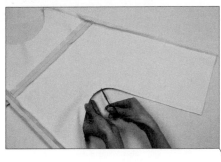

Trim away about half of the seam allowance from the underarm curve and snip into the remaining seam allowance to release the tension. Press open the underarm and side seams as much as you can.

42

You're going to finish your neckline by adding a neckband made of ribbing or any other stretchy fabric. You can use your main fabric, or choose a contrasting fabric.

43

Finish the neckline of your sweater.

You can now try your sweater on. Make any necessary adjustments to the width or the depth of the sleeves by sewing deeper seams to remove fabric, or shallower seams to release fabric. Unpick your initial stitches and re-press your new seams.

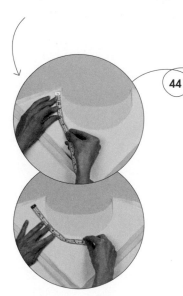

Measure all the way around the neckhole of your sweater – the front and the back!

44

You need to cut a neckband that is shorter than this distance, as you'll be stretching the band out as you sew, forcing it to become as long as the edge you're sewing it to.

If you're using ribbing it is often extremely stretchy. You can see here it becomes 50% bigger when fully stretched, so cut your band about two-thirds of the size of your neckhole measurement.

If you're using a fabric that is less stretchy than ribbing, such as scuba, interlock or sweater fleece, your neckband should be roughly 15% smaller than the full distance round the neck edge.

Your neckband needs to be double the depth you wish it to appear once finished, plus an additional 3cm (1⅛in). Our neckband appears 2.5cm (1in) deep, so we cut a band 8cm (3⅛in) deep.

45

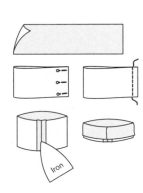

Cut out your strip and fold it in half widthwise, right sides together. Pin and sew the short ends together to make a tube. You can use straight stitch to do this. Press this seam open. Fold the ring of fabric over on itself so you are hiding the wrong side and press it.

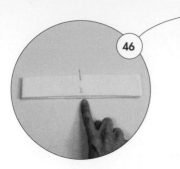

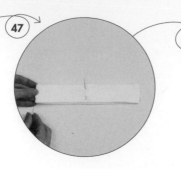

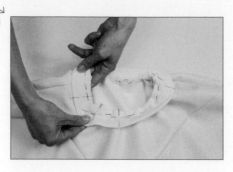

To ensure you sew your ribbing evenly to your neckhole, divide it into sections. Lay the ring of ribbing out with the seam right on the fold at one side. Put a pin into the fold on the other side. Now reposition the band so the marker pin sits right on top of the seam.

Put a marker pin in at each of the folded sides.

You have divided the ring into four equal sections.

Position your neckband over the neckhole of your sweater, with the raw edges of the band sitting on the raw edge of the neckhole. Begin by pinning the seam of your neckband so it sits right at the centre back of your neckhole. Pin the opposite side of the band (marked by a pin) to the centre front of your neckhole. Then pin the two side marker pins so they sit just in front of the shoulder seams. Your front neckline is bigger than your back neckline, so you need more of the neckband to sit at the front than at the back.

Lift the neckband upwards and press it flat, pressing the seam down towards the garment. You can run a line of stitching all the way around your neckhole on your main garment fabric, just under the seam that joins the band to it. This will hold the seam down away from the band and add a nice detail. Make sure you use a stretch stitch so you can get your head through the hole!

Distribute the rest of your neckband evenly between the main anchor points, stretching it to make it match the neckline and pinning it in place. Sew the band to the garment with stretch stitch, stretching it as you sew, but making sure you don't stretch the fabric of your neckline.

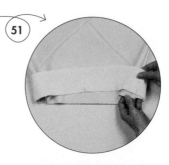

Finish your waist edge and the ends of your sleeves.

You can choose to hem your waist edge and sleeve ends, like our version on page 180, or you can add bands of stretchy fabric, in exactly the same way you did with the neckline.

Mark out and cut out your waistband and cuffs in the same way as the neckband, measuring the full distance around the edge you're applying the band to, then removing either one third of this measurement or 15%, to determine the length of the band you are cutting. It is common for waistbands and cuffs to be deeper than neckbands. Our waistband appears 5.5cm (2⅛in) deep so the strip we cut was 14cm (5½in) deep.

Construct the waistband and cuffs in the same way, folding them in half, sewing the short ends together then folding that ring down on itself to hide the wrong side.

Split your waistband into four parts with marker pins, as you did with the neckband. Arrange your waistband around the bottom edge of your sweater, positioning the two side marker pins over the side seams of the sweater and pinning the band into place there.

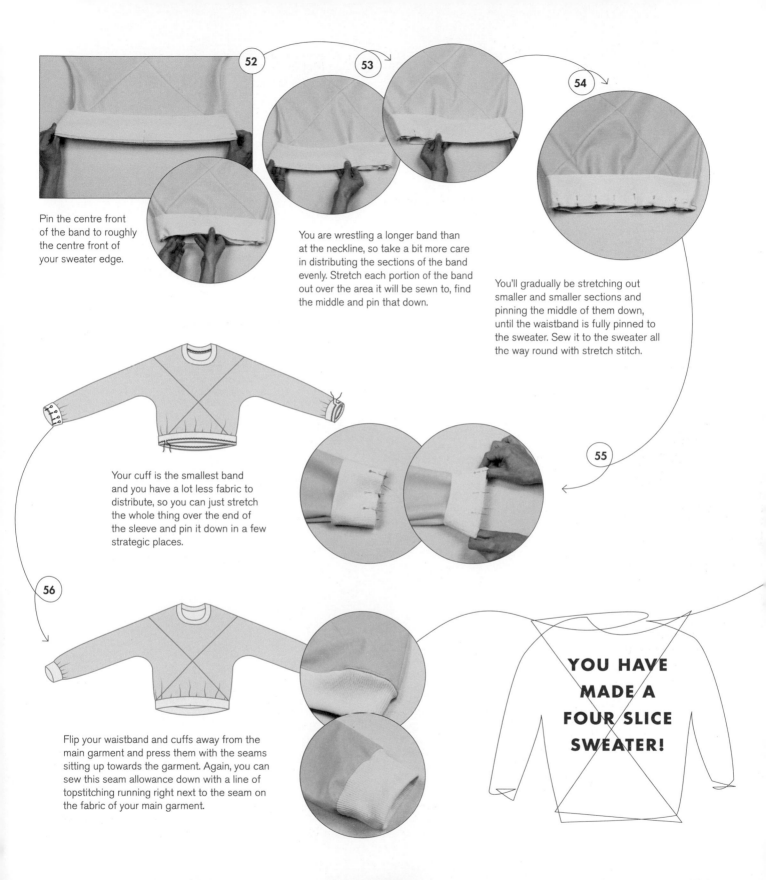

Pin the centre front of the band to roughly the centre front of your sweater edge.

You are wrestling a longer band than at the neckline, so take a bit more care in distributing the sections of the band evenly. Stretch each portion of the band out over the area it will be sewn to, find the middle and pin that down.

You'll gradually be stretching out smaller and smaller sections and pinning the middle of them down, until the waistband is fully pinned to the sweater. Sew it to the sweater all the way round with stretch stitch.

Your cuff is the smallest band and you have a lot less fabric to distribute, so you can just stretch the whole thing over the end of the sleeve and pin it down in a few strategic places.

Flip your waistband and cuffs away from the main garment and press them with the seams sitting up towards the garment. Again, you can sew this seam allowance down with a line of topstitching running right next to the seam on the fabric of your main garment.

YOU HAVE MADE A FOUR SLICE SWEATER!

Four slice sweater

Kristina's version of the sweater is made with three different fabrics. A marble-patterned scuba sits at each side, a heavier quilted black jersey forms the bottom slice and a lighter waffle-textured white jersey sits at the neck, with white ribbing finishing the neckline. The sweater has no additional waistband or cuffs, simply hemmed edges. The sleeves are cropped at three-quarter length.

2

Melody's version of the sweater is also made of three fabrics. The right and lower slices have been cut as one piece from a floral scuba. The left piece is made from a faux fur that has minimal stretch and the upper piece is made from a soft pink fleece. Ribbing has been used to finish the neckline and one sleeve. The other sleeve and the waist edge are finished with bands of scuba.

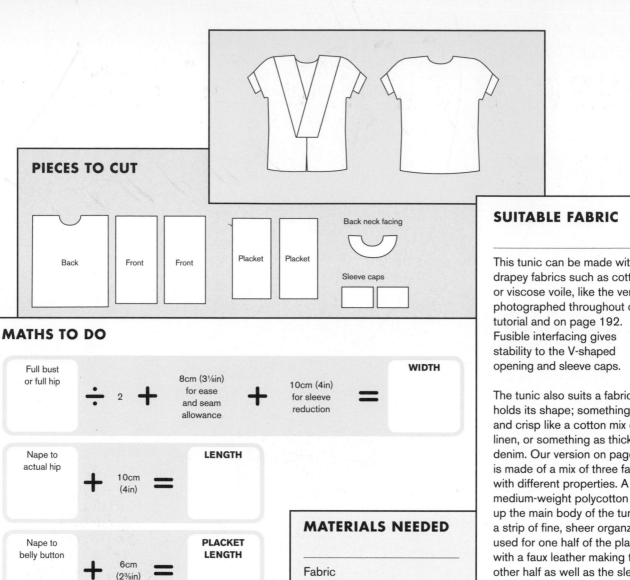

PIECES TO CUT

Back

Front

Front

Placket

Placket

Back neck facing

Sleeve caps

MATHS TO DO

Full bust or full hip $\div$ 2 $+$ 8cm (3⅛in) for ease and seam allowance $+$ 10cm (4in) for sleeve reduction $=$ **WIDTH**

Nape to actual hip $+$ 10cm (4in) $=$ **LENGTH**

Nape to belly button $+$ 6cm (2⅜in) $=$ **PLACKET LENGTH**

BODY MEASUREMENTS NEEDED

Full bust or full hip (whichever is bigger)

Nape of neck to belly button

Nape of neck to actual hip

MATERIALS NEEDED

Fabric

Fusible interfacing

Guide garment – something with a fairly close-fitting neckline

SUITABLE FABRIC

This tunic can be made with drapey fabrics such as cotton or viscose voile, like the version photographed throughout our tutorial and on page 192. Fusible interfacing gives stability to the V-shaped opening and sleeve caps.

The tunic also suits a fabric that holds its shape; something thin and crisp like a cotton mix or linen, or something as thick as denim. Our version on page 193 is made of a mix of three fabrics with different properties. A medium-weight polycotton makes up the main body of the tunic, a strip of fine, sheer organza is used for one half of the placket, with a faux leather making the other half as well as the sleeve caps and bottom band.

Avoid very thick fabrics as creating sharp corners in the placket and sleeve caps will be difficult.

DEEP V TUNIC

This sophisticated tunic evokes the graphic angles of origami. An interfaced placket and sleeve caps add crisp tailoring. Play with the length, taking the hem all the way down beneath your bottom, or cropping it at the hips. Try altering the width of the placket pieces to make them dramatically broad or gracefully narrow. Add a split at the centre front to create a second V-shaped detail.

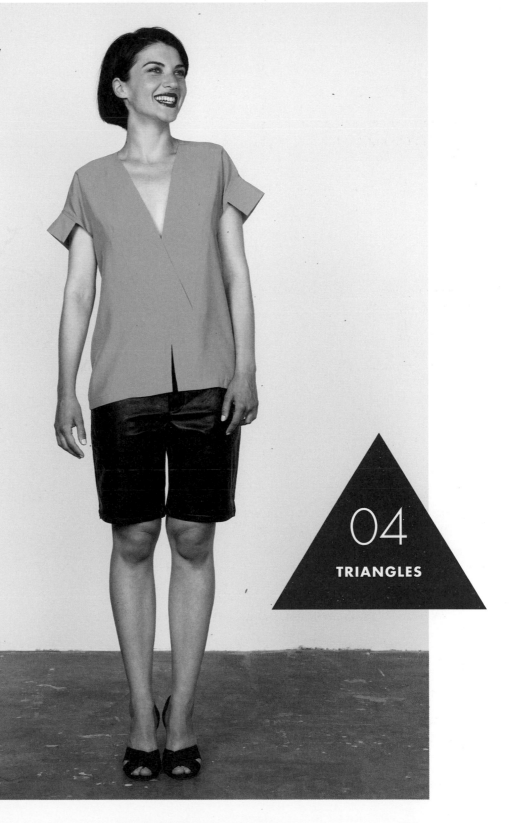

04

TRIANGLES

First, you're going to mark and cut a rectangle (yep, a rectangle!) that will form the back of your tunic.

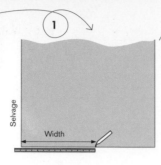

Measure your WIDTH along the bottom edge of your fabric and mark that spot.

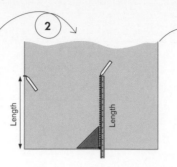

Measure your LENGTH upwards from there and square a line. Measure your LENGTH up the selvage edge of your fabric and mark that spot, then square a line joining the two LENGTH marks. Cut this rectangle out.

Using two fabrics
If you are making the front of your tunic from two contrasting fabrics, you may want to create your back from two halves as well, so that there is no sharp transition between different fabrics at the shoulder seam on one side. If this is the case, simply halve your WIDTH and add 1.5cm (⅝in) to that. Cut two rectangles this size and join them in the same way that you will join your front pieces, as described on page 186.

Now it's time to construct the deep V-shaped placket. This is in fact made of two more rectangles.

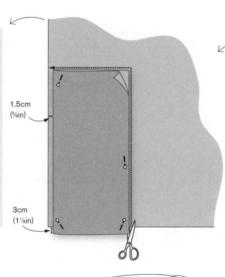

1.5cm (⅝in)

3cm (1⅛in)

Fold your back rectangle in half and position it 1.5cm (⅝in) inland from the side of your fabric, and so that 3cm (1⅛in) hangs over the bottom edge of the fabric.

Pin it to keep it steady and cut around it. Use this piece as a guide to cut a second piece exactly the same.

Now cut the two skinnier rectangles that form the main part of the front of your top.

You need to decide how wide you want each strip of your placket to appear. Your PLACKET WIDTH will be double this plus 3cm (1⅛in). Our version has a 22cm (8⅝in) placket, meaning each placket strip appears 9.5cm (3¾in) deep once the garment is complete. Our version on page 193 has a wider placket, beginning with a PLACKET WIDTH of 27cm (10⅝in). The version on page192 has a much narrower placket, beginning with a PLACKET WIDTH of 16cm (6¼in).

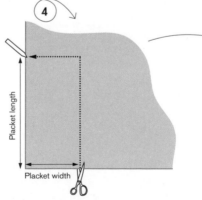

Placket length

Placket width

Mark out a rectangle using your PLACKET WIDTH and PLACKET LENGTH. Cut it out, then use that piece to cut a second piece exactly the same.

If your fabric is drapey or wobbly, cut a piece of fusible interfacing the same size as each of your placket rectangles and bond the interfacing to the wrong side of the fabric with your iron.

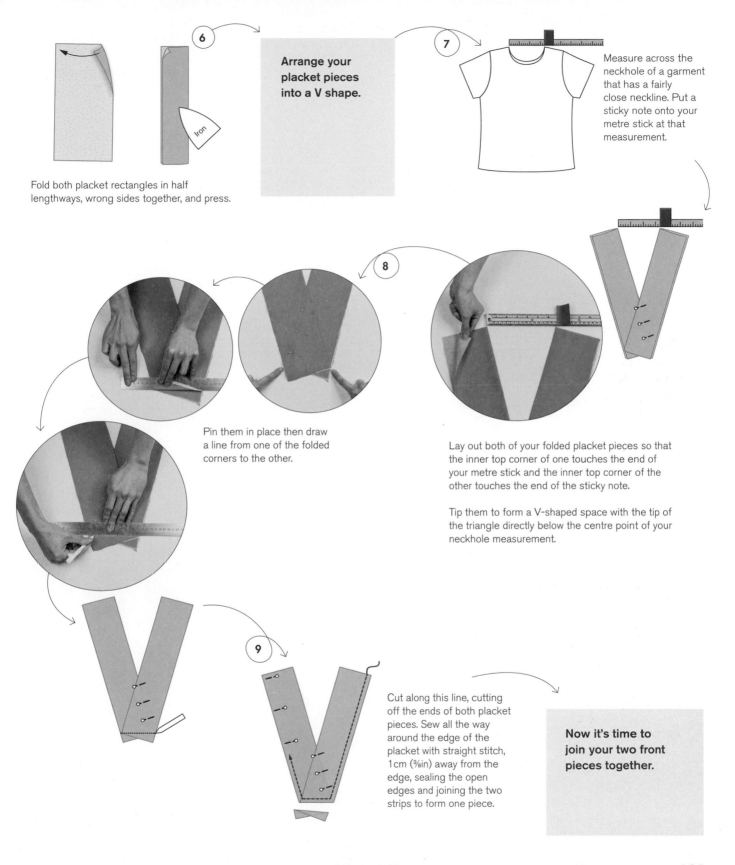

Fold both placket rectangles in half lengthways, wrong sides together, and press.

Arrange your placket pieces into a V shape.

Measure across the neckhole of a garment that has a fairly close neckline. Put a sticky note onto your metre stick at that measurement.

Pin them in place then draw a line from one of the folded corners to the other.

Lay out both of your folded placket pieces so that the inner top corner of one touches the end of your metre stick and the inner top corner of the other touches the end of the sticky note.

Tip them to form a V-shaped space with the tip of the triangle directly below the centre point of your neckhole measurement.

Cut along this line, cutting off the ends of both placket pieces. Sew all the way around the edge of the placket with straight stitch, 1cm (⅜in) away from the edge, sealing the open edges and joining the two strips to form one piece.

Now it's time to join your two front pieces together.

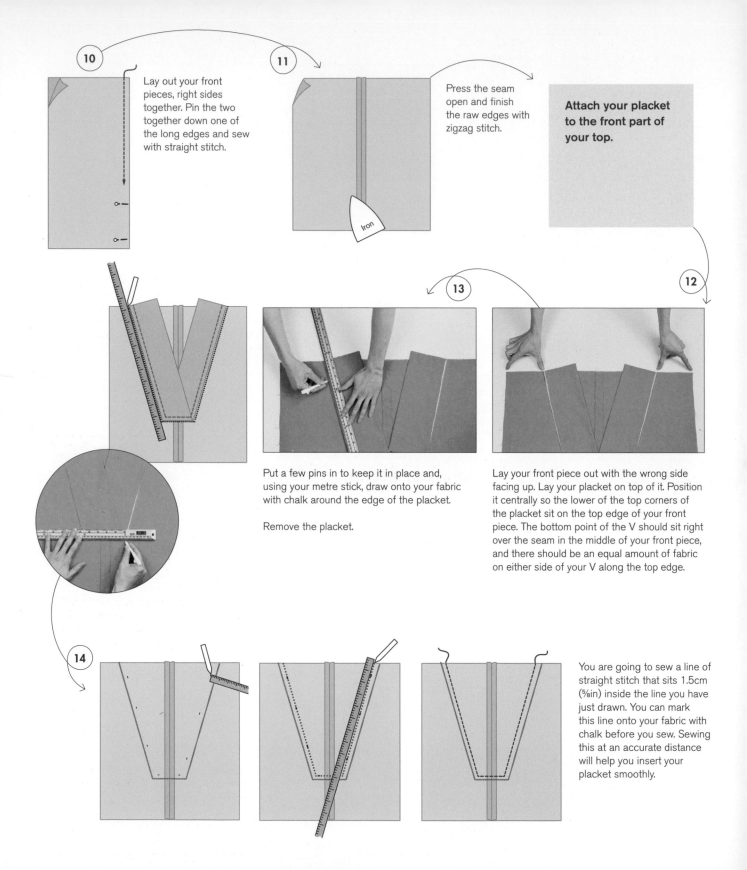

10 Lay out your front pieces, right sides together. Pin the two together down one of the long edges and sew with straight stitch.

11 Press the seam open and finish the raw edges with zigzag stitch.

Iron

Attach your placket to the front part of your top.

13 Put a few pins in to keep it in place and, using your metre stick, draw onto your fabric with chalk around the edge of the placket.

Remove the placket.

12 Lay your front piece out with the wrong side facing up. Lay your placket on top of it. Position it centrally so the lower of the top corners of the placket sit on the top edge of your front piece. The bottom point of the V should sit right over the seam in the middle of your front piece, and there should be an equal amount of fabric on either side of your V along the top edge.

14 You are going to sew a line of straight stitch that sits 1.5cm (⅝in) inside the line you have just drawn. You can mark this line onto your fabric with chalk before you sew. Sewing this at an accurate distance will help you insert your placket smoothly.

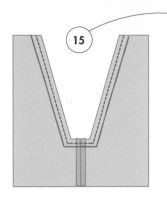

15

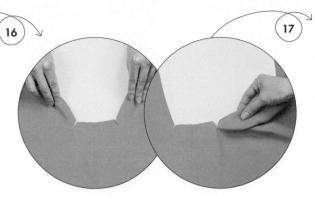

16

17

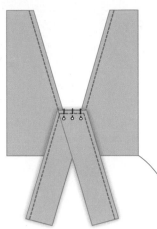

Now cut away the area of fabric inside your stitching, leaving 1.5cm (⅝in) of fabric. Again, mark this if you like, as cutting accurately will help you sew your placket in accurately.

Snip into the two bottom corners, right up to the stitching, as close as you dare. This will allow you to pivot your fabric later on.

18

Flip your front piece over so you are looking at the right side. Turn your V-shaped placket so it is upside down. Pin the bottom of your placket to the bottom of the hole, matching the edges so they sit on top of one another and making sure your placket is positioned centrally.

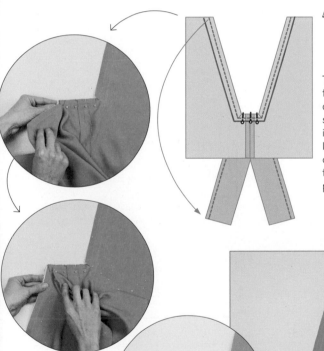

19

Take the left side of your front piece and pull it downwards, pivoting on the snipped corner and twisting it until you can line up the long sloping edge you have cut into your front piece with the long outer edge on your placket. Pin that into place.

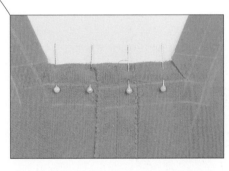

Flip the whole lot over so you are looking at the wrong side (your main front piece will be hiding the placket). Repin the placket in place from this side and remove the pins you originally put in.

It may seem illogical, but unpin the short bottom edge of your placket now!

You're going to sew the placket to the front piece, beginning at the top of the sloping pinned edge.

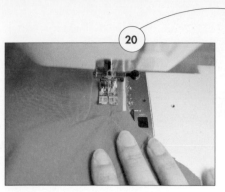

20

Start your stitches at the shoulder edge, sewing down towards the lower tip of the V. Run your stitches just to the left of the line of stitches you can see on your front piece – as close to them as you can!

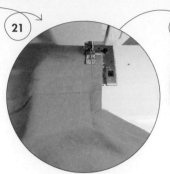

21

Sew until you reach the corner, then with your needle in the down position, lift your machine foot and pivot the whole lot until the short bottom edge of the placket is in the correct position for sewing across. Now twist the fabric of your front piece until the short edges match.

22

Put a couple of pins in to hold the two together. Sew across this short edge until you get to the corner marked by the stitching. Again, with your needle down and the foot lifted, pivot the placket so the last edge is sitting in the right direction for sewing and rearrange the fabric of your front piece to match the placket edge, pivoting it on the snip. Pin and sew up this last edge.

You have inserted your placket.

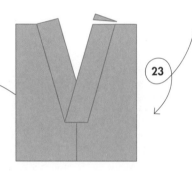

23

Trim away the triangles of fabric that stick up above the top of the shoulder line.

Add a neckline on your back piece.

24

Press the placket flat from the front, using your iron to push the fabric of the front piece away from the placket, especially at the corners. Trim down the seams and zigzag around all three edges.

25

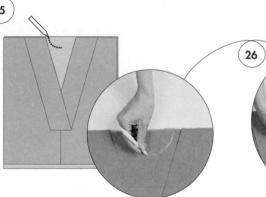

Lay your back piece out with your front piece on top of it, wrong sides together.

Sketch half a neckline, with your chalk marks sitting 1cm (⅜in) away from the edge of the placket.

26

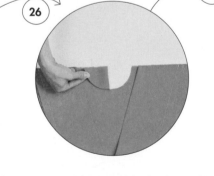

You can use a guide garment to sketch a neckline you like, or freestyle it! Cut the first half of the neckline then fold the flap of fabric over to the other side, making sure the edge is sitting 1cm (⅜in) away from the placket, then cut the second half of the neckline using the flap as a guide.

27

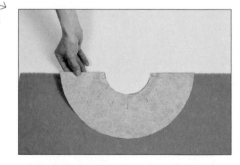

You can finish this back neck edge with bias binding or with facing, as we did. Make your facing the same depth as the width of your placket where it touches the top edge of the top, plus 1cm (⅜in). For instructions on making facing see page 59 of the Deco Drape Dress tutorial. For instructions on using bias binding to finish a neck edge, see pages 88–90 of the Segment Dress tutorial.

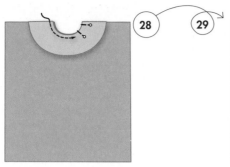

28 **29**

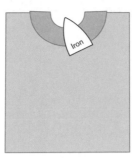

Sew the two together with a 1cm (⅜in) seam allowance then snip into the seam to release tension. Flip the facing to the wrong side of the fabric and press it so it sits flat on the wrong side.

Join your front and back pieces along the shoulder edges.

Pin it to the right side of the garment.

30

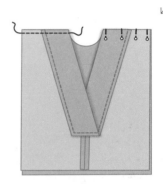

Lay your tunic out, right sides together, and match up the bottom edge of the front and back pieces. This will cause the shoulder seam to sit slightly to the front of the garment. Take your guide garment and position it on top of your tunic, sitting centrally.

Sew up the sides and create sleeves.

Lay out your back piece with your front piece on top, right sides together. Match up the shoulder edges and pin along them. Sew along these pinned edges with straight stitch, running 1cm (⅜in) from the edge, then press the seams open and finish the raw edges with zigzag stitch.

31

32

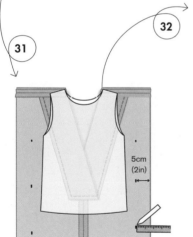

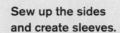

5cm (2in)

Measure 5cm (2in) inwards from the edge a number of times up each side, marking that distance with chalk.

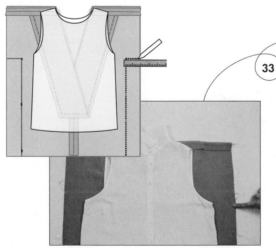

Using your metre stick, join the marks on one side, drawing a line that goes from the bottom of the tunic up to the armpit point of your guide garment. Draw a short line from that point horizontally out to the edge of your fabric.

Repeat this on the other side.

33

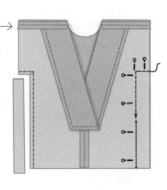

Pin the front to the back of your tunic on both sides, distributing your pins inside the chalk lines you have made. Sew along your chalk lines, pivoting your tunic with the needle in the down position at the armpit point to sew a nice sharp corner.

Trim away the rectangle of fabric on the outside of your stitches, leaving about 1cm (⅜in) of fabric beyond the stitching.

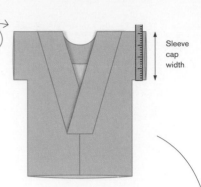

Make sleeve caps for your tunic.

Snip away a small triangle of fabric at the armpit point. See step 48 of the Deco Drape Dress tutorial on page 63 for a close-up photo.

Press the side seams and underarm sleeves open and zigzag all the raw edges.

Each of your sleeve caps is going to be made of a small rectangle of fabric. Measure the depth of one of your sleeves at the front of your garment. This will be your SLEEVE CAP WIDTH.

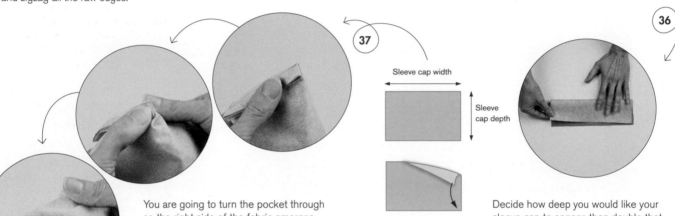

You are going to turn the pocket through so the right side of the fabric emerges. To create sharp corners, fold the seam over towards the inside of the stitches before you turn. Pinch the folded seam as close to the corner as you can, then push it through to the other side. The fold you made will help you push out and shape a crisp corner.

Decide how deep you would like your sleeve cap to appear, then double that depth and add 3cm (1in). Ours appear 5.5cm (2¼in) deep on our finished tunic, so our SLEEVE CAP DEPTH was 14cm (5½in). Cut two identical rectangles using these measurements and two matching pieces of interfacing. Fuse the interfacing to the wrong sides of your rectangles with your iron. Fold the rectangles in half lengthwise, right sides together. Pin, then sew up the two short ends, creating a rectangular pocket.

Lay your garment out, right side out. Fold one of your sleeve caps in half to find the centre. Lay it on top of the sleeve, with the raw edges of the sleeve cap and the sleeve itself matching up, and with the centre fold sitting at the shoulder seam.

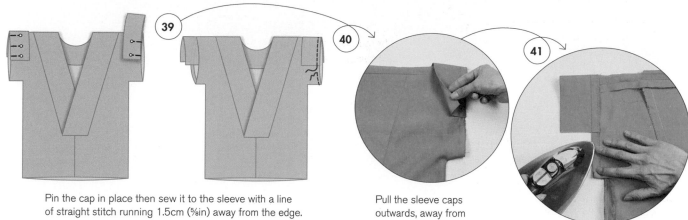

Pin the cap in place then sew it to the sleeve with a line of straight stitch running 1.5cm (⅝in) away from the edge. Continue your stitching all the way around the sleeve until you get back to where you started.

Pull the sleeve caps outwards, away from the tunic.

Turn your tunic inside out and press the hem inwards, using your line of stitching as a guide. The stitching should sit just on the inside of the tunic. Sew the hem down all the way round with straight stitch.

Create a split in the centre front of your garment.

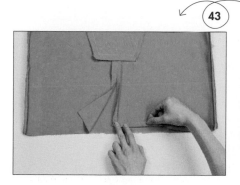

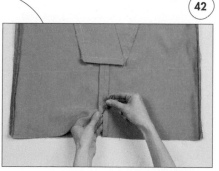

Finally, hem the bottom of your garment. See page 77 of the Shirt Dress tutorial for instructions.

Unpick the central front seam as far up as you would like your split to go. You can choose to leave this seam without a split, like our version on page 192.

To add a border at the hem
You can choose to add an extra strip of fabric to the bottom of your tunic, like our version on page 193.

To do this, create a neat band of fabric in exactly the same way you created your sleeve caps. The band will need to be as long as the full distance around the bottom edge of your tunic, plus 3cm (1⅛in). Pin it to the right side of your tunic all the way round the bottom edge, making sure the neat short edges of the band are in line with the neatly pressed edges of the split at the front of your tunic. Sew the band to the tunic then flip it downwards, pressing the seam upwards.

YOU HAVE MADE A DEEP V TUNIC!

Deep V tunic

Mairead wears a cropped version of the tunic that has no split beneath the placket at the centre front. The placket is made of a light silk with a fusible interfacing backing to ensure it holds its shape. The placket pieces are much narrower than in the other versions of the tunic. Each side of the tunic is made in a contrasting lightweight polyester, and the back is made in two halves so that the fabrics at the front and back blend seamlessly together.

2

Kristina's version of the tunic is made in subtly contrasting fabrics. The main sections of the front and back are made from a matt medium-weight polycotton. One half of the very broad placket is made from a sheer silk organza. The other half is made from a leatherette with a slight sheen. This leatherette was also used to make the sleeve caps and the extra band of fabric around the hem. The tunic has a full split at the centre, from the hem right up to the placket.

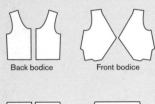

PIECES TO CUT

Back bodice

Front bodice

Skirt back

Skirt back

Skirt front

BODY MEASUREMENTS NEEDED

Full bust

Full under bust

Full waist

Full hip

Waist to full hip

Nape of neck to waist down back

Measure from your waist to where you want your hem to be. Add 3cm (1⅛in) to this. We'll call this your SKIRT LENGTH

MATHS TO DO

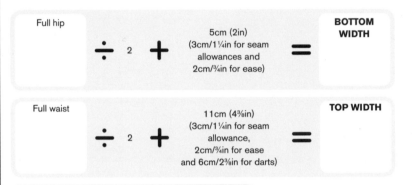

| Full hip | ÷ 2 | + | 5cm (2in) (3cm/1¼in for seam allowances and 2cm/¾in for ease) | = | BOTTOM WIDTH |

| Full waist | ÷ 2 | + | 11cm (4⅜in) (3cm/1¼in for seam allowance, 2cm/¾in for ease and 6cm/2⅜in for darts) | = | TOP WIDTH |

| Waist to full hip | ÷ 2 | = | | | FIRST DART LENGTH |

| FIRST DART LENGTH | + | 2cm (¾in) | = | | SECOND DART LENGTH |

| Nape to waist | + | 3cm (1⅛in) | = | | BACK LENGTH |

| Full bust | − | Full under bust | = | ÷ 4 | = | DART DEPTH |

SUITABLE FABRIC

Something that isn't drapey! Cotton or polycotton are good choices.

MATERIALS NEEDED

Fabric

A long invisible zip

Bias binding (you'll need quite a lot)

Guide garment – a fitted, sleeveless top or dress that isn't stretchy

Newspaper to make template

Large sheet of coloured paper

TRIPLE TRIANGLE DRESS

This design relies on the sewing triangle par excellence – the dart – in order to make the dress fit the body closely. The bodice pieces and waist edge are finished with a bias trim that can be a matching or contrasting colour. The dress fastens at the centre back with an invisible zip.

05

TRIANGLES

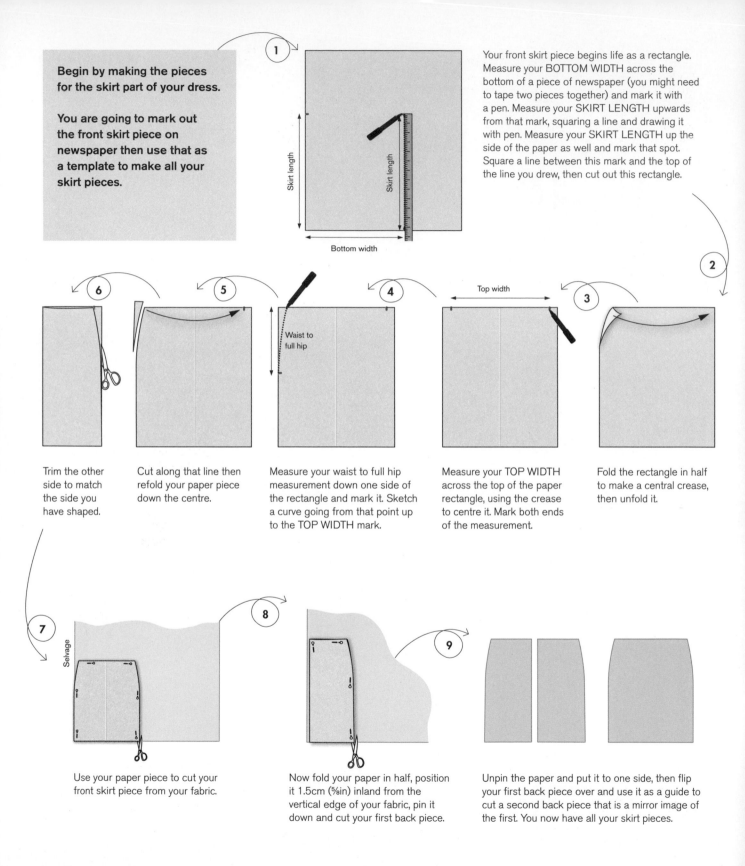

1

Begin by making the pieces for the skirt part of your dress.

You are going to mark out the front skirt piece on newspaper then use that as a template to make all your skirt pieces.

Skirt length

Skirt length

Bottom width

Your front skirt piece begins life as a rectangle. Measure your BOTTOM WIDTH across the bottom of a piece of newspaper (you might need to tape two pieces together) and mark it with a pen. Measure your SKIRT LENGTH upwards from that mark, squaring a line and drawing it with pen. Measure your SKIRT LENGTH up the side of the paper as well and mark that spot. Square a line between this mark and the top of the line you drew, then cut out this rectangle.

2

6

Trim the other side to match the side you have shaped.

5

Cut along that line then refold your paper piece down the centre.

4

Waist to full hip

Measure your waist to full hip measurement down one side of the rectangle and mark it. Sketch a curve going from that point up to the TOP WIDTH mark.

Top width

Measure your TOP WIDTH across the top of the paper rectangle, using the crease to centre it. Mark both ends of the measurement.

3

Fold the rectangle in half to make a central crease, then unfold it.

7

Selvage

Use your paper piece to cut your front skirt piece from your fabric.

8

Now fold your paper in half, position it 1.5cm (⅝in) inland from the vertical edge of your fabric, pin it down and cut your first back piece.

9

Unpin the paper and put it to one side, then flip your first back piece over and use it as a guide to cut a second back piece that is a mirror image of the first. You now have all your skirt pieces.

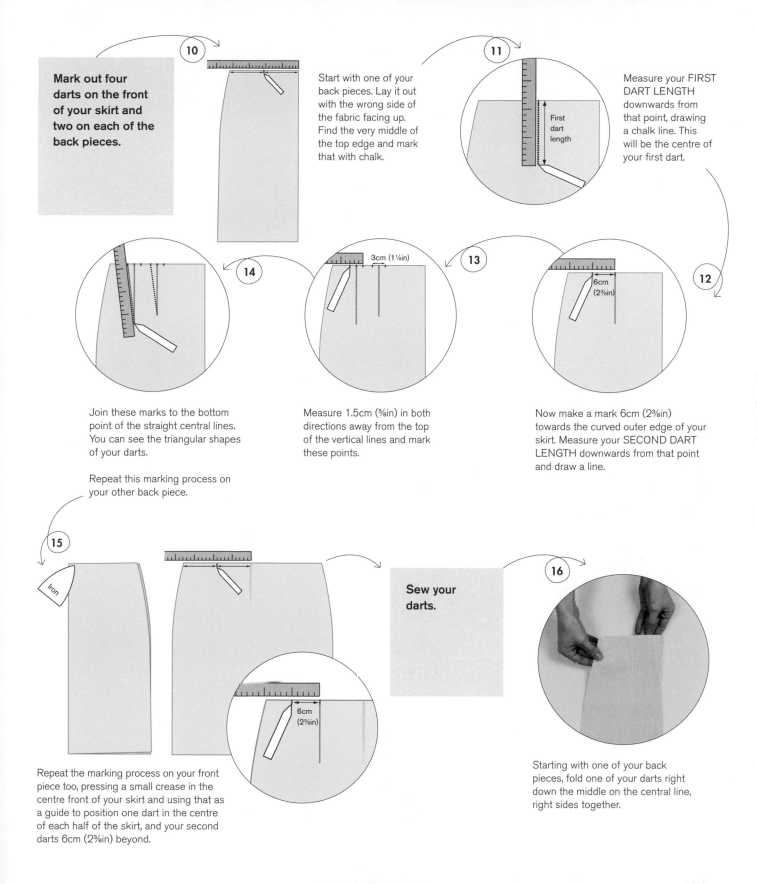

10 Mark out four darts on the front of your skirt and two on each of the back pieces.

11 Start with one of your back pieces. Lay it out with the wrong side of the fabric facing up. Find the very middle of the top edge and mark that with chalk.

Measure your FIRST DART LENGTH downwards from that point, drawing a chalk line. This will be the centre of your first dart.

First dart length

12

6cm (2⅜in)

13

3cm (1⅛in)

Now make a mark 6cm (2⅜in) towards the curved outer edge of your skirt. Measure your SECOND DART LENGTH downwards from that point and draw a line.

Measure 1.5cm (⅝in) in both directions away from the top of the vertical lines and mark these points.

14 Join these marks to the bottom point of the straight central lines. You can see the triangular shapes of your darts.

Repeat this marking process on your other back piece.

15 Iron

6cm (2⅜in)

Repeat the marking process on your front piece too, pressing a small crease in the centre front of your skirt and using that as a guide to position one dart in the centre of each half of the skirt, and your second darts 6cm (2⅜in) beyond.

Sew your darts.

16

Starting with one of your back pieces, fold one of your darts right down the middle on the central line, right sides together.

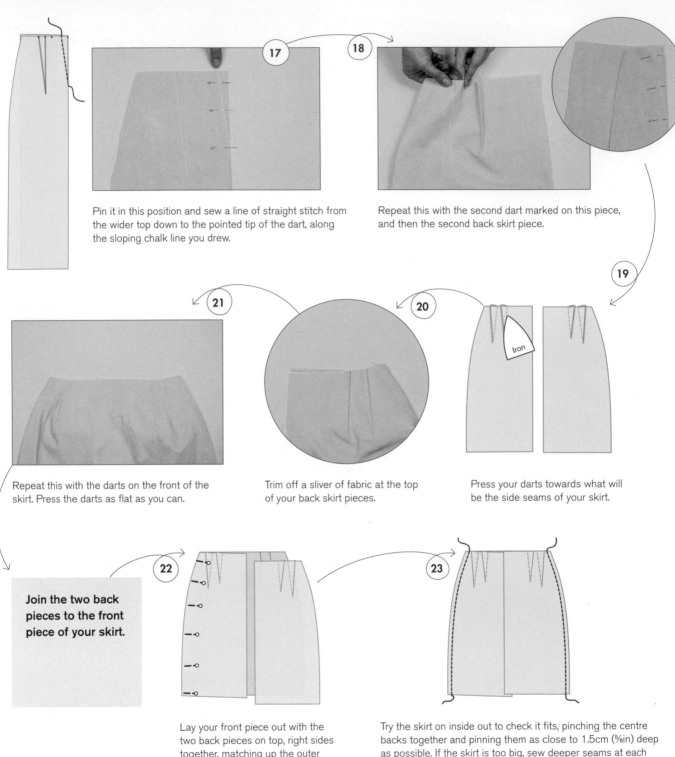

17 **18**

Pin it in this position and sew a line of straight stitch from the wider top down to the pointed tip of the dart, along the sloping chalk line you drew.

Repeat this with the second dart marked on this piece, and then the second back skirt piece.

19

21 **20**

Iron

Repeat this with the darts on the front of the skirt. Press the darts as flat as you can.

Trim off a sliver of fabric at the top of your back skirt pieces.

Press your darts towards what will be the side seams of your skirt.

Join the two back pieces to the front piece of your skirt.

22 **23**

Lay your front piece out with the two back pieces on top, right sides together, matching up the outer edges. Pin then sew them together with straight stitch.

Try the skirt on inside out to check it fits, pinching the centre backs together and pinning them as close to 1.5cm (⅝in) deep as possible. If the skirt is too big, sew deeper seams at each side, unpicking your original stitching. If it is too small, you can sew shallower darts, unpicking your original ones. Once the skirt fits as you want it to, press the side seams open, then neaten the raw edges of the side seams with zigzag stitch.

Now you're going to make the bodice part of your dress. The front and back of the bodice are each made of two pieces. Begin by marking out a paper template that will be used as the basis for all four bodice pieces.

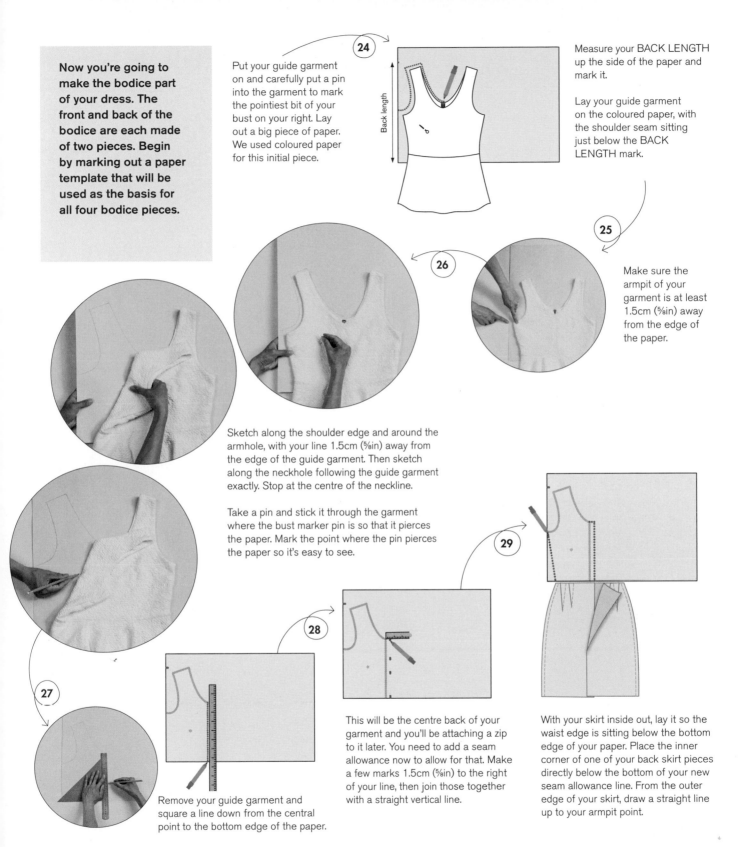

24 Put your guide garment on and carefully put a pin into the garment to mark the pointiest bit of your bust on your right. Lay out a big piece of paper. We used coloured paper for this initial piece.

Measure your BACK LENGTH up the side of the paper and mark it.

Lay your guide garment on the coloured paper, with the shoulder seam sitting just below the BACK LENGTH mark.

25 Make sure the armpit of your garment is at least 1.5cm (⅝in) away from the edge of the paper.

26 Sketch along the shoulder edge and around the armhole, with your line 1.5cm (⅝in) away from the edge of the guide garment. Then sketch along the neckhole following the guide garment exactly. Stop at the centre of the neckline.

Take a pin and stick it through the garment where the bust marker pin is so that it pierces the paper. Mark the point where the pin pierces the paper so it's easy to see.

27 Remove your guide garment and square a line down from the central point to the bottom edge of the paper.

28 This will be the centre back of your garment and you'll be attaching a zip to it later. You need to add a seam allowance now to allow for that. Make a few marks 1.5cm (⅝in) to the right of your line, then join those together with a straight vertical line.

29 With your skirt inside out, lay it so the waist edge is sitting below the bottom edge of your paper. Place the inner corner of one of your back skirt pieces directly below the bottom of your new seam allowance line. From the outer edge of your skirt, draw a straight line up to your armpit point.

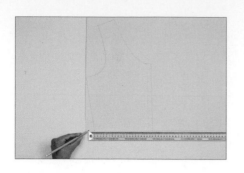

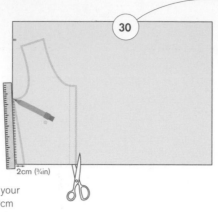

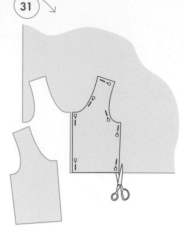

You're going to add a small dart along the waistline of your back piece, so add extra room for this now. Measure 2cm (¾in) outwards from the bottom of the side line and make a mark, then draw a new line from this mark up to the armpit point. Cut out this shape.

Use this paper template to cut your two back pieces from fabric. Make sure you flip the paper so you cut two fabric pieces that are mirror images of each other.

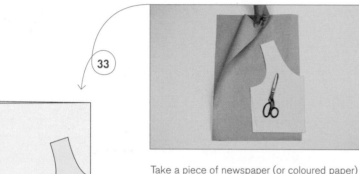

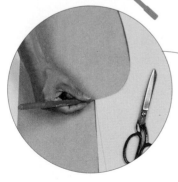

Take a piece of newspaper (or coloured paper) and fold it in half. Lay your paper template onto it. Position your template so the 1.5cm (⅝in) central seam allowance is protruding over the fold. Push it upwards, too, so you have some extra paper under it. You can hold it in place with pins or weigh it down with something heavy like a solid pair of scissors.

Use your paper piece to mark out your front bodice pieces on newspaper.

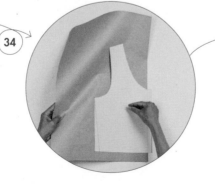

Mark the position of the piece with dots at the armpit point, bottom centre and bottom left corner.

Anchor the paper piece by pushing a pin through the bust point of the coloured paper piece all the way through the newspaper.

Square a line from the bust point down to the waist edge and beyond, onto the newspaper.

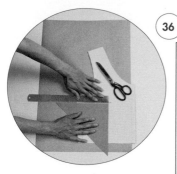

Square a line from the bust point out to the side, extending it beyond the edge again onto the newspaper.

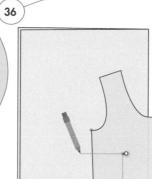

36

37

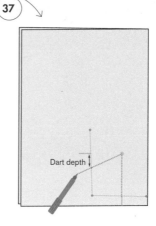

Remove your coloured paper shape and join the dots you made on the newspaper with straight lines.

Measure your full DART DEPTH down the side seam line and make a mark.

Join that mark to your bust point with a straight line, and extend the line beyond the edge of the garment. This will be the centre of your bust dart.

Dart depth

Draw a line joining the bust point to meet the line at the bottom. This will be the centre of your waist dart.

39

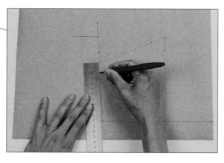

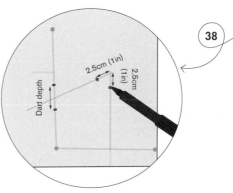

2.5cm (1in)

2.5cm (1in)

Dart depth

38

Make marks 2.5cm (1in) down each dart leg away from the bust point. These will be the actual points of your darts. Mark half the DART DEPTH away at both sides of the central leg of the bust dart.

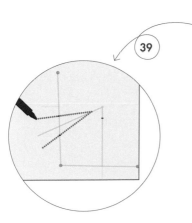

Join those marks to the bust dart point with straight lines.

40

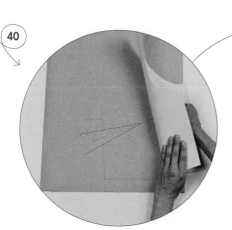

41

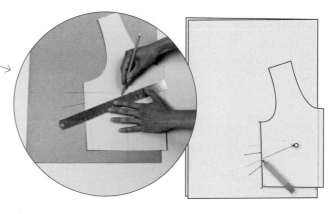

Using the extension of the central dart leg drawn on your newspaper as a guide, draw the central leg of the dart onto your paper template.

Pin your paper template in place again with the bust point pin.

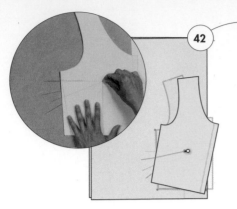
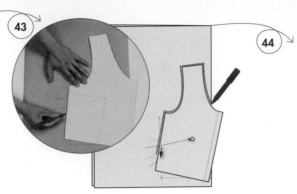

Holding the pin as close to the paper as you can, swivel your coloured template clockwise so that the central leg you just marked now sits in line with the upper leg marked on the newspaper.

Holding the coloured paper in this position, draw from the neckline as shown until you get to the central dart leg on your newspaper.

Next, swivel the coloured paper in the opposite direction, so the central dart leg on the coloured paper is in line with the lower dart leg marked on the newspaper. In this position, draw a line running from the lower dart leg on the newspaper to the outer waist corner of your coloured shape. Remove the coloured paper.

Using a ruler, join up the bottom of this line with the bottom point on the fold of your newspaper.

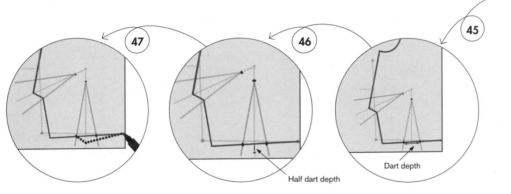

Half dart depth

Dart depth

Then join that mark to the left dart leg and the bottom point on the fold of your newspaper with straight lines.

Add a bit of extra height here so that when you fold this dart you have enough fabric. Measure half your DART DEPTH down the central dart leg from the lowest line and mark that.

Measure your DART DEPTH equally across the central leg of the waist dart and make marks, then join each of those marks to the mark that indicates the point of your waist dart (2.5cm/1in below the actual bust point).

Now you're going to mark the triangular shape of your front piece.

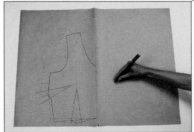

Unfold the newspaper sheet and make a dot at the point where the pin poked through at the back.

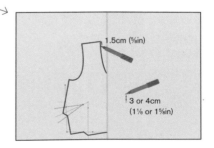

1.5cm (⅝in)

3 or 4cm (1⅛ or 1⅝in)

Make a mark 3 or 4cm (1⅛ or 1⅝in) above that dot. This will be the pointed tip of your triangular front piece. Make another mark 1.5cm (⅝in) away from the shoulder line, along the neckline you've sketched. Now join this line to your triangle tip mark with a straight line.

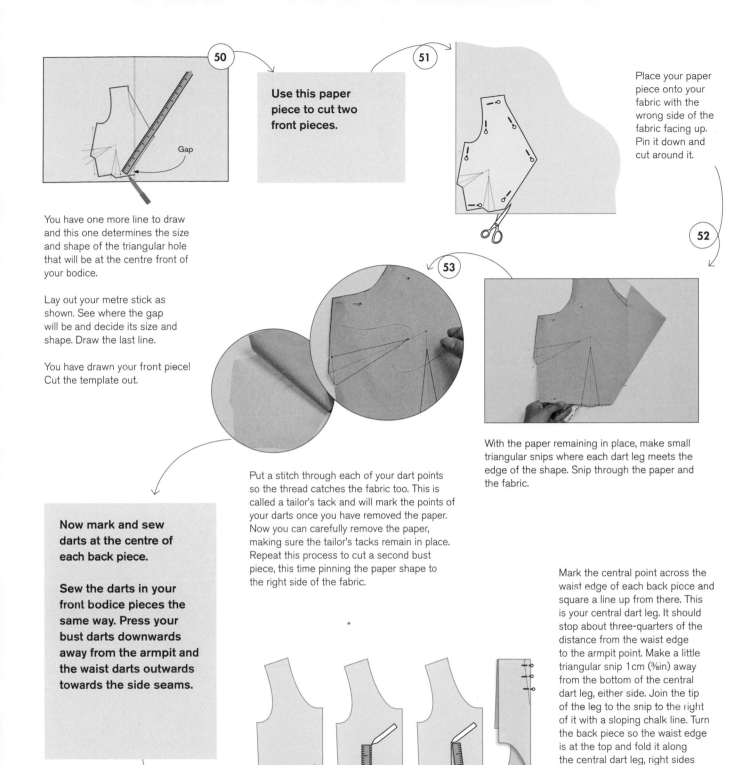

50

You have one more line to draw and this one determines the size and shape of the triangular hole that will be at the centre front of your bodice.

Lay out your metre stick as shown. See where the gap will be and decide its size and shape. Draw the last line.

You have drawn your front piece! Cut the template out.

Gap

51

Use this paper piece to cut two front pieces.

Place your paper piece onto your fabric with the wrong side of the fabric facing up. Pin it down and cut around it.

52

53

With the paper remaining in place, make small triangular snips where each dart leg meets the edge of the shape. Snip through the paper and the fabric.

Put a stitch through each of your dart points so the thread catches the fabric too. This is called a tailor's tack and will mark the points of your darts once you have removed the paper. Now you can carefully remove the paper, making sure the tailor's tacks remain in place. Repeat this process to cut a second bust piece, this time pinning the paper shape to the right side of the fabric.

Mark the central point across the waist edge of each back piece and square a line up from there. This is your central dart leg. It should stop about three-quarters of the distance from the waist edge to the armpit point. Make a little triangular snip 1cm (⅜in) away from the bottom of the central dart leg, either side. Join the tip of the leg to the snip to the right of it with a sloping chalk line. Turn the back piece so the waist edge is at the top and fold it along the central dart leg, right sides together, matching up the snipped holes. Pin in place and sew from the waist edge to the point of the dart, along the sloping line you drew.

Now mark and sew darts at the centre of each back piece.

Sew the darts in your front bodice pieces the same way. Press your bust darts downwards away from the armpit and the waist darts outwards towards the side seams.

54

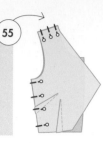

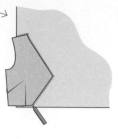
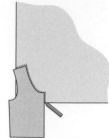

55 Join your fronts and backs together.

Lay out your back pieces with the corresponding front pieces on top of them, right sides together, matching up the sides and the shoulder seams. Pin the sides and the shoulders together, and sew with straight stitch. Try the halves of the bodice on for size and make any adjustments you want, then press the side and shoulder seams open. Zigzag the raw edges.

56 To finish the front bodice edges with facing

This means there will be no visible trim. Use the front and back bodice pieces to sketch facing pieces (see page 59 of the Deco Drape Dress tutorial for detailed instructions). Then sew the fronts and backs of the facing pieces together. Press open the shoulder seams, then sew the facing pieces to the bodice pieces with right sides together, matching up the shoulder seams. Make sure you turn a nice sharp corner at the front point of each bodice piece. Clip into the curved neck edge, then turn the facing to the wrong side of the bodice piece and press it into place at the back. You can sew your bodice pieces directly to your skirt, rather than adding a strip of bias binding across the waistline.

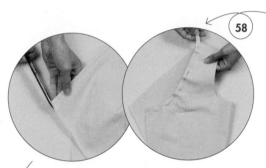

58

Pin the bias binding in place, running it all the way up over the shoulder seam and down to the point of your triangle. Sew it into place here then trim off the end so it runs in line with the edge of the fabric.

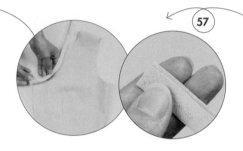

57

You're going to finish the other edges of the bodice with visible bias binding. Press the binding so that one half is slightly deeper than the other. Slip the folded bias over the raw edge of the bodice, starting at the centre back. The deeper side of the bias should sit on the inside.

57 Finish the edges of your bodice with bias binding.

You can finish the armholes by sandwiching the raw edge in the middle of a folded piece of binding, or by sewing the binding to the right side so it is invisible, as described on pages 89–90 of the Segment Dress tutorial.

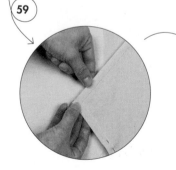

59

Take a new piece of bias and press it in half as before. Tuck the end under and position it so it overlaps the first piece of stitched bias. Wriggle the tuck until the end of the bias is running in line with the edge of the fabric. Sew the binding in place.

60 Join the skirt and the bodice.

To do this you need to add one more strip of bias binding around the waist of your dress. To make it appear the same width as the binding on your bodice, lay the new binding next to the finished binding on your bodice and mark the same depth.

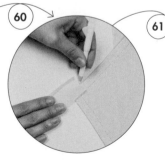

60

You will need to sew your bias binding to your skirt just above this mark. Trim the binding so 1cm (⅜in) remains above the mark you made.

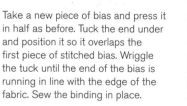

61

Lay your skirt piece out with the right side facing up. Pin the right side of your binding to the right side of the skirt, all the way along the waist edge. Sew them together with a line of straight stitch running about 1cm (⅜in) away from the edge, or just above the mark you made.

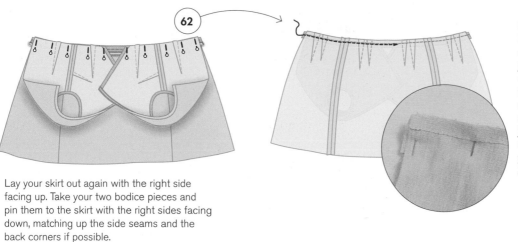

62

Lay your skirt out again with the right side facing up. Take your two bodice pieces and pin them to the skirt with the right sides facing down, matching up the side seams and the back corners if possible.

Flip your skirt over so you are looking at the wrong side and can see the line of stitching that joins the bias binding to the waist edge. You're going to sew from this side, so you can keep an eye on that line of stitching and make sure your new stitches are sitting just fractionally below that. Make sure your pins are accessible so you can remove them as you sew. Zigzag this full edge to neaten.

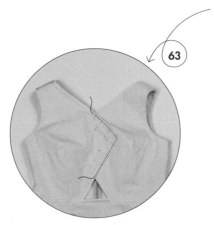

63

Flip the bodice pieces and the binding up. Press the binding up, away from the skirt, and the seam down. You might need to clip into the skirt seam to release some tension.

Sew all the way along the upper edge of the binding, securing it to the bodice pieces. We also sewed a line of topstitching just under the waist seam on the main fabric of the skirt, to hold the waist seam down.

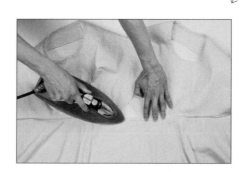

Try your dress on. Ask someone to pin the back for you! Position the front bodice pieces where you want them, so that the tips of the triangles sit level with one another. Pin the overlapping parts of the bodice together.

Take the dress off and put some hand stitches in to hold the front pieces together. For a fast option, sew them together on your machine with the stitches running just inside the bias binding.

Insert an invisible zip at the back of the dress.

64

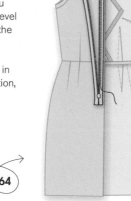

Insert an invisible zip in the same way described on pages 110–12 of the Spot Pocket Skirt tutorial. Your zip should extend from the neck edge at the back to around the bottom points of your darts.

Hem the bottom edge of your dress by zigzagging the raw edge, pressing up an even fold all the way round and sewing it with straight stitch.

YOU HAVE MADE A TRIPLE TRIANGLE DRESS!

Triple triangle dress

1

Karishma's version of the
dress is made in a crisp African
wax-print cotton. The bodice
pieces are finished with facing,
so there is no visible trim. The
lower edges of the bodice pieces
have been cut in line with the
diagonal stripe on the fabric,
creating a wide triangular keyhole
detail. The skirt is longer than
in the other versions, finishing
below the knee.

Technical variations

Linda's version of the Triple Triangle Dress has a short skirt and a bodice made of two contrasting crisp, lightweight fabrics. The overlapping bodice pieces have been cut to create a fairly large triangular keyhole opening. They are finished with a visible bias binding trim.

ACKNOWLEDGEMENTS

Thanks to Helen Rochester for commissioning this book and to everyone at Laurence King for giving me the opportunity to work on a dream project. Special thanks to my editor Clare Double for your natural kindness, patience and thoroughness throughout this very long journey from idea to physical object.

Extra special thanks to Evelin Kasikov, the most wonderful book designer in the world. Thank you for your peaceful, open-minded, intelligent approach to making this book and, above all, thank you for your skills. I am so lucky that Laurence King found you.

Massive thanks to everyone who worked on the photo shoots. Thanks to Haleigh Maskall on hair and make up, for totally 'getting it' and doing an amazing job. Thanks to all my models for being bold, courageous, beautiful women and for letting me prod you while you stood in front of a camera for hours at a time. Special thanks to Andii Melody Mae, Kristina Pringle and Courtney Graham for going above and beyond to help me fit and style your outfits. Huge thanks to Amy Wyatt for flying into my world like a superhero and working your socks off so that the shoots were fun and efficient. Thanks to Suzie Kemner for stepping in to lend a hand, too. Extra special thanks to Victoria Siddle for your energy, obsessive attention to detail, sense of humour and skill behind the lens, all of which created an outstanding set of photos. Thanks to Natsue and Matt Golden at the Russian Club for supporting us throughout the preparations for the shoot and for providing us with such a stunning location.

Big thanks to two wonderful fabric shops in London: Ray Stitch for kindly giving me the beautiful blue bamboo jersey to make the Drip Drape Skirt and baby pink cotton to make the Shirt Dress; and the Village Haberdashery, for kindly giving me a selection of gorgeous kona cottons, with which I made the mint green Insert Skirt and the pale blue Segment Dress.

Enormous thanks to the global sewing community that I am so proud to be a part of. You are all the best. Thanks for being there! Special thanks to all of you who popped up on Instagram and Twitter, helping me with fabric choices and generally giving me encouraging words through the power of the internet.

Thanks to my wonderful instruction testers Kirsty Fife and Fooniks, and special thanks to Clare Szabo. Clare, your methodical approach to sewing and generosity in giving me such detailed feedback on the Four Slice Sweater should win an award! Thank you for playing a major part in making those instructions work. Big thanks to Kerrie Curzon, my trusty friend and sewing rock. Thanks to my clever friend Andy Hopwood for helping me with maths.

Finally, thanks to all my friends and family, to my colleagues at Bag Books and to my bandmates Oli Don and Owain Paciusko from Giant Burger, and Lisa Lavery and Lucy Pereira from Melge, for supporting me and putting up with me being only partially mentally present on many occasions. Special thanks to Joel Shea for supporting me while I did my thing, and for distracting me with laughter at all the right moments.

TECHNIQUE INDEX